The Roads to Congress 2010

The Roads to Congress 2010

Edited by
Sean D. Foreman and Robert Dewhirst

LEXINGTON BOOKS
Lanham • Boulder • New York • Toronto • Plymouth, UK

Published by Lexington Books
A wholly owned subsidiary of The Rowman & Littlefield Publishing Group, Inc.
4501 Forbes Boulevard, Suite 200, Lanham, Maryland 20706
www.lexingtonbooks.com

Estover Road, Plymouth PL6 7PY, United Kingdom

British Library Cataloguing in Publication Information Available

Library of Congress Cataloging-in-Publication Data

Foreman, Sean D., 1969–
  The roads to Congress 2010/edited by Sean D. Foreman and Robert Dewhirst.
    p. cm.
  Includes index.
  ISBN 978-0-7391-6944-5 (cloth : alk. paper)—ISBN 978-0-7391-6945-2 (electronic)
    1. United States. Congress—Elections, 2010—Case studies.   2. Political
campaigns—United States—History—21st century—Case studies.   3. Elections—
United States—History—21st century—Case studies.   I. Dewhirst, Robert E.   II. Title.
  JK19682010.F67 2011
  324.973'0932—dc23   2011030732

Printed in the United States of America

Contents

List of Tables, Figures, and Charts

TABLES

ix

FIGURES

CHARTS

Preface

Sean D. Foreman and Robert Dewhirst

There are indeed many "roads to Congress" traveled by hopeful candidates every two years as all 435 seats in the House of Representatives and about one third of the 100 seats in the Senate are up for the selection of American voters. The 2010 congressional campaigns were but the latest chapter in the nation's continuing saga of self-government. Moreover, with the presidency not on the ballot, public attention was focused entirely on relatively local House and Senate contests.

Readers of this book will follow the path of seven House and six Senate races from inception to election postmortem. The following chapters are both narrative and analysis of an array of interesting and diverse contests from throughout the country. Each entry was written by one or more experts living in the state or region of the contest. The authors provide succinct and highly readable chapters meant to illustrate the distinctive nature of the campaigns they are examining. Readers will see individual campaigns and elections up close and be able to compare and contrast one from another because of the common format employed throughout the book. Taken together, the chapters reveal that the roads to Congress, while similar in so many ways, each follow a unique route to Capitol Hill.

Sean Foreman would like to thank Richard Newell, Julian Wynter-Anderson, and Michael Worley for their research assistance. He is grateful for the support of the Department of History and Political Science and the College of Arts and Sciences at Barry University. Foreman sends a thank you to Ol' Dewhirst and all of the contributors who made the book possible, and to Robert Watson for handing this project to him. Most of all, Foreman gives sincere thanks to his wife, Hadley, and son, Luke, for their patience and support during the writing and editing of this volume.

Dewhirst would like to thank Sean Foreman for his tireless work on the manuscript and making certain chapter authors and co-editor alike kept on task and on time (for the most part). His energy, good humor, and attention to detail were essential for the successful completion of this project.

Part I

2010 Congressional Elections

Chapter 1

A Third "Wave" Election in a Row

The House Turns Republican while the Senate Stays Democratic

Sean D. Foreman

On November 4, 2008, Barack Obama, a first-term Democratic Senator from Illinois, was elected as U.S. president. Democrats also gained 23 seats in the House of Representatives and nine in the U.S. Senate to build on the majorities they attained in the 2006 midterm elections. After two cycles of Democratic victories, President Obama and the Democratic majority in the 111th Congress, led by House Speaker Nancy Pelosi (D-CA) and Senate Majority Leader Harry Reid (D-NV), embarked on an ambitious agenda, partly driven by ideological design, and partly pushed by economic necessity.

Soon after Obama was inaugurated on January 20, 2009, Republicans and conservatives focused on preparing for the 2010 elections and doing what they could to take back power. They hoped to continue the historical trend where the president's party usually loses seats in his first midterm election and sought to block Obama's political success to set the stage for their potential return to majority status in the 112th Congress.

One of the first actions of the Obama administration was to gain support for the American Recovery and Reinvestment Act of 2009, also known as the economic stimulus package, which passed with no Republican support in the House and only three Republican votes in the Senate. Much of the next year focused on debates and town hall meetings about health care reform, leading up to a major reform law passed in March 2010.

DEMOCRATIC WAVE INTERRUPTED

Democrats initially enjoyed a filibuster proof majority with 60 votes in the Senate—58 Democrats and two Independents (Senators Joe Lieberman of

Connecticut and Bernard Sanders of Vermont) that caucused with the Democrats. But the first blow to that supermajority was the special election to fill the seat held by Edward "Ted" Kennedy of Massachusetts, for 47 years who died August 25, 2009. It was popularly referred to as "Kennedy's seat," but State Senator Scott Brown called it "the people's seat" and, by driving around the state in his old pickup truck dressed in casual clothes with rolled up sleeves, he surprised Democratic candidate Martha Coakley, the commonwealth's Attorney General, in a January 2010 special election.[1] Brown's win was the third major GOP victory since Obama's election after Republicans wrested control of governor's mansions in Virginia and New Jersey in November 2009.

The Republican brand had been declared all but dead after the 2006 and 2008 Congressional sweeps for the Democrats. But they bounced back fueled by voter anger at federal spending. *Time* magazine had declared the Grand Old Party's symbolic elephant an endangered species in May 2009. But fortified by an angry and bitter Tea Party movement, the GOP looked well-nourished while Blue-Dog Democrats appeared to be the dying breed, as several conservative Democrats lost their jobs in the 2010 contests.

The Tea Party movement—signifying "taxed enough already" and using the 1775 Boston Tea Party as a motivating theme—formed in early 2009 and picked up steam over the next year and a half. Groups of citizens largely organized at the grassroots level formed organizations and held rallies and protests around the country. Their main issues were opposition to the rising federal deficit and national debt, wasteful government spending, and high tax rates. The Tea Party movement quickly gained followers and plenty of media attention. Eventually some prominent Republican politicians attached their fundraising abilities and celebrity status to candidates running under Tea Party labels around the country. There were signs that 2010 was shaping up as an anti-establishment and an anti-Democrat year.

Gallup polls showed that only 21 percent of Americans surveyed believed that America was headed in the right direction in October 2010. This was much lower than the 35 percent in 2006 when Democrats regained the majority in Congress and the 30 percent just prior to the 1994 elections when Republicans supplanted decades of Democrats in majority rule.[2] Congressional job approval dipped to 16 percent in March 2010 and ticked up slightly to 21 percent in October. It dropped again to 17 percent soon after the midterm elections.[3] This general discontent led to enthusiasm among Republicans to vote in November. *USA Today*/Gallup polls found about 53 percent of registered voters were enthusiastic to vote. Not surprisingly, 63 percent of Republicans and Republican-leaners were excited to vote while 44 percent of Democrats and Democratic-leaners were eager, leading to a so-called enthusiasm gap favoring the party out of power.[4]

The wave of 2010 discontent claimed Democratic causalities nationally. Republicans captured 6 governor's seats, including key electoral states Michigan, Ohio, Pennsylvania, and Wisconsin, and gained more than 600 seats in the 50 state legislatures. Republicans gained 63 seats in the House and 6 in the Senate. The Democratic House losses were 9 more than the 54 seats lost in the 1994 Midterm election that ushered in the so-called Republican Revolution. The 6 Senate seats were short of what most analysts expected going into November but enough to make the upper chamber more competitive and responsive to bi-partisan efforts. Voter turnout was around 40 percent, which is average for the last few decades of midterm elections.

THE ROADS TO CONGRESS

There are many roads to the U.S. Congress. Every 2 years there are 435 separate races for seats in the House of Representatives. In most years, more than 90 percent of them are safely guarded or even uncontested. Usually one-third of the Senate is up for election. Due to filling partial terms from appointments due to deaths or presidential nominations, there were 37 seats up for grabs in 2010. Add to that the sundry and sordid candidates that offered themselves for office and this election season was one of the most fascinating in recent memory.

Several prominent incumbents lost their primary bids. Arlen Specter, a five-term Republican from Pennsylvania, became a Democrat in mid-2009 to avoid a GOP primary challenge. Instead, he lost his Democratic bid despite (or because of) White House support. Three-term Republican Senator Bob Bennett from Utah, a stalwart conservative, lost a party convention vote to an even more conservative candidate. Congressman Alan Mollohan of West Virginia's First District, a 14-term Democrat, lost his party support in a nasty primary race.

Despite all of the "anti-incumbent" rhetoric in the media, the reelection rate in the general election was still relatively high. There were 51 defeated incumbents in the House out of 390 members that ran for reelection. That is an 86.9 percent reelection rate, the lowest since 1964's 86.6 percent and below the 93 percent reelection success of House members since 1954. Two Senate Democrats, Blanche Lincoln (Arkansas) and Russ Feingold (Wisconsin), lost reelection.

The biggest House losers were the Blue Dog Democrats. Allen Boyd of Florida, Chet Edwards in Texas, and four committee chairs lost. House Budget Chair John Spratt lost a South Carolina district that had voted for conservative Democrats for decades. Edwards, a 30-year House veteran, lost by 25 percent to Tea Party–supported businessman Bill Flores.

Scott Murphy (NY-20) won a special election in 2009 and, after an early lead in the 2010 polls, lost by nearly 11 percent of the vote (Chapter 6). Gene Taylor (MS-4), a 10-term incumbent conservative Democrat, lost by nearly 10,000 votes (Chapter 7). In Southern Virginia, Democrat Tom Perriello defeated conservative Democrat-turned-Republican Virgil Goode in 2008 only to lose to Republican state senator Robert Hurt in 2010 (Chapter 8).

THE ROLE OF MONEY

Money is always a dominant theme in elections. This cycle, several self-funded candidates spent huge sums but were unable to buy their way into the exclusive Senate club. Carly Fiorina, former Hewlett Packard CEO, spent $5.5 million of her own money to win a competitive Republican primary in California. She lent her campaign less ($1 million) in the general election and was outraised and outspent in her bid for the Senate seat against 3-term incumbent Barbara Boxer (Chapter 10). Linda McMahon, CEO of WWE (the sports entertainment company), spent $50 million of her own money in Connecticut but lost to state Attorney General Richard Blumenthal (Chapter 12). Real estate investor Jeff Greene spent $23 million trying to win the Democratic nomination for Senate in Florida and lost the primary to Congressman Kendrick Meek. That Senate seat was won by Marco Rubio, who used Tea Party support to drive Governor Charlie Crist from the Republican Party and then defeat both Crist and Meek (Chapter 13). Beyond individual contributions, unlimited amounts of corporate expenditures were allowed to influence elections after the *Citizens United v. Federal Election Commission* (2010) decision by the U.S. Supreme Court.

TEA PARTY IMPACT

Tea Party–affiliated candidates in the general election won 50 percent of their Senate races (5 out of 10) while just 42 out of 130 candidates that identified with the Tea Party won in the House (32 percent). Some argued that the Tea Party movement cost the Republicans three seats that otherwise would have been ripe for takeover by more moderate Republicans. Harry Reid survived a challenge in Nevada against Tea Party–backed Sharron Angle. In Delaware, Christine O'Donnell defeated longtime House member and former governor Mike Castle in the primary. With O'Donnell's nomination, that seat, long held by Vice President Joe Biden, went from one that Republicans expected to pick up to one the Democrats held. Colorado saw Ken Buck lose a narrow race to Senator Mike Bennett after both survived tough primary challenges (Chapter 11).

One of the most watched races was in Alaska where Joe Miller, backed by the Tea Party, defeated incumbent Lisa Murkowski in the Republican primary. Murkowski refused to back Miller and ran as a write-in candidate. She prevailed to become the first person elected to the Senate as a write-in candidate since Strom Thurmond of South Carolina in 1954 (Chapter 9).

Nancy Pelosi was the face of Congress and, along with President Obama and Reid, became the focus of Tea Party anger. Conservatives planned for a "Pelosi pink slip party" to send her packing from the Speaker's office after four tumultuous years. She was safe to be easily reelected in her home San Francisco district. But dozens of conservative candidates ran their contests against both their Democratic opponents and Pelosi. She was portrayed as the villain of a Congress that had record low approval ratings. Still, after Democrats lost 63 seats and Pelosi lost the speakership, she said that she had no regrets about her efforts as Speaker.

The election results reflected the rejection of certain policies of President Obama and Pelosi's leadership in Congress. Thirty-two members of the House who voted for the health care law lost reelection. Thirty-one newly elected House GOP freshmen are from districts that President Obama won in 2008. In 11 races that were rematches of 2008, the Republican candidates won 8 of them.

There were a few bright spots for Democrats. Reid held on in Nevada, and Democrats kept the Colorado, Connecticut, and Delaware Senate seats that were under attack. Standard bearers Barney Frank and Charlie Rangel held on to their congressional seats, either of which would have been a major symbolic loss for their party. Many voices pointed out that the country did not vote for Republicans as much as they voted against Democrats.

THE ROAD AHEAD

The 112th Congress witnessed the largest freshman class since 1950. There are 96 new members, of which 87 are Republicans. Nearly one in four of the newcomers have no political experience. This allows more chances for newcomers to make an immediate impact and to move into leadership roles quicker than at other points in history. It also may bring unconventional methods of governing and communication with constituents.

The following chapters provide a sampling of some key races from 2010. They include stories that illustrate the role of the Tea Party; the impact of key policies like the stimulus package, the bank and auto bailouts, and the health care law; the importance of campaign financing; newcomers running for office; and old timers fighting for their political lives. Each of them takes the reader on the campaign trail and illuminates various roads to Congress.

NOTES

1. Cooper, Michael. "G.O.P. Senate Victory Stuns Democrats." *New York Times*, January 19, 2010. www.nytimes.com/2010/01/20/us/politics/20election.html.

2. Gallup 1. "U.S. Satisfaction on Pace to Be Lowest in Midterm Election Year." www.gallup.com/poll/143840/Satisfaction-Pace-Lowest-Midterm-Election-Year.aspx.

3. Gallup 2. "Congressional Approval at 17 Percent after Elections." www.gallup.com/poll/144419/Congressional-Approval-Elections.aspx.

4. Gallup 3. "Record Midterm Enthusiasm as Voters Head to Polls." www.gallup.com/poll/144152/record-midterm-enthusiasm-voters-head-polls.aspx.

Part II

U.S. House of Representatives Elections

Chapter 2

Florida District 8 Race (Webster v. Grayson)

No Magic Kingdom for the Incumbent

Peter Bergerson and Margaret Banyan

Daniel Webster
Party: Republican
Age: 61
Sex: Male
Race: Caucasian
Religion: Southern Baptist
Education: Georgia Institute of Technology
Occupation: Family owned heating and air conditioning business
Political Experience: Florida House of Representatives, (1980–2000); Florida House Speaker, (1996–1998); Florida Senate, (1998–2000)

Alan Grayson
Party: Democrat
Age: 52
Sex: Male
Race: Caucasian
Religion: Judaism
Education: A.B Harvard; J.D. Harvard; M.A. Harvard
Occupation: Attorney
Political Experience: U.S. House of Representatives, (2009–11)

In 2010, the road to the House of Representatives from Disney World and central Florida is much like Florida weather: folks often say that if you don't like it, stick around, it will change. That might also apply to Florida Congressional District 8. If candidates or residents do not like the district, they only have to wait around awhile, because it is sure to be redrawn and with it resident preferences. The 2010 election and the 8th Congressional District is

11

a story about political culture and the candidates' ability to adjust their style to a fickle boundary.

Fluid district boundary lines have consequences that shape the political culture of a district. Boundaries shape congressional campaigns, issues, candidate behavior, and voter decisions. The classic work of Richard Fenno, Jr.[1] brings clarity on how a district's composition plays a critical role in how a representative interprets his "reelection constituency," "primary constituency" and performs his "home style" behavior. This chapter will use Fenno's lens to analyze the District 8 candidate race between incumbent Alan Grayson (D) and challenger Daniel Webster (R). The analysis will outline the District's characteristics, voting patterns, candidates, campaign financing, campaign issues, and election results. The chapter will conclude with several observations about the district, its people, and the campaign.

CHARACTERISTICS OF FLORIDA DISTRICT 8

To understand the dynamics of the 2010 District 8 race, it is important to understand the characteristics of the district itself, including its history and voting patterns. The demographics of the 8th District are not entirely dissimilar to those of the population of Florida as a whole. However, its history is unique, as are some key characteristics of the electorate.

Figure 2.1   Florida Congressional District 8

Congressional District 8

nationalatlas.gov™

8 — Congressional District
Orange — County

Florida (25 Districts)

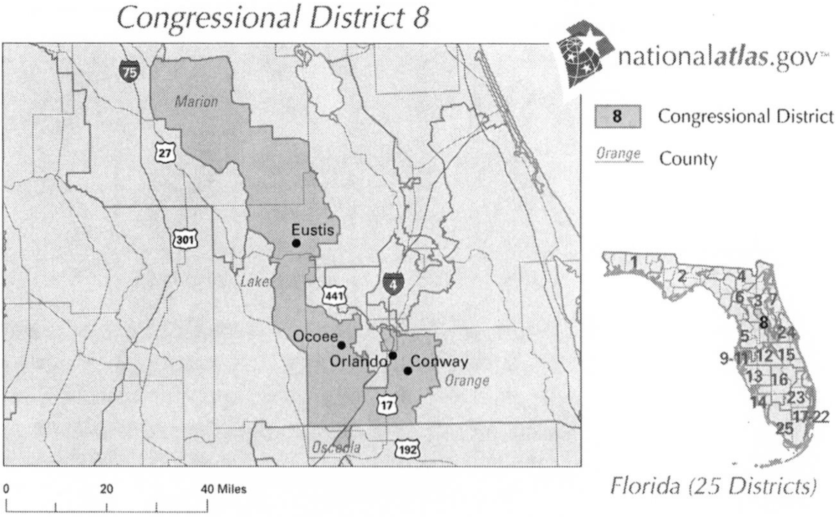

DEMOGRAPHICS

District 8 encompasses 4 counties, 15 municipalities, and 1,158 square miles. The district includes parts of Orlando, Walt Disney World, and the Disney town of Celebration. The racial and ethnic composition of the district is somewhat similar to the state of Florida, but some small differences are indicative of the people that settle in the area. The district is less white than the state as a whole; with District 8 having 76.8 percent whites compared to 78.2 percent in the state. It also has significantly less African Americans; with 9.6 percent compared to 16.1 percent in the state. Yet, there are more Asians than the state average; with 4.1 percent residing in the district compared to 2.7 percent throughout the state. The district also has 1.9 percent more Latinos than the state average.[2]

The district's industries are also revealing. The district has 1.6 percent more people working in the professional, scientific, management, and administration and 6 percent more in the arts, entertainment, recreational, and accommodation industries.[3] This difference is likely due to the major recreational attractions of Walt Disney World, Universal Studios, and SeaWorld.

The population of District 8 is also younger and more educated than the rest of the state. There are 9 percent more 19–64 year old working age residents in the district and many less (4.1 percent) of retirement age. Residents are also more educated; the district has 3 percent more residents with a high school degree or higher and 3.6 percent more that have a bachelor's degree or higher.[4] Clearly, a younger and more educated population is attracted to the area, due in large part to the industries in the general area. Even though the district is not home to NASA, it, and other aero-space and high technology industries are within a comfortable driving distance and attract employees to the geographic area.

Despite differences in the population and industries, housing values are strikingly similar when compared to the state. The median house value in the 2005–2009 Census estimates was $219,900 in District 8 and $211,300 in Florida. However, the length of time that residents have lived in the district is striking. More than one-third of residents moved to their current house in 2005 or later. Another third moved to their current location prior to 2000. In the last 10 years, 66.7 percent of current residents moved to their current household. While these statistics do not account for how many residents moved from within or without the district in the last ten years, in 2009, nearly 8 percent of the population were new to the county, state, or to the United States.[5] By any calculation the Disney district is populated by young, educated, diverse newcomers.

REDISTRICTING AND VOTER REGISTRATION

One of the interesting problems with District 8 is tied to its lack of political maturity and inconsistent boundary lines—its history is that it has no history. Since 1971, parts of District 8 have been redistricted five times. In 1971 it was District 12 on Florida's Gulf Coast; in 1973–1977 it was redistricted from District 6 on Florida's East Coast; from 1977–1983 it was redistricted from District 10; and in 2001 was redistricted from District 5. In 2010, District 8 was carved from three counties in the center of the state resembling a reverse "J"-like vertical figure.

Analysts have argued that the district had become more liberal, citing the district's 52 percent vote in favor of President Barak Obama.[6] The rampant redistricting and significant growth in newcomers may indeed affect registration. One way to assess the claim is to compare voter registration. At the book closing for the 2010 general election, District 8 was 38 percent Republican, 40 percent Democrat, 19 percent No Party Affiliation, and 4 percent all other minor parties.[7] As a whole, Florida voters in the 2010 election were 36 percent Republican, 41 percent Democrat, and 19.5 percent No Party Affiliation. When compared to the state, District 8 was not necessarily more liberal, indeed it had more registered Republicans.

VOTING PATTERNS

The claim that the district had turned liberal also overlooked its historical voting patterns. The 2008 election results were more likely a short term adjustment, rather than a trend. Though the district has transitioned from the 12th, 6th, 10th, 5th, to the 8th, it is interesting to observe the party affiliation of those elected to the U.S. House of Representatives. Since 1953, the district elected Republican leaders for 32 years, while they elected Democrats for 26 years. The Democrats predominantly held power in the early years of the district, coinciding with the time in which Southern Democrats were a major political factor. The State Senate history since 2002 shows a similar pattern with Republicans holding office over the entire time period. The State House shows a different pattern, with Democrats holding a large electoral majority since 2000. The general voting pattern of the district, while varied, is predominately Republican, especially since 1983 onward. The support for Obama and Grayson was likely due to other trends than the history of the district, as we discuss below.

POLITICAL CLIMATE

The election in Florida's 8th Congressional District was considered one of the most competitive House races nationally in 2010. While traditionally conservative, the District was somewhat more moderate in the 2008 election. Yet, Charlie Cook a nationally recognized election analyst and author of the *Cook Report* labeled the Grayson-Webster race as "leans Republican" and CNN considered the contest as a "race to watch."[8] Meanwhile Politico identified Grayson as one of the "besieged incumbents" who "tops the hit list" by hostile outside groups such as the U.S. Chamber of Commerce, the 60 Plus Association and the National Republican Congressional Committee. Political handicappers considered this race as "ground zero" for the Republican's efforts to win a majority in the House.[9] Entering the 2010 election cycle, Alan Grayson was running for reelection as a freshman congressman, in a politically competitive swing district with a national political bounty on his seat. Yet, David Mayhew argued that incumbents have a built in advantage of being able to advertise their activities as a "promissory representative," claim credit for Federal programs (i.e. "pork") for their district, and take popular positions that reflect district values.[10] Each of these strategies usually contributes to incumbents over whelming reelection. This seemed to be the case for Grayson, who, according to Nate Silver of FiveThirtyEight and the New York Times had at one time almost a 59 percent chance of winning.[11]

Meanwhile, Webster's tough four- way primary in August made Grayson look like a strong candidate for reelection. Within this political climate, the general election challengers each brought something unique to the table.

THE CANDIDATES

Alan Grayson

Alan Grayson grew up in the tenements in the Bronx borough of New York City, where his life was hard and "[one] had be a fighter to survive."[12] His parents were teachers. A childhood illness left a lasting impression as his mother took him to the hospital four times a week for treatment. He states that without health coverage, he would not have survived. A very bright student, Grayson attended Harvard College and earned both his law degree and master's degree in government in 1983. Following law school he was a legal assistant at the D.C. Court of Appeals, working with judges Ruth Bader Ginsburg, Robert Bork and Antonin Scalia. In 1985, Grayson joined a Washington law firm in which Justice Ginsburg's husband was a partner. Grayson specialized in government-contracting law during his time with the firm, leaving in 1990 to start IDT Corporation, a telecommunications company. In 1991, Grayson also became a founding partner in Grayson and Kubli, a law firm based in Vienna, Virginia. Grayson continued his previous work of representing government contractors in cases against the government. After the U.S. invasion of Iraq in 2003, however, Grayson began taking on more whistle-blowing cases involving contractor fraud against the United States. Shortly thereafter Grayson moved to the Orlando area to pursue a political career.[13]

In 2006, as a political newcomer to Florida's 8th Congressional District, Grayson ran an unsuccessful bid for the Democratic nomination. Two years later, he earned his party's nomination and defeated four-term Republican incumbent Ric Keller. In Congress, Grayson served on the House Committee on Financial Services, the House Committee on Science and Technology, the Financial Services Subcommittee on Oversight and Investigations, and the Science and Technology Subcommittee on Investigations and Oversight. These rather sedate committee assignments did not fit Grayson's character. Unlike many new members he did not settle for being a back bencher resigned to obscurity as a freshman congressman. As a newly sworn Congressman he became the focus of national attention. *The New Republic* reported that "almost immediately after arriving in Congress, Grayson shot to stardom as a darling of the liberal blogosphere" known for his aggressive politics, embrace of YouTube culture and controversial sound bites.[14] *The New York Times* noted that, "Mr. Grayson has catapulted himself to national renown for outlandish rhetoric and a pugilistic political style that makes him seem less staid lawmaker than a character on the lam from one of his Orlando district's theme parks."[15] Even among his Democratic colleagues, Grayson acquired the political idiom known as a wing nut—an outspoken ideological extremist.

Daniel Webster

Daniel Webster was born in 1949 in Charleston, West Virginia. He is a distant relative of the antebellum politician and orator Daniel Webster. His family moved to Orlando when he was seven, after a doctor recommended a change of climate as a cure for Webster's sinus problems. He was an excellent student and attended the Georgia Institute of Technology, where he graduated with a B.S. in electrical engineering in 1971. He was active in Tau Kappa Epsilon fraternity and student government where he was the student chaplain. Since college Webster has worked in the family air conditioning and heating business; he presently owns and operates it. Webster lives in Winter Park. Webster was attracted to politics the same year Ronald Reagan ran for the presidency.[16]

In 1980, Webster was elected to the Florida state house, which was under Democratic control at the time. During his 18 years in the Florida House of

Representatives, Webster became the speaker in 1996, the first Republican to do so in 122 years. In 1998, Webster was elected to the Florida State Senate. After 28 years of service in the Florida legislature, he retired in 2008. Among his notable legislative activities, as a state senator, Webster sponsored State Bill 804 that was aimed at keeping Terri Schiavo on her feeding tube. Schiavo was brain-damaged after suffering cardiac arrest in 1990, and her husband's choice to remove her feeding tube precipitated a long-legal battle at the state and federal level. Webster describes his leadership style as the . . . quiet conservative . . . who has proven himself to be a true statesman, standing on principles and steadily advancing conservative values."[17] As a 54-year resident of central Florida, he is the consummate political insider whose 28 years in the state legislature had embedded him in the political fabric of the area with a legacy of trust and accountability to the voters. Webster's community stature was bolstered through his membership on the Board of Trustees of the University of Central Florida. Perhaps more importantly, Webster brought to the campaign his staunch conservative political credentials, openly devout Christian beliefs, and claim to "greatly respect the Tea Party Movement."[18]

CAMPAIGN STRATEGIES

Richard J. Fenno, Jr. argues that what and who a legislator "sees" as his district will shape a representative's perceptions and determine his campaign strategy.[19] Fenno defines this as "home style" behavior, the person-to- person style of how a member presents himself to the voters. It is affected by the nature of the congressmen's geographical constituency, the candidate's per-ception of the voters, and who he/she thinks shapes their primary constituents. Fenno suggests that incumbents seek to leave the "correct impression"— to present themselves in such a way as to accrue favorable responses from the voters. Fenno writes that successful incumbents understand that voters are continually sizing up the candidate or measuring their behavior and actions from the perspective of the political culture. Thus, elections are a "matter of place" or location. The location incorporates unique district characteristics, which define base voters and shape voter choices. In a similar vein, Jane Mansbridge writes that a legislator's model of representation can be classified as promissory, anticipatory, gyroscopic, or surrogate representation.[20]

The candidate's behaviors represented both Fenno's and Mansbridge's models—but they could not have been more different. As the Democrat incumbent, Grayson chose the role of a surrogate representative, one in which Mansbridge defined, "as representation by a representative with whom no one has electoral relationship" and typically appeals to voters outside of the district. Edmund Burke referred to this as "virtual" representation, by that he meant elected officials who focus on morally right issues rather than the good of the whole.[21] Surrogate representation is when legislators represent constituencies that did not elect them.[22] During Grayson's two years in office he took on the role of representing causes not in tune with his reelection constituencies. Clearly, Grayson's rhetoric did not fit the political values of the 8th District, particularly in an environment of political uncertainty.

While Grayson launched a tirade against the excesses of Wall Street and the Federal Reserve, Former Florida Speaker of the House Daniel Webster employed a campaign strategy that was honed by a quarter of a century of experience in Florida politics. Webster employed what Mansbridge called a "promissory representation" strategy, which evaluates candidates on their past performance in keeping campaign promises.[23] Webster used a classic principal-agent model where the voters are the principal and the legislator is their agent. Webster understood the importance of making explicit and implicit promises to the electorate. His previous campaigns taught him the electoral value of positioning himself so the voters understood they would have both legal as well as moral control over him as their elected official. Webster centered his campaign strategy on the ideal of traditional accountability, keeping promises to voters and building trust. This perspective was also articulated in his website that boldly states, "Honor, Principle, Leadership You Can Trust."[24]

CAMPAIGN FINANCING

One of the more interesting aspects of this campaign was that Webster won, despite Grayson's massive campaign war chest. During the 2010 season, Grayson's campaign expended $5.5 million compared to Webster's $1.7 million.[25] The candidate's coffers do not tell the whole story, however. Grayson's 8th District and Susan Kosmas' 24th District seats were considered to be endangered and targeted early on by the conservative opposition. The opposition believed that they could leverage their funding better because both seats were in the same media market. They also knew that the Webster would be at a funding disadvantage due to a costly primary. The U.S. Chamber of Commerce funded ads attacking Grayson as a "big mouth" and "extreme" and spent more than $1 million to defeat the Democrats.[26]

CAMPAIGN ISSUES

In the final six weeks key issues of a campaign can be the most important decision time in the mind of the electorate, particularly for swing or independent voters. In competitive elections, factors that impact on an election's outcome include turnout, party organization, party unity, and candidate personalities. The fine points of key policy issues such as health care or Social Security often lose out to a tsunami of 30-second radio and television advertisements. In some elections a candidate's behavior becomes the deciding issue. A major campaign blunder or untoward candidate behavior can lead to redefining the outcome of the election.

ADVERTISEMENTS

Perhaps the most significant turning point in the campaign was Grayson's notorious *Taliban Dan* television attack ad in September. While leading in the polls, incumbent Grayson released a commercial which featured Taliban fighters and linked Webster to extreme biblical spousal relationships. The video showed footage of Webster speaking to a Christian organization and saying the phrase: "[W]ives, submit yourself to your own husband . . . she should submit to me." A fact check group provided evidence showing that Webster's comments were completely taken out of context. Grayson's strategy of going into attack mode backfired. Polls taken after the ad and the subsequent clearing of Webster showed an electoral reversal of fortunes. Grayson trailed 35 percent to Webster's 43 percent.[27] Sensing a dramatic shift in voter opinion, Webster never looked back. Entering October as the front runner, Webster traveled the district and basically provided audiences with his conservative philosophy, family values stump speech, which included less government control in people's life, welfare reform, focus on job training and education, a strong right-to-life position, and the right for parents to home school their children. Within one week, Grayson had gone from a "59 percent chance of winning to less than 40 percent chance. . . ."[28] The race was also characterized by a lack of a debate. Each side refused a debate among the main candidates, with Webster's side commenting, "[a] debate with Alan Grayson will be nothing more than gutter politics" and Grayson's side calling Webster a "religious nut" and a "draft dodger."[29, 30]

CANDIDATE ISSUES IN COMPARISON

The issues that each candidate supported in their stump speeches were characteristically along party lines. Table 2.1 outlines the issues each candidate supported. Grayson supported the Democratic administration's initiatives for health care, stimulus spending, and green energy. Webster,

Table 2.1.   Florida 8th District Candidate Issues in Comparison

Issue	Grayson	Webster
Government spending	Spending cuts	Spending cuts, balanced budget, and line item veto
Education	Federal funding for schools. Attracted $240 million for Orange, Lake, and Marion County Schools	Family initiatives, including the right for parents to home-school their children. Support education as a means of economic development
Regulation	Concerned about offshore drilling in Florida as a risk to environment and tourist economy	Favored eliminating excessive burdens on Florida's businesses and entrepreneurs
Women's issues and right to life	Strong support of women's rights and equal pay	Strong right-to-life candidate
Social issues		Less government control in people's life and supported right to keep and bear arms
Health care	Outspoken advocate of health care reform and the Patient Protection and Affordable Health Care Act	De-fund and repeal the Obama health care plan
Banking regulation	Opposed huge bonuses for bailed out bank CEOs and voted against every bank bailout	
Stimulus and federal spending	Advocated "green" development, American Clean Energy and Security Act of 2009, and the American Recovery and Reinvestment Act of 2009	Reforms to Florida's welfare system, reducing the emphasis on cash payouts and more focus on job training and education
Taxes		Supported elimination of the "death tax", capital gains tax, dividends and interest taxes.

on the other hand, carried the water for the Republican issues. He supported less government regulation in business, but more social control in the area of family and abortion. It is doubtful that any of the issues that the candidates proposed defined the race. More likely, Grayson's erratic behavior and short relationship with an incoherent district were significant factors in his defeat.

CONCLUSION

The election results demonstrated Webster's big success. Webster won 56.1 percent of the vote; Grayson carried 38.2 percent; and the other candidates shared the remaining 5.7 percent.[31] The 2010 Congressional election in Florida's 8th Congressional District resolved around the "home style" behavior of the candidates, their perceived partisan nature of mid-term voters, and how each candidate defined their representational role and voter perception of the candidates. This was especially important in a district with little consistent identity, either with candidates or their fellow voters. Further, the Grayson-Webster campaign and election illustrates how "home style" behavior contributed to an incumbent's defeat.

Grayson had lost his constituency. His core loyalists who elected him two years earlier had lost trust over the course of his tenure in office due to his outspoken style and seemingly erratic behavior. Grayson also had miscalculated his constituency. Believing that his adherence to national party-line politics held sway with his home-town voters was in error. Grayson mistakenly defined his representational role as a policy entrepreneur. The issues he advocated as a congressman took national precedence over 8th District issues. His campaign reinforces in the voters mind his self-defined role as a "surrogate." Thus, Grayson, chose to campaign on the idea that it was more important to "save the world, before he saved his seat" and his role as a surrogate for national causes contributed to his defeat. Grayson showed that he was not in tune with his electorate by his comment at the Florida Democratic Party convention, "[s]cientists have studied for years this difficult question of why some people have a conscience and some do not. . . . Some people are called Democrats, and some people are called Republicans."[32] Further, Grayson's verbal attacks on the opposition party alienated Republican voters when he characterized them as "foot-dragging, knuckle-dragging Neanderthals, who know nothing but 'no.'"[33] In a historically Republican-leaning district with 19 percent registered independents, this is not good politics.

Meanwhile, Webster followed a campaign playbook based on a solid grasp of the political competitiveness of the district and knowledge of its hybrid political party composition and voting habits. Webster took the opportunity to campaign as the delegate and to employ a "home style" behavior based on promissory representation. This style was a natural fit for Webster who had nearly three decades of public service in the Florida legislature. He was a legislator who believed in the grass roots, "citizen legislature" reflecting Jacksonian Era local populist issues. His reputation as a state legislator was that of a "work horse" and not a "show horse." This instilled voter confidence and reinforcement that he would be their advocate in Washington.

The voter perceptions of the candidates were also instrumental in the outcome. Campaigns are composed of watchers, talkers, cue takers and what Mansbridge called "anticipatory voters."[34] Mansbridge argued that causal relationships exist between the preferences of the candidates and the outcome of an election. She suggests that relationships that develop between the representative's period of service and the next election are critical to his/her reelection. The level of trust is based on looking backward at the candidate's record. Grayson's record of service to the district did not fit the perceptions the voters had of what their representative should be. Nor did he have the kind of long-standing history that Webster shared with Florida voters. Grayson relished the national exposure as an ideological political gadfly. He was seen as one who brought attention to himself for outlandish comments and policy proposals that did not reflect the voter values. Subsequently, Daniel Webster was seen by voters as a pinnacle of the virtues of a public servant, one in which they could place their confidence, trust and vote. In addition, the political elites in the district and state, including former governor Jeb Bush, touted Webster as 'one of them' a proven leader who shares their conservative values. The prophetic message of the campaign was best provided by Rep. Chris Van Hollen (D) of Maryland, who headed the House Democrats' campaign operations. He cautioned Grayson, "[j]ust make sure your style goes over as well with your constituents as it may with a lot of people outside of the district."[35] Clearly, this was a message Alan Grayson missed and Daniel Webster understood.

NOTES

1. Richard J. Feeno Jr., "U.S. House Members in Their Constituencies: An Exploration," *American Political Science Review,* 71, no. 3, (September 1977): 883–918.

2. United States Census, "2005–2009 American Community Survey 5-Year Estimates: Population 1 Year and Over in the United States," factfinder.census.gov/servlet/DatasetMainPageServlet?_lang=en&_ts=311768292570&_ds_name=ACS_2009_5YR_G00_&_program= (accessed December 30, 2010).

3. United States Census, "2005–2009 American Community Survey 5-Year Estimates."

4. United States Census, "2005–2009."

5. United States Census, "2005–2009."

6. Chloe Cotton, "Rose Report: Redistricting in Florida: Part Two," rosereport.org/20100216/redistricting-in-florida-part-two/ (accessed December 31, 2010).

7. Florida Department of State: Division of Elections, General Election: County Voter Registration by Congressional District (Report) (Tallahassee, FL: Florida Department of State, October 4, 2010).

8. CNN Politics, "Election Center: The Results," www.cnn.com/ELECTION/2010/results/full/#H (accessed December 31, 2010).

9. Alex Isenstadt, and John Bresnahan, "Republicans Target Six Vulnerable Democrats," Politico, www.politico.com/news/stories/1010/43309.html (accessed December 31, 2010).

10. David Mayhew, *Congress: The Electoral Connection,* (New Haven, CT: Yale University Press, 1974).

11. Scott Harris, Big Shift by Analyst in Alan Grayson-Dan Webster Race, www.cfnews13.com/article/news/2010/october/158012/Big-shift-by-analyst-in-Alan-Grayson-Dan-Webster-race (accessed December 31, 2010).

12. King World News Broadcast, "Alan Grayson," kingworldnews.com/kingworldnews/Broadcast/Entries/2009/10/2_Congressman_Alan_Grayson.html (accessed December 31, 2010).

13. Alan Grayson, "Congressman Alan Grayson: Proudly Serving Florida's 8th District" *Biography,* alangrayson.house.gov/Biography/ (accessed January 2, 2011).

14. Marin Cogan, "Pajamas Government," *The New Republic,* www.tnr.com/article/politics/pajamas-government (accessed December 31, 2010).

15. David M. Herszenhorn, "Alan Grayson, the Liberal's Problem Child," *New York Times,* www.nytimes.com/2009/11/01/weekinreview/01herszenhorn.html?_r=2 (accessed December 31, 2010).

16. Daniel Webster for Congress, "About Daniel," www.electwebster.com/about-daniel-webster (accessed December 31, 2010).

17. Daniel Webster for Congress, "About Daniel."

18. Tim Padgett, "Florida's 8th Congressional District: Alan Grayson vs. Daniel Webster, Time.com, www.time.com/time/specials/packages/article/0,28804,2019138_2019132_2019776,00.html (accessed December 31, 2010).

19. Richard J. Feeno Jr., "U.S. House Members in Their Constituencies: An Exploration."

20. Jane Mansbridge, "Rethinking Representation," *American Political Science Review,* 97, no. 4, (2003): 515–529.

21. Mansbridge, "Rethinking Representation," p. 516.

22. Edmund Burke, *The Works of the Right Honorable Edmund Burke*, Vol. 2, (Boston: Little Brown, 1792), p. 19.

23. Mansbridge, "Rethinking Representation."

24. Daniel Webster for Congress, "About Daniel."

25. United States Federal Election Commission, "Campaign Finance Reports and Data/Data Search/Summary Reports Search," www.fec.gov/finance/disclosure/srssea.shtml (accessed December 31, 2010).

26. Alex Isenstadt, and John Bresnahan, "Republicans Target Six Vulnerable Democrats."

27. Stephanie Condon, "'Taliban Dan' Ad Spurs Debate over Dan Webster," CBS News.com www.cbsnews.com/8301-503544_162-20017949-503544.html (accessed December 31, 2010).

28. Scott Harris, "Big Shift by Analyst in Alan Grayson-Dan Webster Race," www.cfnews13.com/article/news/2010/october/158012/Big-shift-by-analyst-in-Alan-Grayson-Dan-Webster-race (accessed December 31, 2010).

29. Mike Lafferty, "Dan Webster Will Not Debate Alan Grayson," blogs. orlandosentinel.com/orlando_opinionators/2010/10/dan-webster-will-not-debate-alan-grayson.html (accessed December 31, 2010).

30. Alex Isenstadt, "Grayson Compares Foe to Taliban," Politico, blogs. orlandosentinel.com/orlando_opinionators/2010/10/dan-webster-will-not-debate-alan-grayson.html (accessed December 31, 2010).

31. Florida Department of State: Division of Elections, General Election Official Results: United States Representative," (Tallahassee, FL: Florida Department of State, November 2, 2010), enight.elections.myflorida.com/Index.asp?ElectionDate= 11/2/2010&DATAMODE= (accessed December 31, 2010).

32. Eric Kleefeld, "Grayson Explains What It Means To Be a Democrat: 'We Have A Conscience,'" tpmdc.talkingpointsmemo.com/2009/10/grayson-explains-what-it-means-to-be-a-democrat-we-have-a-conscience.php (accessed December 31, 2010).

33. Bernie Becker, "Pelosi Plays Down Grayson Remark," The Caucus: The Politics and Government Blog of The Times, October 1, 2009, thecaucus.blogs. nytimes.com/2009/10/01/pelosi-plays-down-grayson-remark/ (accessed December 31, 2010).

34. Mansbridge, "Rethinking Representation."

35. David M. Herszenhorn, "Alan Grayson, the Liberal's Problem Child."

Chapter 3

Illinois District 14 Race (Hultgren v. Foster)

A National Referendum against the President and Incumbents

Jeffrey Ashley and Joshua Whitney

Randy Hultgren
Party: Republican
Age: 44
Sex: Male
Race: Caucasian
Religion: Christian
Education: Ph.D., (Chicago-Kent College of Law, 1993) B.A. (Bethel College, 1988)
Occupation: Attorney; Investment Advisor
Political Experience: Member, DuPage County Board (1994–99); Illinois State House of Representatives (1999–2007); Illinois State Senate (2007–2010)

Bill Foster
Party: Democrat
Age: 54
Sex: Male
Race: Caucasian
Religion: Not Stated
Education: Ph.D., Physics (Harvard, 1984); B.S. (University of Wisconsin, 1975)
Occupation: Cofounder, Electronic Theater Controls (1975); Scientist, Fermi Lab (1984) *Political Experience:* U.S. House of Representatives (2008–2011)

The 14th Congressional District has historically been recognized as one of disparate political ideals. While it has shown traditional Republican views more common in the central and southern parts of the state, it also maintains strong Democratic ties to Chicago and other urban areas. This district has seen significant growth that has changed the political balance as well as the demographics of the region in general. Though the district encompasses large rural areas in the west, it also has seen major growth in Kendall County and the eastern urban areas. In the past, this district stayed relatively true to its downstate identity and roots. While the district has often been represented by Republicans, changing demographics suggest that this particular seat could be in-flux for the foreseeable future.

CHARACTERISTICS OF THE DISTRICT

Party Balance

Despite more recent events, this district has been a Republican stronghold for many decades. It has traditional ties to the Republican Party that stretch back to the Nineteenth Century and has remained one of the strongest areas of Republican support for nearly the entire twentieth century.[1] Though it has voted strongly for Republican presidents in the past, scoring an R +1 on the Cook Partisan Voting Index, it went strongly for Barack Obama in the 2008 elections in addition to supporting a Democrat for its representative.[2] This change is not, however, guaranteed to last given the strong Republican support in the area and its frequent support of Republican gubernatorial and

Figure 3.1   Illinois Congressional District 14

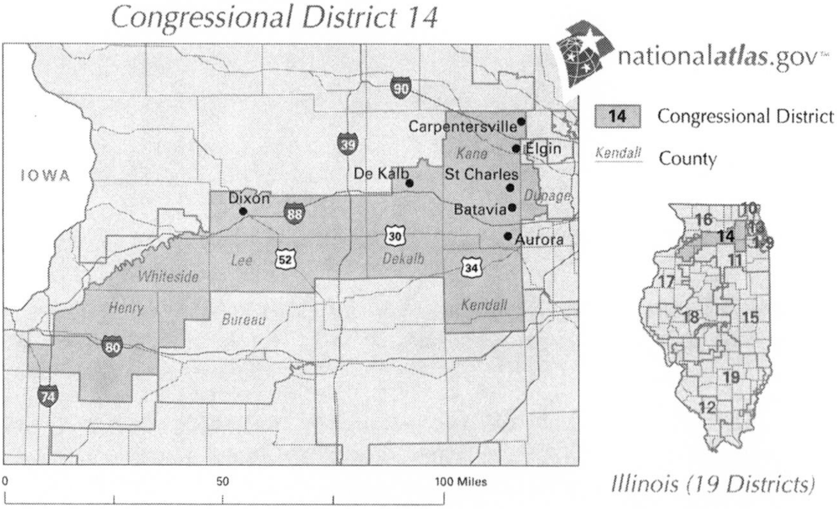

presidential candidates. It also could be vulnerable to re-districting as Illinois lost a congressional seat after the 2010 Census was published.

Electoral and Voting History

Former Speaker of the House Dennis Hastert (R-IL) loomed large over the district's political scene for many years. He served, accidentally as some would have it, from 1999–2007 and maintained the dominance of the Republican Party in this district with little challenge. His tenure as Speaker, the longest in history for a Republican, meant that the district gained significant access to pork barrel projects and this deepened GOP support. The demographics of the region have complicated this support however. In recent years, Kendall County has enjoyed tremendous growth and the population has changed its characteristics. Despite considerable Republican dominance, this district has shown some signs of growing Democratic support.

Demographic Character of the Electorate

The 14th District is predominantly white and middle class, though the white racial composition has slipped significantly from 80.8 to 68.7 percent in the last few years.[3] It also has a large upper middle class with a median income of over $67,000. While the district has also enjoyed population growth over 20 percent, much of this growth has come from increases in the Hispanic population. This also means that it's the fastest growing district in Illinois and could assume more importance given the loss of a congressional district due to changing national demographics. While this growth has certainly made the district more important politically, it has not meant that the district has lost the 'small town' feel that attracts many of its newcomers. In fact, the 14th District still draws many from the city of Chicago and other parts of the state due to its high number of white collar jobs and its higher performing schools.[4]

Major Urban Areas and Employment/Occupational Characteristics

The eight counties that comprise the 14th District stretch from the outskirts of Chicago encompassing Kane, Kendall and DuPage counties to the western part of the state within a few miles of the Mississippi River in Henry County. This geographically large district also has diverse industries contributing to its prosperity. Health care and education occupy the largest section of the economy at over 18 percent with manufacturing following close behind at 16.5 percent.[5] It is worth noting that manufacturing has continued to decline in this area; falling nearly one percentage point between 2006 and 2008. Despite this downturn, manufacturing is still a potent force in occupations with 60.2 percent white collar, 22.8 percent blue collar and 16 percent service oriented.[6]

The cities of Elgin and Aurora make up the largest concentrations of manufacturing in the district. Aurora has long surpassed Rockford as the second largest city in Illinois with a population of 172,950 that continues to rise. Aurora has also surpassed Rockford's manufacturing capacity and boasts lower unemployment. The district also contains some of the most productive soil in the world and includes the city of DeKalb where Northern Illinois University is located and the Fox River Valley, which is home to many manufacturing areas.

Key Voting Blocks

The largest voting block in this district, as with many others, is the unaffiliated (independent) voter. Despite being a Republican stronghold, historically, this district has undergone changes that brought a Democrat to office for the first time in decades in 2008. It also voted strongly for Barack Obama for president. Part of the changing demographics is explained by the increase in the Hispanic population in the urban areas such as Elgin and Aurora.[7] This population growth in Kane County alone now encompasses 27.7 percent of the overall population. As in 2008, this expansion of Hispanic voters has importance due to their identity as swing voters as well as a group that is greatly interested in immigration politics and policy.

THE CANDIDATES

Bill Foster

Bill Foster had surprised many with his narrow win of this district in the special election of March 2008 and his victory in the general election later in November. Foster's victory was surprising not only because the 14th District had traditionally been a Republican stronghold but also because he knew that his chances for victory were slim.[8] Despite the odds, the Fermilab scientist defeated his multiple Democratic rivals in the primary and narrowly defeated Jim Oberweis to win the seat. Foster had gained significant aid in his campaign from Senator Richard Durbin (D-IL) and campaign contributions from the Democratic Congressional Campaign Committee (DCCC). He also gained timely support from Senator Barack Obama as his bid for the White House gathered strength in mid 2008.[9] After Foster won the seat, he attained a seat on the Financial Services Committee where he supported the financial bailout and approved restored funding for Fermilab. Foster also secured earmarks for his district, something Hastert had proved adept at as well, in the form of education funding totaling $100,000 in 2010.[10]

Foster had tried to work as a centrist Democrat, fully aware that far left leaning politics could negatively affect him in subsequent elections. His support of small business, through the Small Business Jobs Act and his aid in securing funding for Northern Illinois University, which was targeted to also create jobs, showed more dedication to his district rather than to a particular partisan ideology.[11] This particular funding was connected to the National Recovery Act, which Foster had voted for. In many ways, Foster's political life was tied to that of his fellow Illinois politician, Barack Obama.

Obama's meteoric rise to national prominence and the White House had helped numerous Democrats win seats in the 111th Congress. Bill Foster was one of those who had garnered support from Obama's campaign in the form of votes and increased funding from the DCCC. As President Obama's fortunes rose or fell nationally, it became increasingly likely that Democratic politicians whom had ridden his coattails would have to deal with the consequences in November of 2010. As the race began in earnest, multiple issues such as the healthcare debate, the stimulus legislation and the rising Tea Party movement exerted significant pressures on an incumbent Congressman whom had won a race in a traditionally Republican district. The national mood did not appear promising.

Randy Hultgren

The Republican Primary for the 14th District assumed many aspects of the 2008 primary with two prominent names battling, not only for the congressional seat, but also for the national goals of the Republican party; repudiation of President Obama's agenda and policies. Randy Hultgren and Ethan Hastert emerged as the two Republican favored candidates for the primary. While they shared similar views on many issues, the differences in experience proved decisive to victory.

Ethan Hastert brought his father's prominent name back to 14th District politics. It was thought at the time that his name and the known leanings of the district could help raise larger sums of money for the general election campaign. Hastert also had to keep some distance from his father's name due to controversy over financial benefits he had received after he left office.[12] Hastert also had to overcome inexperience; he had never served as an elected official. Name recognition and its' financial benefits were his most prominent advantages.

Randy Hultgren, by contrast, had a long career of public service in the Illinois General Assembly. He had taken an early stand against the national healthcare legislation and became a Tea Party favorite fairly early in the contest. Despite this, Hultgren did suffer from lack of name recognition and, subsequently, had more difficulty in raising funds equal to his less-experienced opponent.[13] Campaign funding would continue to be an issue for Hultgren throughout the primary and general election. Hultgren trumpeted his record in the General Assembly in contrast to Hastert's inexperience. He also allegedly engaged in back-handed tactics versus Hastert by suggesting the young hopeful had engaged in human trafficking; something he later apologized for.[14] Despite this, both candidates agreed on several issues.

Healthcare, job creation and government spending were the most prominent issues during the primary. Each candidate agreed that the national healthcare policy was not needed, that the federal stimulus package was a failure and that the United States needed to refocus its efforts in the war in Afghanistan.[15] While Hastert had to battle against his inexperience, Hultgren had to negotiate around the budgetary disaster that Illinois had endured for many years. His involvement in the General Assembly brought both rewards in the form of experience and baggage due to the financial instability of the state; something that could potentially be magnified by the public's anger over spending in Washington D.C. Both candidates identified job creation as a top priority, but they differed on how to go about it. Hastert stood against any sort of tax credits or programs to stimulate the economy opting for non-government interference in business affairs. Hultgren opted for extension of tax credits to businesses to help stimulate new job growth.[16]

The primary was less close than one might imagine given the newcomer status that each candidate possessed. Hastert's campaign financing became one issue that caused him considerable trouble; he failed to report contributions from an employee of his father.[17] In the end, Hultgren's experience trumped Hastert's name recognition and contributions and brought him to victory with a margin of 34,735, 55 percent, to 28,745, 45 percent.[18] Despite the controversy over the human trafficking charges leveled at his law firm, Hastert pledged to support Hultgren's bid for the district seat. This had the added advantage of shoring up financial support against a Democratic opponent that had already raised considerable funds.[19]

CAMPAIGN ISSUES

Taxes, immigration, government spending, Social Security, concerns over corruption, and the rising Tea Party movement were identified early as the key issues for this race. Similar to the last 14th District elections between Oberweis and Foster, this election also showed itself to be a proxy for the national elections at large where anti-incumbency became a driving force among the electorate. In February, Gallup showed that the two parties were virtually tied with one another in terms of preference of candidates for Congress.[20] The American electorate was also decidedly negative in its views of Congress in general. A wave of anti "big government," which increased dramatically after the unpopular bank bailouts and the debate over healthcare, had far reaching consequences for the 2010 elections in the form of the Tea Party movement. Gallup also showed, early in the campaign, that voter enthusiasm was highest amongst conservative voters across the nation.[21] Republican voter turnout had been low in the 2008 race and had been one of many reasons why Oberweis lost. In the 14th District, therefore, higher Republican turnout and the national mood concerning the economic downturn had direct local consequences.

Healthcare

Bill Foster had voted for the Patient Protection and Affordable Care Act and was proud of achieving this goal of President Obama's. Foster defended his support by pointing out that it would help protect families and small businesses from increasing costs.[22] Randy Hultgren took a far different view of the new law. He believed it to be badly flawed and hurtful to small businesses, especially the 1099 provision that involved providing reports to the IRS for any transactions over $600.[23] Hultgren frequently stated that he would have voted against the new law and, were he victorious, would vote to repeal it in the new Congress. The health care act also met mixed reactions in Illinois amongst the voters. As the campaign moved on, the specifics of the health care reform became less of an issue than the idea that the federal government was spending beyond its means; especially at a time of increasing unemployment.

The Economy

The state of the economy was the most important issue of the 2010 elections. Americans were concerned over the economy more than healthcare, the budget deficit or terrorism.[24] The fact that unemployment kept rising, even more so in Illinois, encouraged the view that Congress's efforts had been largely unsuccessful at best. Job growth in Illinois was negligible in the first half of 2010.[25] Hultgren attacked Foster's statements about lower unemployment in Illinois as "living in a fantasy world" and that the policies in Washington created by "liberals" were the reason for one in ten from the 14th District being out of work.[26]

Foster, the former small businessman, had tried to defend his support of the TARP funding and bailouts; this was an area that received special attention by Hultgren. Hultgren stressed that bailouts of Fannie Mae and banks were doing more to damage the economy and raise the federal debt. He argued instead for cutting taxes, especially the higher ones on business as a better strategy for economic growth.[27] While this was not a view that Hultgren shared alone, it was echoed in a large number of other districts, it was in direct contrast to Foster's views and actions that supported government spending on recovery and ending the so-called Bush tax cuts. He also stressed that job creation was the area that Congress should have focused on above all other issues.

Social Security

Social Security has been a congressional issue for many elections. In 2010, there were new fears that the fund would be depleted or privatized. Foster tried to assure retirees that Social Security would be made secure and that he would always vote against privatization stating that "retirees need an income that they can depend on."[28] Hultgren agreed with Foster on the need to protect Social Security, but that Democratic spending and bailouts had jeopardized the future of meeting the needs of future retirees. Later, both candidates attempted to clarify their positions but actually succeeded in contradicting themselves. Foster said that small changes could be needed to save Social Security and that small cuts in benefits could be necessary.[29] Hultgren came under fire for a previous interview, conducted in December 2009, which showed his possible support *for* privatization of benefits or raising the retirement age.[30] Hultgren later tried to retract these statements maintaining that he did not favor any cuts to the program. He maintained that the current spending levels of congressional bills were the greatest threat to the solvency of Social Security.

Immigration

Illegal immigration and the U.S. immigration policy had been a major issue during the previous campaign between Oberweis and Foster. By 2010, a new law in Arizona and a lack of coherent policy at the national level meant that this issue was still important and controversial. Foster had embraced a stance of reform for current laws while also pushing for legal application for citizenship by all immigrants and punishments for those breaking the law or businesses that employed illegal workers.[31] Foster did not, however provide specific solutions for the immigration debate; he was not the only Democrat nationally to have trouble with this issue.

Hultgren took the view that border security needed better funding and support. He also disagreed with the idea of raising the cap on legal immigration rather than tackling the issue of the large numbers of undocumented workers already in the country.[32] Neither candidate made major campaign promises in regard to this issue especially given the strength of the Hispanic voters in the district where the issue was a complicated one. Later in the campaign, these rather vague views were never truly clarified. Both Foster and Hultgren avoided committing strongly to an immigration policy. Both advanced the idea of cracking down on illegal hiring by businesses and that immigrants needed to learn English. Foster also supported the idea of a national "ID" card to provide verification of citizenship.[33] Hultgren, by contrast, was uncommitted to any hard-line stance other than to improve border security and streamlining the current bureaucracy involved with legal immigration. As is apparent, each candidate reflected the split in his respective party over immigration. In the end, the attention paid to this issue may have been inconsequential as this issue lost its' priority in polls conducted near Election Day.[34]

Corruption

Corruption was less a national issue for this district than it was a local one. During the previous two years, Illinois governor Rod Blagojevich had made headlines due to his appointment of Roland Burris to fill Barack Obama's previous Senate seat and his own charges of corruption and malfeasance that resulted in a federal corruption trial during the campaign. Illinois voters had soured considerably on much of the political landscape both at the state and federal levels. While there were no corruption charges leveled at Foster or Hultgren, in real terms it meant that each candidate had a high level of skepticism that they had to overcome; especially when it came to previous votes.

The budgetary situation in Illinois, one of the worst in the nation, also became an issue for Hultgren. He had to defend himself during the election for many of the budget votes that had taken place in the Illinois general assembly.[35] He had voted against income and property taxes but had also supported the smoking ban and supported the capital bill that was to be funded by expanded video gambling; something that Republicans had traditionally been against. His social views were not always in agreement with the voters of Illinois either: he had voted against medical marijuana and stem cell research while supporting a moment of silence in schools and vouchers for students to attend private schools.[36]

Foster had to defend his votes as well. While in Congress, he had voted for the controversial health care reform law, federal stimulus package, and the bank bailouts. Foster defended his votes by explaining that if TARP and health care reform were not passed then the increased costs to the nation would have been far worse.[37] He countered those that disagreed with the spending in Washington by stating his opposition to the budget plans that had been submitted during his term. Foster was very conscious of people's concerns over the national debt, and he emphasized that he wanted to see this addressed before he would support a budget plan.[38] Despite this concern, Foster had a tough road to travel as American confidence and approval for Congress had continued to dwindle to the point where only about one quarter of the electorate thought that the 111th Congress had actually accomplished positive legislation.[39]

CAMPAIGN STRATEGY

Almost as soon as Hultgren had won the primary, Democratic criticism began to be leveled at him for his stances and past voting record. The DCCC started the negative campaigning with an attack on Hultgren's views on taxes; something that was already identified as a key voting issue. The DCCC claimed, following charges used by Hastert, that Hultgren's real record included voting for tax *increases* in Illinois rather than any cuts.[40] As the recession continued to take its toll and criticism mounted over government spending and the national healthcare plan it became clear that the issues of 2008, such as the Iraq War, would assume less importance than economic issues in 2010.

Foster chose to stand on the successes, as he saw them, which had been attained over the past two years. TARP funding, bank bailouts, health care reform, and a strategy to end American involvement in Iraq were, despite public consternation, notable achievements. As an incumbent, Foster knew that he could rely on larger funding than in the previous election. As a former small businessman, he was conscious of the need to explain his votes to the district and couch them in terms that would address these concerns. Hultgren, based on the lack of popularity of this particular Congress, needed to attack many of those same votes to show that he understood the frustration of Illinois voters; regardless of their views on key legislation. The Tea Party movement helped to provide a new avenue of attack for Hultgren, and he embraced it accordingly. The fact that Illinois was facing increasing job losses only helped to feed these attacks. Both candidates recognized that foreign policy issues, such as Afghanistan, were not going to have the same importance with the dire financial situation at both the national and state levels.

Media

Both candidates realized that the stakes were quite high for this district, and that it would be a close race. Subsequently, negative campaigning took over almost immediately. Not only were there attacks by the DCCC on Hultgren on the day after his victory in the primary, as mentioned above, there were negative campaign commercials and charges leveled throughout the campaign.

Unlike the previous election, when Oberweis and Foster had agreed late in the contest to restrict negative campaigning, no such détente was reached in 2010. Each candidate used the one year anniversary of the passage of the federal stimulus package to highlight their differences on taxes.

Hultgren stated that this anniversary showed Democrats to be out of touch with the voters in Illinois by increasing spending, imposing an energy tax and discussing transfer of Guantanamo Bay prisoners to Illinois rather than focus on job creation and debt relief.[41] Foster defended his votes by saying that the increased spending had helped the people of his district, regardless of the increased borrowing that could result from cash-strapped state governments. Foster also tried to emphasize that the stimulus package had helped to halt job losses, or at least to prevent larger losses were it not passed.[42] While he recognized that it was not a perfect solution to the financial crisis, Foster maintained that it was a positive development. It would seem that the voters were as split in their view of this as they were on other issues. The economy remained the top issue for the campaign up to Election Day.[43]

While campaign commercials retained their mostly typical negative character throughout the campaign, as with 2008 the "robo-calls" and flyers exposed the very negative tenor to the campaign and provided less than savory views of the two candidates. Independent firms conducted anonymous phone polls in the 14th District that drew fire from Foster's campaign. The group We Ask America had conducted a poll that showed a majority of voters were unfavorable to Foster over his vote in favor of the health care reform bill.[44] Though it was difficult to prove that the data had been manipulated, the tactics were hardly unique. Though each candidate tried to appear positive during the campaign, their comments and the media scrutiny of this close race meant that each statement and action would eventually become a campaign issue; even if only for a moment.

Foster attacked Hultgren as in favor of "toxic assets" that helped to lead to the housing market meltdown in 2008–2010. This charge came from Hultgren being connected to sales involving the firm Performance Trust TALF Fund, Ltd. The firm had engaged in real-estate sales and Foster characterized these as contributory to the housing meltdown with Hultgren gaining a salary from the same firm.[45] While Hultgren denied any wrongdoing, he claimed to be an ambassador for the company and had nothing to do with its business practices, he ran ads claiming that Foster's ads were lies, and the negative tone continued. There was no evidence of any wrongdoing by Hultgren in connection to this firm.

Hultgren had to defend himself, similarly to the primary race, from illegal campaign contributions. A $2000 campaign donation made from Hultgren's state campaign was made to his congressional campaign, and this is illegal under federal law. Foster's campaign lost no time in attacking Hultgren for this contribution.[46] Hultgren apologized for the mistake and treated it as such; the money was simply returned. This episode was indicative of the race as regards funding, however. Earlier in the year, both Foster and Hultgren had taken shots at one another over campaign contributions: Foster was attacked for a donation made by Charles Rangel (D-NY) during his corruption investigation.[47] The Republican Party in Illinois also did its best to portray Foster as another supporter of Speaker Nancy Pelosi (D-CA) and charged that he had voted with her over 90 percent of the time.

Financing

Campaign financing was one of the most important aspects to this campaign, though not in conventional ways. Foster managed to out-raise Hultgren for nearly the entire campaign.[48] Despite this, the actual amounts that each candidate had spent and raised were quite closer. Early in the campaign, Hultgren benefited greatly from the perception that he could beat Foster and due to the unpopular votes that Foster had supported. Hultgren out-raised Foster by over $100,000 in the first quarter of the campaign.[49] Foster had to make a special loan to his campaign and carried considerable more debt as the campaign dragged on. As the campaign neared the final month, Foster started to out-raise and outspend Hultgren in the district, though Hultgren saw increases as the end neared.

The various PACs that supported each candidate helped to make this race one of the most highly funded in Illinois to the tune of over $4 million raised between Foster and Hultgren. As the election drew near, and Democrats realized just how vulnerable this seat truly was, millions of dollars poured in to try and shore up Foster's campaign.[50] The DCCC also attempted to shore up support, in conjunction with national efforts, by enlisting Michelle Obama to stump for Illinois Democrats that were in danger of losing seats. The first lady attempted to galvanize support for Foster and several other Democratic hopefuls such as Senate candidate Alexi Giannoulias.[51]

Grassroots Efforts

No discussion of the 2010 campaigns is complete without mentioning the impact of the Tea Party movement. This grass-roots movement, though it had significant funding from interest groups, made a point of attacking incumbent candidates throughout the country. Bill Foster, due to his votes for health care reform, TARP and bank bailouts, was a target in Illinois especially due to his relatively close win over Oberweis two years earlier. His support for many of the policies of President Obama also made him a target. Randy Hultgren made great use of this anger; drawing support from conservative blogs and benefiting from Tea Party endorsements.[52] As Election Day approached, polling showed that this movement had at least achieved one thing: many races were very close with the distinct possibility of the Republicans taking control of at least one house of Congress.[53]

ELECTION RESULTS

After all of the punditry, controversy over campaign contributions, mud-slinging, and the Tea Party, the voters of Illinois had their say in the 14th District. Despite endorsement of Bill Foster by the many newspapers in the region, *The Chicago Tribune* and *Chicago Daily Herald* among them, Randy Hultgren rode the wave of anti-incumbency to a victory in Illinois. He won the contest by a margin of 51.4 percent to 45 percent or nearly 13,000 votes. Bill Foster had been unable to overcome all of the obstacles to his reelection regardless of the support of the White House, endorsements by major and smaller newspapers and a nearly two-to-one advantage in campaign financing. The financial situation of the 14th District, and the nation at-large, was far too negative to overcome.

Unlike in 2008, when the groundswell of support for Barack Obama translated to success for many other Democrats; the 2010 elections saw an opposite effect. President Obama's approval had declined throughout the year. Regardless of whether or not the nation's woes were the fault of the President and his party, voters had come to believe that another "change" was necessary in Washington and incumbents were the favored targets. It was no secret that Democratic seats in Congress were vulnerable.[54] When the election ended, this was proven beyond a doubt.

NOTES

1. Michael Barone with Richard E. Cohen, *Almanac of American Politics 2010*, 526.
2. Barone and Cohen, *Almanac of American Politics 2010*, 525.
3. Barone and Cohen, *Almanac of American Politics 2010*, 526.
4. Leslie Mann, "Oswego working to keep small town charm," *Chicago Tribune*, June 19, 2008.

5. United States Bureau of the Census, 2008 American Community Survey. factfinder.census.gov/servlet/ADPTable?_bm=y&-geo_id=50000US1714&-qr_name=ACS_2008_3YR_G00_DP3YR3&-context=adp&-ds_name=&-tree_id=3308&-_lang=en&-redoLog=false&-format=

6. United States Bureau of the Census, 2008 American Community Survey.

7. United States Bureau of the Census, 2008 American Community Survey. www.factfinder.census.gov/servlet/ADPTable?_bm=y&-geo_id=16000US1703012&-qr_name=ACS_2009_5YR_G00_DP5YR5&-context=adp&-ds_name=&-tree_id=5309&-_lang=en&-redoLog=false&-format=

8. Barone, 527.

9. Barone, 527.

10. James Fuller, "Foster delivers education message at Glenwood School, a few packages," *Chicago Daily Herald,* January 8, 2010.

11. U.S. Congressman Bill Foster, "Rep. Foster helps to Create 300 Jobs, Grow Local Economy," September 13, 2010, foster.house.gov.

12. James Fuller, "Hastert, Hultgren carry GOP hope in 14th Congressional District," *Chicago Daily Herald,* January 31, 2010.

13. Fuller, "Hastert, "Hultgren carry GOP"

14. Fuller, "Hastert, "Hultgren carry GOP"

15. Fuller, "Hastert, "Hultgren carry GOP"

16. James Fuller, "14th District candidates disagree on job creation," *Chicago Daily Herald,* January 18, 2010.

17. Jameel Naqvi, "Fox Valley voters to decide primary races," February 1, 2010.

18. James Fuller, "Hastert's son loses race to Hultgren," *Chicago Daily Herald,* February 3, 2010.

19. Fuller, "Hastert's son loses race to Hultgren,"

20. Gallup, "Parties Tied in 2010 Midterm Election Preferences," February 9, 2010.

21. Gallup, "Conservatives Most Enthusiastic About Voting In 2010 Midterm," May 18, 2010.

22. "Rep. Foster Announces Health Insurance Reform Provisions That Will Immediately Go Into Effect," Bill Foster. Gov, March 23, 2010.

23. James Fuller, "Hultgren, Marks take firm stance on repealing new health care reform law," *Chicago Daily Herald,* August 8, 2010.

24. Gallup, "Voters Rate Economy For Top Issue of 2010," April 8, 2010.

25. USA Today, "Recession's effects hit majority in U.S.," September 26, 2010.

26. James Fuller, "14th District candidates speak out on unemployment," *Chicago Daily Herald,* June 26, 2010.

27. James Fuller, "14th Congressional seat candidates' questionnaire," *Chicago Daily Herald,* October 27, 2010.

28. James Fuller, "14th Congressional candidates jump into Social Security debate," *Chicago Daily Herald,* August 17, 2010.

29. James Fuller, "Foster, Hultgren try to clear up positions on Social Security," *Chicago Daily Herald,* August 25, 2010.

30. Fuller, "Foster, Hultgren try to clear up positions on Social Security,"

31. James Fuller, "Immigration reform an issue to avoid for some 14th Cong. candidates," *Chicago Daily Herald,* September 18, 2010.

32. Fuller, "Immigration reform an issue to avoid for some 14th Cong. candidates,"

33. James Fuller, "Foster, Hultgren expound on immigration stances," *Chicago Daily Herald,* October 24, 2010.

34. Gallup, "Economy Top Issue for Voters; Size of Gov't May Be More Pivotal," October 26, 2010.

35. James Fuller, "Hultgren explains budget role, unpopular votes," *Chicago Daily Herald,* October 23, 2010.

36. Fuller, "Hultgren explains budget role, unpopular votes,"

37. James Fuller, "Foster explains unpopular votes at session with business owners," *Chicago Daily Herald,* April 8, 2010.

38. Fuller, "Foster explains unpopular votes at session with business owners,"

39. Gallup, "One in 4 Say Congress Accomplished More Than Usual This Year," October 29, 2010.

40. James Fuller, "Democrats waste no time in launching attack on Hultgren," *Chicago Daily Herald,* February 3, 2010.

41. James Fuller, "Foster, Hultgren clash on impact of stimulus in 14th district," *Chicago Daily Herald,* February 18, 2010.

42. Fuller, "Foster, Hultgren clash on impact of stimulus in 14th district,"

43. Gallup, "Economy Top Issue for Voters; Size of Gov't May Be More Pivotal,"

44. James Fuller, "Firm behind Foster health care phone poll won't apologize," *Chicago Daily Herald,* March 26, 2010.

45. James Fuller, "Getting to the bottom of Foster's 'toxic assets' claims about Hultgren," *Chicago Daily Herald,* October 2, 2010.

46. James Fuller, "Hultgren apologizes for illegal campaign contributions," *Chicago Daily Herald,* September 9, 2010.

47. Fuller, "Hultgren apologizes for illegal campaign contributions,"

48. James Fuller, "Foster outraises Hultgren in 14th District race," *Chicago Daily Herald,* October 18, 2010.

49. James Fuller, "Hultgren has best financial quarter, but still lagging behind Foster," *Chicago Daily Herald,* April 22, 2010.

50. Joseph Ryan and Ray Gibson, "National Democrats doubling down on two suburban congressional contests," *Chicago Tribune,* October 24, 2010.

51. Christi Parsons and Michael A. Memoli, "First Lady comes home for Democrats," *Chicago Tribune,* October 12, 2010.

52. Randy Hultgren for Congress.com.

53. Trisha Miller, "Hultgren Poll Shows Him Leading Foster in Illinois," *Roll Call,* October 6, 2010.

54. Associated Press, "Democrats fight to keep 3 Illinois Congressional seats," *Chicago Daily Herald,* November 2, 2010.

Chapter 4

Illinois District 11 Race (Kinzinger v. Halvorson)

A Freshman Incumbent Does Not Survive the Tsunami

William K. Hall

Adam Kinzinger
Party: Republican
Age: 32
Sex: Male
Race: Caucasian
Religion: Protestant
Occupation: Captain, U.S. Air Force
Political Experience: McLean County Board (1998–2003)

Debbie Halvorson
Party: Democrat
Age: 52
Sex: Female
Race: Caucasian
Religion: Lutheran
Occupation: Sales
Political Experience: Crete Township Clerk (1993–1996); Illinois State Senate (1997–2008); U.S. House of Representatives (2009–2011)

CHARACTERISTICS OF ILLINOIS DISTRICT 11

Party Balance

The eight-county 11th Congressional District of Illinois leans Republican. Several of the northern counties in the 11th are Republican strongholds, and there are substantial numbers of Republicans in each of the District's eight

Figure 4.1   Illinois Congressional District 11

Congressional District 11

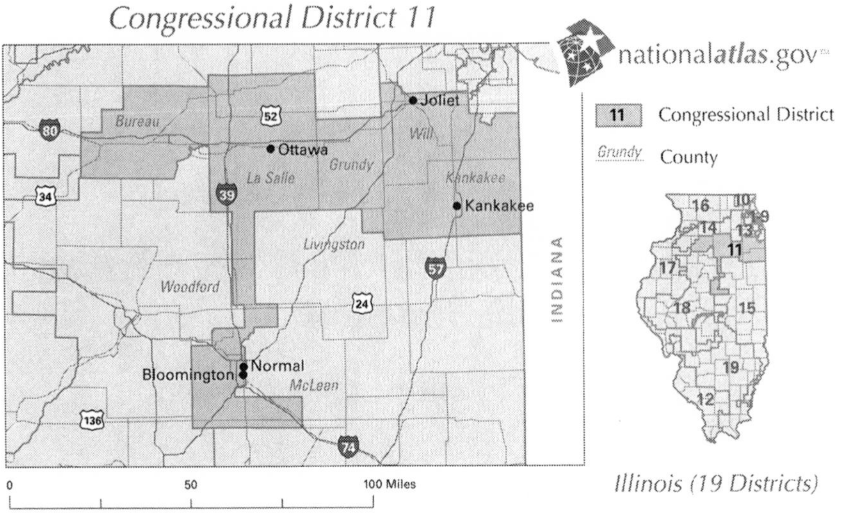

counties. Although the District leans Republican, it is not a district which can be taken for granted by GOP candidates.

Voting and Electoral History

The reapportionment of Illinois congressional districts in 1991 created the main elements of the present 11th District. The reapportionment of 2001 made it possible for Republicans to continue to elect a Republican to the 11th District House seat. The Illinois General Assembly, faced with the loss of one of the State's U.S. House seats opted to strengthen the electoral position of as many of the House incumbents as possible, regardless of party affiliation. Eighteen of the incumbents were either in the same political shape they had been in prior to the 2001 reapportionment or ended up in a stronger position, In order to "lose" a seat, two southern/central Illinois incumbents found themselves battling each other for the 19th seat, and Congressman John Shimkus (R-20th) dueled Congressman David Phelps (D-19th) to see who would be the 19th House member from Illinois. Shimkus won the battle of the incumbents.

For 14 years prior to the 2008 election, the 11th District was represented by Jerry Weller (R-Morris). Weller, first elected in the Republican wave election of 1994, decided not to seek reelection in 2008 because of questions raised over some Central American land deals. Over his seven successful election bids, Weller only once polled less than 55 percent of the vote, and in 2002, he garnered 64 percent of the vote.[1] Following Weller's retirement, Democrat Debbie Halvorson won the open seat in 2008 in the Obama/Democrat wave election of 2008.

President George W. Bush had carried the 11th twice and Barack Obama carried the 11th in 2008 with 53 percent of the vote.[2] That was well below his 62.7 percent for the State of Illinois.

Demographic Character of the Electorate

The 11th District is 80 percent white, 8 percent African-American, and 9.8 percent Latino. According to 2000 census data, the median household income for the District was above the U.S. median income.

The 11th District is partly suburban, partly exurban, and partly rural in character. The Chicago area commuters of Will and Kankakee counties, the rich and fertile farmland of the middle and southern part of the district, and the communities of Bloomington/Normal, headquarters for two of America's largest insurance companies and a state university illustrate the diversity of the 11th District.

Key Voting Blocs

The farm vote is important in the 11th, as is the vote of its union members and their families. Small businesses abound in the district, and there are many white collar jobs in the district.

Major Urban Areas and Employment/Occupational Characteristics

The District is 78 percent urban and 22 percent rural. Blue collar workers make up 28 percent of the workforce with white collar workers making up an additional 55.5 percent. The largest cities in the 11th include Joliet, Kankakee, Ottawa, and Bloomington/Normal.

THE CANDIDATES

Debbie Halvorson

Congresswoman Debbie Halvorson (D-Crete) was elected in 2008. Recruited by the national Democratic Party, she ran against Jerry Weber, who had no money, no name recognition, and no chance to be nominated. His primary election expenditures totaled $17,550.[3]

Halvorson, a former Mary Kay salesperson, had been the Township Clerk for Crete Township (1993–1996), and a member of the Illinois State Senate (1997–2008). She served as Majority Leader from 2005 until she left the State Senate to go to Washington.

The Republicans would have a three-candidate race to nominate someone for the open seat from the 11th. The winner was Tim Baldermann, Mayor of New Lenox and the Police Chief of Chicago Ridge. Baldermann would emerge from the February primary with 60 percent of the vote. However, he dropped out of the race in late February citing the unexpected time demands on him and the daunting task of raising significant campaign funds. Two months would pass before the Republicans settled on Marty Ozinga as the party's official nominee. It was hoped that the cement company magnate would be able to self-fund much of his campaign against Halvorson. Ozinga did provide nearly a third of his campaign war chest of $1,969,365.

Halvorson had decided to make the race in what would turn out to be a very good year for Democratic candidates running for Congress. She raised $2,317,193 for her campaign, more than half of that amount coming from PACs. Riding the Democratic wave, Halvorson would defeat Ozinga with 58 percent of the vote to Ozinga's 34 percent and 7 percent for Jason Wallace, Green Party candidate. Halvorson would run more strongly in the 11th than Barack Obama. He won only 53 percent of the vote in the 11th District while carrying his home state with 62.7 percent of the vote. Halvorson would carry all eight of the counties in the 11th District. That it is not easy for a Democrat to win a congressional election in the 11th is evident in comparing Halvorson's and Obama's vote total for the District.

Halvorson struck a moderate/liberal pose on many of the important issues facing the nation, and she strongly endorsed some sort of national healthcare plan. The sharp downtown in the economy came during the 2008 campaign, but how severe the downturn and how drastic the effects were not evident until late in the 2008 campaign season.

Upon taking her seat, Congresswoman Halvorson was appointed to serve on the Agriculture Committee, the Small Business Committee, and the Veterans' Affairs Committee. Her committee assignments seemed to position her well for the first campaign to retain her seat.

When she faced reelection, Congresswoman Halvorson would be an incumbent with the many blessings thought to accompany that station in political life. Her race to keep her seat in 2010, however, would not be fought in such positive circumstances as her first race in 2008. The nation had turned against the Democrats and the President, and Democrats across the nation were scrambling to keep their House and Senate seats. The "Yes We Can" euphoria of 2008 quickly gave way to the new economic and political realities of 2010.

Adam Kinzinger

Kinzinger, a 32-year old former Air Force pilot tossed his hat into the ring in 2009 in an effort to return the 11th District seat to the GOP. Twelve years before, while a 20-year old college student at Illinois State University, Kinzinger ran for the McLean County Board in 1998 and defeated a 12-year Democratic incumbent in the process. Following reelection in 2002, he would resign from the Board in 2003 to enlist in the Air Force where he served in the Air Force Special Ops, the Air Combat Command, the Air Mobility Command, and the Air National Guard.

In 2007, he was credited with saving the life of a young woman who was being violently attacked on a street in Milwaukee. According to his campaign biography, Kinzinger wrestled a knife away from the young woman's attacker and pinned him to the ground until the police arrived.

In the 2010 Republican primary, Kinzinger would face four opponents. Two of the four were underfunded (one raised $13,799 and the other $6,208). The other two candidates in the Republican primary reported raising no money for their campaigns. Kinzinger finished the primary with 63.7 percent of the vote. Dave White came in second with 10.4 percent of the vote, followed by David McAloon with 9.6 percent, Henry W. Meers, Jr., with 9.0 percent and Darrel Miller with 7.3 percent.[4] Although the primary competition was not much of a problem for Kinzinger, the fact that there were candidates to defeat on the road to winning his party's nomination gave Kinzinger the legitimate excuse he needed to get out and campaign throughout the district.

CAMPAIGN ISSUES

Jobs

Like several hundred other congressional districts, the Illinois 11th was hard hit in terms of unemployment. A number of factories and manufacturing companies cut back on their workforce numbers. Some closed. White collar employees were as hard hit by job losses as factory workers. Companies were cutting back, not expanding. Unemployment in the District topped 10 percent. Republican congressional candidates across the nation argued that unemployment was as bad as it was because both Congress and the Obama Administration had spent too little time creating jobs. The attack on the Democratic efforts to deal with job losses and high unemployment and the personal misery such numbers created was a telling one in that Democrats controlled both ends of Pennsylvania Avenue, making it very difficult to assign blame elsewhere. The economic downturn had proven to be much more difficult to reverse and much slower to respond to government efforts to right the nation's economic ship.

Television commercials that aired in the 11th District were similar to commercials aired in other districts and states. In this case, Halvorson was blamed for the entirety of the unemployment problem in Illinois. No matter that she represented only 1/19 of the State's people. It was an argument with legs, and it gained traction in the 11th District.

Government Spending

Many Americans and many Illinoisans were upset by the various spending programs advocated and passed by the Obama Administration. The $787 billion stimulus recovery package was said by some to be legislation the government could not afford.

Illinois, with many roads and bridges in serious need of replacement or repair, felt that if the government was intent on spending serious amounts of money in a stimulus package, more should have gone to infrastructure improvements. The stimulus package became one part of a larger picture that included bailouts for banks (that one really grated on some 11th District residents), the TARP program, and the cash-for-clunkers program that suggested the federal government was spending a lot of money that it did not have and that the bill for each of those programs and other spending programs would have to paid by citizens' children and grandchildren. Republicans preached spending only what you have. Democrats were accused of spending without regard to whether the government had the money or not.

National Healthcare

The national healthcare plan (nicknamed Obamacare by opponents), passed by Congress and signed into law by the President was perhaps the ultimate symbol for those who worried about a federal government throwing all fiscal restraints to the winds. The 2,000 page piece of legislation was little understood by members of Congress or members of the public. The bill was passed with Democrats providing almost every single vote for its passage. No one knew with certainty how much the program would cost when fully implemented in 2014. No one knew the effects of the bill on healthcare costs. In fact, one of the criticisms often leveled at Obamacare was that the program did not do nearly enough to help contain and hold down health care costs which were spiraling out of control. Without Republican support in Congress, Obamacare became the Democrats' answer to the many problems with health care in America.

Without Republican support, Obamacare was going to be under attack by an entire political party as one more example of the party in power misreading the electoral mandate of the 2008 election. Republican congressional candidates cultivated the image of Obamacare as yet another federal government program the nation could ill afford. Members of the Tea Party often took the lead across the nation's congressional districts and it was true for the 11th District in Illinois.

All three of these major issues were related to a larger and more important question—how much power should the federal government have? The question, as old as the Republic itself, is often the basis for political campaigns. With Republicans shouting "fiscal insanity," this larger issue summarizes the crux of the 2010 campaign.

Congresswoman Halvorson often found herself on the defensive in terms of defending the actions of the Democrats in Washington. Republicans sensed the uncertainty about, if not outright opposition of the public to many of the laws passed by the Democrats in Congress.

CAMPAIGN STRATEGY

Media

Both candidates made full use of the various media resources in the district. Television was expensive because of the proximity of Chicago to the district. Television ads were prohibitively expensive, but both candidates spent considerable resources advertising in the vote-rich northern counties.

Both candidates also made press releases to the print and electronic media a regular staple for their campaigns. Both campaigns used press releases for purposes of attacking their opponent as well as for answering the attacks on them by their opponent.

Both campaigns also made full use of the various social media including Facebook, and other social networking sites. Blogs, expressing various opinions, were a common fact of life in this race. Everyone it seemed had an opinion and felt an obligation to share that opinion, regardless of how thoughtfully (or not) it had been reached. If one set up an ongoing Google search for either "Debbie Halvorson" or "Adam Kinzinger," one's mailbox would soon overflow with the constant "publications" cited daily in such a search. Over the course of the final three months of the general election campaign, the author was showered with more than 400 articles on each of the two finalists.

Image and Advertising

The Halvorson camp sought to portray their candidate as what she was—the incumbent Congresswoman. They hoped to make the accomplishments of her first two years acceptable in the eyes of the voters and convey an image of her as a responsive, thoughtful, accessible, problem-solving public official.

This approach had several problems inherent in it. For one, as the Congress became less popular (approval ratings in the teens), as the Democratic President's approval ratings dropped, as some of the legislation passed by the 111th Congress came under fire, touting your service as an incumbent was not the jewel it might be expected to be normally.

Kinzinger was portrayed by Halvorson as too young and too inexperienced to serve in Congress. In a not-so-subtle swipe at Kinzinger's youth, Halvorson called him too young and when challenged, she maintained she had not meant that he was too young (in age), but rather his youth limited his vision. According to a Kinzinger press release, Halvorson's campaign manager noted that "Seniors have real issues about someone who has never come close to being in their shoes talking about their retirement security."[5]

Finance

The race for the 11th District was not cheap, but it was far from the top tier of House race expenditures. Congresswoman Halvorson raised $2,702,605. Kinzinger raised $1,836,389.[6] Even though that means the incumbent outraised her challenger by nearly $900,000, that didn't mean the challenger was underfunded or financially handicapped in this race. Numerous studies of congressional elections note that challengers need not keep pace with the funds raised by the incumbent, but challengers must raise significant funds so as to be competitive.[7] Adam Kinzinger certainly did that.

As might be expected, Halvorson raised a greater portion of her campaign funds from political action committees (44 percent) than did her challenger who raised only 22.9 percent from political action committees. Neither candidate received much in the way of funds from their political party. Halvorson received $14,092 from her party, Kinzinger $7,625 from his. Halvorson received no cash from party committees, but she was given services as resources.

Halvorson received little in the way of contributions from the Democratic Party, in the beginning because she did not seem to need such contributions. Later on, the Party was trying to spend its funds where the chances of success were the greatest and Halvorson appeared to have a lesser chance of victory than some other races where Democrats ended up putting their money.

Grassroots

Halvorson was popular with most Democrats and some independents in the District who had helped elect her in 2008. She had been a dependable vote for the President's programs, voting with her party in the House 92 percent of the time.

The Republicans portrayed that slavish devotion to all things Democratic as doing whatever Speaker Pelosi asked of her. They attacked her for her lack of independence. It was that lack of independence that would hurt her with independent voters who had given her their votes in 2008. Although she had voted against the wishes of party leadership on occasion, such occasions got lost in the barrage of advertising which painted her as a "tool" of the President and Speaker Pelosi.

One sensed throughout this campaign that 11th District Democrats didn't see this race as a potential loss until late in the campaign. They seemed blinded by the 58 percent of the vote gained by Halvorson in her initial race in 2008. She seemed to Democrats that she had acquitted herself well in her freshman term in the House. This would prove to be a dangerous interpretation of the 2008 results since even though Halvorson ran up a sizeable victory margin in 2008, she was still representing a center-right district, a Republican-leaning district. That would seem to suggest that she needed to display a streak of independence and needed to take some political/issue positions which could be showcased as moderate.

Kinzinger on the other hand benefited from the rise of the Tea Party, a set of groups across the nation which generally supported a leaner, less costly, smaller federal government. They ended up being the "true believers" of the 2010 elections. Liberals spent too much time ridiculing the Tea Party and not enough time noticing what the Tea Party was accomplishing.

A Tea Party-supported candidate won the governorship of Virginia in November 2009 and another Tea Party-supported candidate ousted the Democratic governor of New Jersey the same day. The Tea Party scored one of its biggest victories when the candidate it supported, Scott Brown, won the U.S. Senate seat in Massachusetts in January 2010, the first Republican Senate win in Massachusetts in decades.

In the 11th District, the Tea Party was particularly active in Will and Kankakee counties, two of the larger counties in the District. Several large Tea Party rallies were held in Will County late in the campaign.[8]

The fact that Halvorson was nearly unopposed for renomination coupled with the fact that Kinzinger cruised to the Republican nomination by defeating four other Republican candidates, speaks to the fact that both of the nominees for the 11th District seat had maximized their grassroots support and each had become their party's official nominee easily.

Bases of Support

Halvorson was again able to garner the support of the major groups in the Democratic coalition. She got the votes of labor union members; she was still preferred by the Democratic liberals in the District. Minorities in the District still saw her as the better of the two choices. She scored high on the list with the District's veterans because of the work she had done for their interests in her two years in the House.

However, the problem for Halvorson was the same problem facing other 2008 Democratic congressional winners. While she was still popular with the Democratic bases of support, many Democrats who voted for both Senator Obama and Debbie Halvorson in 2008 seemed less likely to vote at all in the off-year election of 2010. Younger voters, minority voters, and other weaker-affiliation Democratic supporters showed far less enthusiasm and interest in the election of 2010 than they had two years earlier. They seemed much less likely to turn out to vote and were less likely to vote Democrat. Halvorson had been elected to the House in an election in which the tide favored Democratic candidates up and down the ballot.

An important key to winning would be to get the same voters out to vote in an election in which the President was not standing for reelection and in an election in which the President's job approval ratings were lower than his disapproval ratings.

There was an additional problem facing the Halvorson campaign. Many of those who considered themselves independents were deserting Democratic candidates in 2010. They had voted for Democrats across the country in 2008 congressional races, but 2010 was different. Whereas independents had elected many Democrats to the Senate and House in 2008, or made their margins of victory larger than they otherwise would have been, there was a change of mind among independents.

Halvorson was faced not only with holding the support of Democratic voters and getting them out to vote, she was faced as well as appealing to a different breed of voter—the independent. That would prove a difficult assignment. In 2008, Obama had carried the independent vote by 8 percent. When the votes were tabulated in 2010, Democratic House candidates lost the independent vote by 18 percent.

Kinzinger had a different problem with his bases of support. He first had to convince Republicans and especially conservatives that he was a good choice. It was not a question of whether he was preferable to re-electing Halvorson. It was a question of whether his appeal was sufficient to get Republicans and conservatives to the polls in November. Plus, he had to demonstrate that he could defeat Halvorson in head-to-head competition. He sounded all the right notes for the District's Republicans. He supported many of the positions taken by Republican candidates across the nation—America needs a leaner, less active, less expensive federal government. He said over and over that we needed to bring the nation's fiscal house into order. Those statements were music to conservatives' ears. Republicans found in Adam Kinzinger a candidate they could support willingly and with enthusiasm.

However, Kinzinger also had to reach out to independents, to sound the right notes for them—not too conservative, but fiscally responsible. He had to seem as though he was the candidate who would rein in runaway federal spending and he had to do all of this without seeming "dangerously conservative."

ELECTION RESULTS

The election of 2010 turned out to be the third "wave election" in a row. The first two wave elections had helped the Democrats into office. Democrats gained 31 House seats in 2006 and regained the House majority they had lost in 1994. In 2008, they added 23 more seats to their House majority. In the third wave election of 2010, the tide swept Republicans into office and swept Democrats out. Republicans gained 63 seats in the House, more than recovering from their losses in 2006 and 2008. Debbie Halvorson who rode the second wave to victory with 58 percent of the vote in 2008 went out with the tide as Adam Kinzinger ran up 57.4 percent of the vote in Halvorson's initial reelection bid. Across the country, fifty House Democratic incumbents were defeated including three committee chairs. In Illinois, four Democratic incumbents including Halvorson were voted out. It was perhaps less a "wave election" and more of a political tsunami. Congresswoman Halvorson was not yet positioned to withstand such a political tsunami.

One of the reasons Kinzinger defeated Halvorson was that he ran a better campaign with fewer internal campaign problems. His campaign manager, Erik Rayman, had cut his teeth in the Aaron Schock campaign of 2008 in the 18th Congressional District. He brought order and a sense of purpose to a campaign that was struggling to gain its sea legs in the early months of 2010. On the other hand, Halvorson fired her campaign manager in August. Travis Worl, had been a staffer for Hillary Clinton's presidential campaign. His firing was likely prompted by the continuing bad news from polls taken in the District. He would be replaced by Julie Merz, a former aide to Speaker Nancy Pelosi. Since Republicans had substituted Pelosi as their political arch-villain rather than directly attacking the President of the United States, this presented another front for conservatives to attack.

Another reason for Kinzinger's victory was the fact that he seemed the more open and accessible of the two candidates. Halvorson had promised to hold town hall meetings before deciding how to vote on the health care bill. She failed to do so. Kinzinger frequently criticized her for hiding from the voters.

The two candidates debated each other in a public debate forum only once during the campaign. Kinzinger had wanted a sizeable number of debates/joint appearances. Halvorson seemed to prefer more "controlled" public appearances, either phone-in town hall meetings, or appearances in union halls. By doing so, she opened herself up to Kinzinger's charges that she was unwilling to face the voters and explain her voting record. At one point, Halvorson said she had "a huge job to do" before politics. The problem with her claim was that within three days, she had time to bring Majority Leader Steny Hoyer to her district for a fund-raiser.

Kinzinger claimed to have held town hall meetings with total attendance of 3,000+ focusing on the health care proposal put forward by President Obama. Halvorson, noting the rather destructive meetings held by members of Congress elsewhere in the country argued that she did not want to go to town hall meetings where a vocal minority would dominate and disrupt. The two candidates did appear together in a radio debate late in the campaign. The fact that Halvorson had responsibilities during the times the House was in session did not explain her apparent reluctance to make public appearances. She maintained that she was able to know what her constituents were thinking without having large, impersonal public town hall meetings. It seems likely that Kinzinger scored some political points in this appearance dispute.

Kinzinger benefited from a substantial number of newspaper endorsements. He was endorsed by the *Chicago Sun-Times, Chicago Tribune, South Town Star,* and the *Bloomington Pantagraph*, among others. Kinzinger was also endorsed by the *City News,* an African-American newspaper serving the northeastern part of the 11th District. The newspaper accused Halvorson of "hiding and running," and said of Kinzinger: "The *City News* also believes that Adam Kinzinger can and will make a positive difference in people's lives. . . . A vote for Adam Kinzinger as Congressman . . . is a vote for the African-American community."[9]

Many voters in the 11th District felt that their Congresswoman was too beholden to the House Democratic leadership and too inattentive to the concerns of the residents of the 11th District. If they did not reach that conclusion on their own, Adam Kinzinger was constantly reminding them of that state of affairs.

With the exception of her fine work in behalf of veterans, Halvorson had not yet had time to establish her congressional credentials. Because the Party needed her vote in the House on important legislation, she was seen as not independent enough. Like many other congressional Democrats, she found that she had far less flexibility than she had expected and hoped. She had not carved out a niche as an independent thinker. She came off as a too-willing participant in the various programs put forward by the Obama Administration.

Kinzinger tried to portray Halvorson as an "extreme liberal." She returned the favor by referring to him as outside the conservative mainstream. Whether either charge stuck, she likely suffered more from having the charge made than did Kinzinger. As is true of any challenger, he had no voting record to explain, or defend.

It is interesting to note that nonpartisan publications pointed out that Democratic attacks on Republican congressional candidates seemed to fall on deaf ears.[10] According to Nathan Gonzales, "Democrats thought GOP challengers were simply too flawed to be acceptable alternatives to voters who wanted change. But as Republicans learned in 2006 and 2008, the messenger and the audience matter just as much, if not more, than the message when it comes to political attacks. The Republicans seemed better prepared to answer the Democratic attacks and that too contributed to the lessening of their impact.

There seems to be no single issue or incident that signaled the end of Halvorson's stay in the House. It was a combination of factors, almost all of them negatively impacting Halvorson's reelection campaign. The mood of the country and of the 11th District had soured on Democrats and their plans for the nation. The Kinzinger campaign ran more smoothly and with fewer hiccups than the Halvorson campaign. Campaign gaffes were held to a minimum by the Kinzinger campaign. Kinzinger was able to campaign on issues and positions endorsed by more citizens of the 11th District. He did not have to support votes he had cast. He was not a member of the party which had enjoyed two successful elections in a row, but was experiencing a downturn in its fortunes. It was an off-year election and in such elections, it is very important to get out the "right voters." The mood of Americans across the nation was one of dissatisfaction and they voted that dissatisfaction by turning out large numbers of Democratic office-holders, up and down the ballot.

CONCLUSION

It does not seem that Congresswoman Halvorson was defeated because she was a Democrat. It seemed that she was defeated because she seemed willing to do whatever the Washington, D.C. wing of the party asked of her. She came off to many voters in the 11th as too liberal and not independent enough. If she believed that the 58 percent of the vote she garnered in 2008 was a mandate to be "liberal" in the truest sense, she probably misread the mandate. It would have been more accurate according to hindsight to interpret her win as a victory for a moderate-liberal Democratic voice from central Illinois.

Voters who sent her to Congress in 2008, thought they were getting a center-left member of the House who would at times stand up for what she believed and occasionally vote against her Party and its leadership. The Kinzinger campaign successfully convinced 11th District voters that what they hoped for in voting for Halvorson two years ago was not what they got.

That, coupled with the tide sweeping the nation, was enough to send Halvorson along with three House colleagues from districts in Illinois down to electoral defeat. In comedy as in politics, it is said, timing is everything. If that is true, clearly this election year was not the best time to be a Democratic member of the U.S. House of Representatives seeking reelection.

NOTES

1. *Almanac of American Politics*, 1998, 2004, 2008.

2. *Almanac of American Politics*, 2008.

3. Federal Election Commission, 2008 House Campaign Finance Record for 11th Illinois House District.

4. Illinois Board of Elections, Results for 2010 Republican Primary in 11th Congressional District.

5. Kinzinger press release, "Adam Kinzinger Among GOP Young Guns taking aim at Democratic seats," August 11, 2010.

6. Federal Election Commission, 2010 House Campaign Finance Record for 11th Illinois House District.

7. The Politics of Congressional Elections, pp. 45–51.

8. "Tea Party rallies in Will County," *Plainfield Sun*, October 28, 2010.

9. Quote in a press release from the Kinzinger for Congress headquarters, June 22, 2010.

10. Nathan Gonzales, "Democratic Attacks Fell on Deaf Ears This Fall," *Roll Call*, November 30, 2010.

Chapter 5

Mississippi District 4 Race (Palazzo v. Taylor)

A Conservative Democrat Loses to a More Conservative Republican

Tom Lansford

Steven Palazzo
Party: Republican
Age: 40
Sex: Male
Race: White
Religion: Roman Catholic
Education: University of Southern Mississippi (accounting, both undergraduate and graduate)
Occupation: Certified Public Accountant
Political Experience: State Representative (2006–2011)

Gary Eugene "Gene" Taylor
Party: Democrat
Age: 57
Sex: Male
Race: White
Religion: Roman Catholic
Education: Tulane University (political science and history undergraduate degree); University of Southern Mississippi (business and economics graduate)
Occupation: Salesman
Political Experience: State Senator (1983–1989); U.S. Representative (1989–2011)

CHARACTERISTICS OF MISSISSIPPI DISTRICT 4

Mississippi is one of the more conservative states in the United States and has voted Republican in every presidential election since 1980. District 4 is the most conservative of Mississippi's four congressional districts, and had not voted for the Democratic presidential candidate since 1956. However, moderate to conservative "Blue Dog" Democrats remain competitive in the district by emphasizing conservative positions on economic and security policy. This anomaly was personified by maverick Representative Gene Taylor (D-MS) who represented the area for more than 20 years and who was well known for voting with the Republicans on key issues. The district encompasses the coastal region of Mississippi and includes 12 counties and parts of three others for a total of 9,536 square miles. It was formed following the 2000 census when Mississippi lost one congressional seat and is based mainly on what was previously Mississippi's 5th District. Like other districts in Mississippi, the 4th District seldom turns incumbents out of office. Incumbency is historically a major advantage in congressional elections in the area.

Party Balance

District 4 has become increasingly Republican as the result of demographic trends and the 2000 redistricting. Prior to the 2010 election, the Cook Voting Index rated the area as one of the two most heavily Republican districts

Figure 5.1   Mississippi Congressional District 4

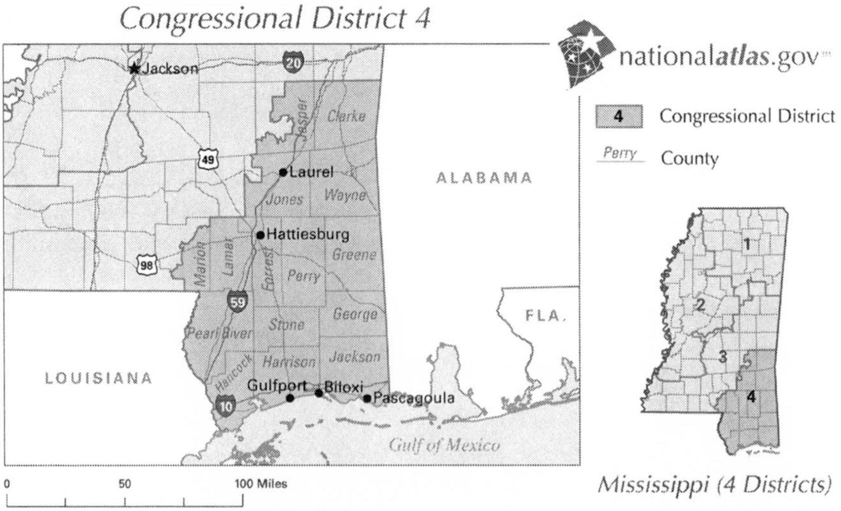

represented by a Democrat (the other being Texas 17).[1] In 2008, the district was 38 percent Republican and 30 percent Democrat. Harrison, Jackson, and Lamar counties had the highest number and percentage of Republican voters. However, even Democrats in the region have had a history of voting Republican in national and state elections, although both parties have been very competitive at the local level.

Voting and Electoral History

Voters in the district overwhelmingly have supported Republican presidential and senatorial candidates. In 2004 and 2008, the 4th District led the other Mississippian districts in voting for GOP candidates. In 2004, incumbent president George W. Bush won the district with 68 percent of the vote to 31 percent for his Democratic challenger, Sen. John Kerry (D-MA), while Sen. John McCain (R-AZ) won the area with 67.3 percent to 31.8 percent for Sen. Barack Obama (D-IL) in 2008. In the 2008 balloting, Sen. McCain won Greene, Lamar, Stone, and Perry counties in the district with more than 70 percent of the vote, and George and Pearl River counties with more than 80 percent of the vote. Support for Republican senatorial candidates averaged more than 60 percent in 2002, 2006 and 2008. Nonetheless, Rep. Taylor was able to convincingly win reelection after he first gained office in 1983. After the consolidation of the 4th and 5th Districts in 2000, Taylor averaged more than 70 percent of the vote in his reelection bids, and secured 74.5 percent of the vote in 2008.

Demographic Character of the Electorate

In 2010, the district had a population of approximately 715,000, of which 53.7 percent was urban, and 46.3 percent rural. Like many other areas of southeastern states, the growth of the suburbs in the three coastal counties and in Lamar and Stone counties has resulted in a growing base for the Republican Party. The median household income was $35,056, well below the national average, and the poverty rate was 15.6 percent, although both rates varied widely across the counties. The unemployment rate ranged from a low of 7.1 percent in Lamar County to a high of 12 percent in Greene County, with an average of 9.5 percent, below the state average of 9.8 percent, but above the national average of 9.3 percent. The population was concentrated in the three coastal counties, Hancock, Harrison and Jackson. The district had the highest percentage of whites among Mississippi's electoral districts. It was 75.3 percent white, 22.6 percent African American, and 2 percent Hispanic, with small Asian and Native-American populations. The Hispanic population swelled after Hurricane Katrina in 2005, but declined as reconstruction projects along the coast slowed during the subsequent economic downturn. The Asian population was located mainly along the coast and included a significant Vietnamese-American community.

Key Voting Blocs

There are three main voting blocs in the district. The first is the growing Republican-leaning suburbanites in the coastal areas and Lamar and Stone counties. Although conservative in most areas of economic, social and foreign and security policy, there is a divide among the Republican base between the more moderate three coastal counties, with cultural ties and affinities with New Orleans, and the more traditionally right-of-center northern counties of the district (often referred to as the "Pinebelt"). The second group is the African American community, which makes up the main base of the Democratic Party. African Americans voted overwhelmingly for Democrats at the state and national level in 2006 and 2008. Rural Southern Democrats make up the third and final bloc. They typically have conservative views on most social issues, ranging from abortion to capital punishment to gun control. However, the group tends to be more centrist on economic issues and foreign policy. The rural Democrats often emerge as the main swing vote between the Republicans and the Democratic base.

Major Urban Areas and Employment/Occupational Characteristics

The main urban areas are the cities of Gulfport, Biloxi, Hattiesburg (respectively, the second, third and fourth largest cities in Mississippi), and Pascagoula. In 2009, Harrison County on the coast had the second largest population among Mississippi's counties with 171,875. Both Gulfport, population approximately 71,100, and Biloxi, population 50,640, are located in Harrison County. Hattiesburg, home to the University of Southern Mississippi, has a population of 44,770, while Pascagoula has 26,200. Some 51.9 percent of the population is engaged in white collar or management jobs, while 30.6 percent are in manufacturing or agriculture, and the remaining 18.4 percent are in the service sector.

There are several main employment sectors in the district. Along the coast, casino gaming and tourism are a combined $20 billion industry. Manufacturing centers include the Northrup Gruman shipyard in Pascagoula and a growing aerospace sector centered at the Stennis Aerospace center in Hancock County. Kessler Air Force Base, a large military training facility, is Biloxi's largest employer with an economic impact of $1.4 billion in

2010. Mississippi's congressional delegation has historically been effective at protecting, or enhancing, the large military and defense-industrial presence statewide and especially in District 4. In the rural counties, agriculture remains an important economic sector, as does commercial fishing along the coast.

THE CANDIDATES

Major Republicans in the region avoided challenging the popular Taylor who cruised to reelection 10 terms by emphasizing his fiscal and social conservatism. Steven Palazzo had only entered public office in 2006 and was relatively unknown. In addition, there were very few policy differences between the two candidates. Besides Taylor and Palazzo, Kenneth "Tim" Hampton ran as a Libertarian, and Anna Jewel Revies was a Reform Party candidate. Neither Hampton nor Revies had a major impact on the election.

Gene Taylor

Gary Eugene "Gene" Taylor was born in New Orleans on September 17, 1953. He joined the Coast Guard Reserve in 1971 and served until 1984, rising to command a search and rescue vessel. Meanwhile, Taylor graduated from Tulane University in 1974 and went to work as a sales representative for a shipping company. He entered politics in 1981 when he was elected to the city council of Bay St. Louis as a Democrat. Two years later, Taylor was elected to the state senate. He quickly established a reputation as a maverick, willing to challenge party leadership when he disagreed on policy issues. Taylor also became known as a staunch conservative on economic and social matters.

Popular Republican Rep. Trent Lott (R-MS) was elected to the U.S. Senate in 1988, and Taylor campaigned unsuccessfully for his seat, losing to Larkin Smith. When Smith died in a plane crash the following year, Taylor won the special election to replace him. Taylor emerged as a leading member of the conservative Blue Dog coalition. Taylor voted to impeach Bill Clinton but rebuffed repeated Republican overtures to switch parties. He was a vocal critic of the Bush tax cuts because of their impact on the deficit and of the Bush administration's oversight of the Hurricane Katrina response and recovery.

Taylor was a member of the House Armed Services Committee and the Transportation and Infrastructure Committee. He was chair of the Subcommittee on Seapower and Expeditionary Forces. Taylor did not face an opponent in the 2010 Democratic primary.

Steven Palazzo

Steven McCarty Palazzo was born on February 21, 1970 in Gulfport, Mississippi. Palazzo joined the Marine Corps in 1988, serving in the 1991 Gulf War. He later attended the University of Southern Mississippi where he earned an undergraduate degree in accounting in 1994 and a master of public accountancy in 1996. He joined the National Guard in 1997. Palazzo launched a successful accounting firm in Gulfport.

In 2006, he won a special election to the Mississippi state house as a Republican, representing a district in Harrison County along the Gulf coast. He served on a number of committees, including Banking and Financial Services, Juvenile Justice, and Wildlife and Fisheries. In 2009, the Mississippi Wildlife Federation named Palazzo its elected official of the year. While in Jackson, Palazzo developed a reputation as a staunch states' rights advocate and one of the most conservative members of the conservative Mississippi House of Representatives.

In the Republican primary, Palazzo faced Joe Tegerdine, an Oregon native and political newcomer who moved to Petal, Mississippi in 2007. Tegerdine, a successful businessman, advocated a libertarian approach to most social policies, but his short time in Mississippi undercut his attractiveness to some Republican voters in the district, as did his Mormon faith in the mainly Catholic and Baptist region. Tegerdine was endorsed by the Tea Party, while Palazzo was supported by the stalwarts of the Republican Party. The primary campaign was highly negative. Palazzo raised about $125,000 for his primary effort, while his opponent brought in approximately $60,000. Palazzo defeated Tegerdine in the June 1 balloting, with 57 percent of the vote.

CAMPAIGN ISSUES

The two candidates had similar stances on most major issues, including opposition to the federal stimulus package and the 2010 federal healthcare reform act. Both candidates asserted they were anti-abortion, anti-gun control and in favor of limited government. Nonetheless, differences over policy specifics did materialize, while Taylor's party affiliation emerged as the main issue in the campaign as the Palazzo campaign endeavored to tie the incumbent to the unpopular Speaker of the House, Rep. Nancy Pelosi (D-CA).

Tax Cuts

The most significant policy disagreement between the two candidates was whether or not to extend the Bush-era tax cuts. Taylor voted against the tax cuts in 2001, and then opposed extending the majority of the tax revisions in 2010, arguing that the country could not avoid the reductions that contributed to the growing deficit and debt. The incumbent contended that the country needed to both eliminate most of the tax cuts and undertake deep cuts in spending in an effort to achieve a balanced budget.

Palazzo countered that increasing taxes during an economic downturn would further depress the economy and that spending cuts should be the primary focus for deficit reduction efforts. The challenger announced that he had supported the original Bush tax cuts, which he believed were responsible for economic growth in the post-2001 era.

Insurance Reform

Another substantive difference between the two candidates was insurance reform, a topic of keen interest in the hurricane-ravaged Gulf coast region. Following Hurricane Katrina, Taylor, who lost his home in the storm, developed a proposal for an all-perils insurance system that would operate along similar lines as the existing national flood insurance program and act as an insurer of last-resort when private carriers declined to provide wind or other coverage to areas. The House repeatedly failed to advance Taylor's Multiperil Insurance Act, which faced resistance from both Democrats and Republicans because of cost, and was opposed by the President Barak Obama's administration. Taylor asserted that as one of the reasons for his dissatisfaction with Pelosi.

During the campaign, Palazzo criticized Taylor's inability to secure support for the measure, despite his party's control of Congress, asserted that the failure was an indication of the veteran Democrat's limited effectiveness in the House. Palazzo endorsed a much more limited reform that emphasized a public-private partnership.

The War in Afghanistan

While the two candidates held similar views on the war on terror and the conflict in Afghanistan, Taylor supported the troop surges in Iraq and Afghanistan, but was increasingly hesitant about the ability of the United States to defeat the Taliban in Afghanistan. The congressman's main concern was the reliability of U.S.-backed regimes in Kabul and Islamabad. Taylor contended that corruption and drug-trafficking had undermined the popularity and capabilities of the government of Afghan President Hamid Karzai.

Palazzo cautioned against an early withdrawal from Afghanistan before the Taliban and al Qaeda were defeated. He asserted that Afghanistan remained the central front in the war on terror and that it was necessary for U.S. and allied troops to fight the Taliban in Afghanistan in order to prevent terrorists from regaining a base from which to conduct further attacks against the United States. During the campaign's sole debate, Palazzo stated "I want our troops home as fast as possible, but it doesn't need to be the politicians in Washington, D.C. We need to listen to generals on the ground and commanders because they know best. And I want to keep this fight in their backyard and not in my backyard."[2]

Obama and Pelosi

The core issue in the campaign was Taylor's party affiliation. The incumbent stressed his reputation as a maverick and his willingness to buck the party and vote in line with his conservative constituents while his challenger attempted to link Taylor with Democratic leaders including Obama and Pelosi who were very unpopular in South Mississippi (Obama's approval rating declined to 37 percent in Mississippi prior to the 2010 balloting). Consequently, the issue and the campaign became intertwined as Palazzo's main campaign slogan was "Fire Pelosi," and the challenger emphasized that a vote for him was a vote against the Democratic speaker and national policies that were unpopular in the district, including healthcare reform and the economic stimulus package.

Taylor had to defend his conservative credentials while not alienating the more liberal base of the Democratic party in South Mississippi. In an extraordinary act of distancing his campaign from the national party, Taylor admitted to a reporter at the end of October 2010 that he had voted for Sen. McCain in the 2008 presidential election. Taylor downplayed his decision by stating, "I know John McCain. I don't know Barack Obama," and declaring that the vote was not a surprise to those who knew the incumbent.[3] Taylor also pledged to not support Rep. Pelosi if she sought reelection as Speaker of the House, but instead back a more moderate Democrat such as Rep. Ike Skelton (D-MO) (Skelton was also defeated in the 2010 balloting).

CAMPAIGN STRATEGY

Media

Both campaigns were highly negative and notable for attack ads. Palazzo's media strategy revolved around efforts to link Taylor to the national Democratic Party. Footage of Taylor voting for Pelosi for House speaker in 2009, and receiving a round of applause from fellow Democrats, featured prominently in campaign ads and websites. In addition, the Palazzo campaign charged that despite Taylor's assertions of independence, the incumbent voted with his party the majority of the time. In a database that analyzed the votes of incumbent members of Congress, the *Washington Post* found that Taylor voted with his party 77.3 percent of the time.[4]

Taylor doggedly emphasized his votes against major legislation such as healthcare reform, cap-and-trade, and the stimulus packages as proof that his stance on major issues coincided with those of his constituency. The Taylor campaign also highlighted the importance of the congressman's seniority and what the potential loss of clout would mean for shipbuilding and military facilities in the region.

The candidates had one debate on October 29, 2010 in a local television station, without an audience. The debate was simulcast on both television and radio, with questions from viewers. Both candidates claimed victory and simultaneously charged the other campaign with avoiding efforts to hold additional debates.

Image and Advertising

Both campaigns used multiple forms of advertising, ranging from television to websites. Taylor's campaign emphasized the congressman's conservative credentials. Taylor secured the endorsement of a number of conservative groups, including the National Rifle Association, the Veterans of Foreign Wars and the National Right to Life Committee. He also secured the endorsement of the region's major newspaper, the *Sun Herald*. Central to the Taylor campaign was the importance of seniority in advocating for the interests of the district. The campaign asserted that if the Democrats remained in control of Congress, Palazzo would have little influence, and even if Republicans gained control of the House, Palazzo would be too junior to be appointed to any important committees. Meanwhile, the campaign ran a series of ads that highlighted the $3.7 billion in funding for defense projects that the congressman had secured for south Mississippi in 2010.

Taylor ran a range of negative advertisements against his challenger. For instance, the Taylor camp accused Palazzo of being funded by the insurance industry in a series of ads. In addition, Taylor highlighted votes Palazzo had made in the state house that would reduce pension benefits for state employees, arguing that the challenger was out of touch with the needs of the working class.

Palazzo's campaign emphasized his record as a conservative state legislator and combat veteran. Palazzo had the backing of both state and national Republican leaders. For instance, he was endorsed by Sarah Palin, who provided a recorded telephone message for voters. He also secured the backing of former Speaker of the House and conservative pundit Newt Gingrich. Meanwhile, national and state Republican officials stumped for the challenger. A week before the election, Tegerdine, Palazzo's opponent in the primary, endorsed Taylor. The former Tea Party candidate defended his action as a stand against the Republican party establishment that backed Palazzo. Throughout the campaign, Palazzo ran negative advertisements attempting to link Taylor with liberal Democrats.

The challenger also argued that Taylor's party affiliation prevented the incumbent from effectively representing the district. The Palazzo camp contended that the Blue Dog Taylor would never gain senior leadership positions in the House because of the liberal nature of the Democratic leaders, nor enjoy the support of other Democrats in advancing his bills. Palazzo asserted that Taylor had been marginalized when Republicans controlled the chamber, and that was unlikely to change if Republicans regained control of the House.

Campaign Finance

Taylor began the campaign with a monetary advantage. He had not faced a primary challenge and had an efficient fundraising network in place. However, since the congressman had not faced significant challenges in his recent elections, he had not built a large war chest. Meanwhile, the race was not initially seen as competitive by the national parties and it was late in the cycle before Taylor and Palazzo began to receive substantial funds from their respective national organizations.

During the campaign, Taylor raised $858,398, of which $403,696 came from individuals, and $451,867 came from political action committees (PACs). Funds in Taylor's war chest allowed the incumbent to spend $933,480 in the election, and end with the campaign with $144,398 in cash and no debt. Palazzo brought in $1,049,581, the majority, $799,308 from individuals, and $200,399 from PACs. Palazzo spent $1,018,077, and finished his bid with $31,504 in cash and no debt. The two minor party candidates raised less than $5,000 each.

Grassroots Campaign Efforts

Palazzo's "Fire Pelosi" slogan proved popular in the conservative district. Palazzo's campaign developed a strong grass-roots network throughout the district, bolstered by a strong, existing Republican Party network. Taylor's grassroots efforts were constrained by his attempts to distance himself from the national Democratic Party. The congressman had to compete with Palazzo for moderate to conservative voters and convince them that he would be a better advocate for their values and interests than the Republican Palazzo. However, Taylor's emphasis on conservatism likely depressed voter turnout among liberals.

Bases of Support

Palazzo enjoyed the support of the state's powerful Republican Party. Prior to the election, Republicans controlled seven of the eight statewide offices in Mississippi and Republican Governor Haley Barbour enjoyed a 70 percent approval rating. Palazzo was able to capitalize on anti-incumbency sentiment and the broader dissatisfaction with the national Democratic Party leadership. Polls showed that prior to the election, the challenger enjoyed strong support in the rural counties, while Taylor polled ahead of Palazzo in the three Coastal counties.

ELECTION RESULTS

A week before the election, CBS News continued to rate the district as a "probable Democratic hold."[5] Both candidates reported internal polling that gave them a slight lead over their opponent. Turnout was expected to play a major role in the election with higher turnout likely to favor the challenger. Preliminary results affirmed that turnout was 8 percent higher in the 2010 balloting over 2006.

Palazzo won the election with 105,613 votes or 51.93 percent, to Taylor's 95,243 or 46.83 percent. Hampton secured 1,741 or 0.86 percent of the vote, while Revies received 787 votes, or 0.39 percent. As expected Taylor did well in the three coastal counties, but his margins of victory were not as high as anticipated. For instance, in Harrison County, the most populous in the district, Taylor received 24,845 votes to Palazzo's 17,917. In his home county, Hancock, Taylor gained 6,487 to Palazzo's 5,266. Jackson County, the home of the Pascagoula Shipyard, was also a disappointment to the incumbent. He received 18,463 to the challenger's 17,588. In the interior Pine Belt areas, Palazzo won the majority of counties and with significant margins of victory. In Lamar County, Palazzo secured 11,484 to Taylor's 5,546, while in Jones County, the challenger received 11,834 to 7,513, and Palazzo got 10,570 in Pearl River County to 4,678 to Taylor.

CONCLUSION

Taylor's defeat was part of a broader national trend which saw moderate to conservative Democrats lose to Republicans. In Mississippi, besides Taylor's loss, Rep. Travis Childers (D-MS), another Blue Dog Democrat who represented the state's 1st District also lost his seat. Long-time Republican State Senator Alan Nunnelee defeated Childers, who had been in office since 2008, 55.3 percent to 40.7 percent in a district that was also traditionally Republican. Senator Roger Wicker (R-MS) had represented the district for 12 years before being appointed to the Senate in 2007 and the seat was historically a safe one for the GOP. Meanwhile, incumbents Bennie Thompson (D-MS) and Greg Harper (R-MS) were reelected by large margins in safe districts. Thompson had been in office since 1993 in the state's only majority African-American district. Harper was elected in 2008 to replace Rep. Chip Pickering (R-MS) who retired after twelve years in office. Following the 2010 balloting, Mississippi's House delegation was transformed from three Democrats and one Republican to three Republicans and one Democrat.

NOTES

1. Cook Political Report, "Partisan Voting Index: Districts of the 111th Congress," pp. 2A, 6–8.

2. Steven Palazzo, quoted in Doug Walker, "Taylor, Palazzo Square Off in First and Only Debate," *WLOX* (October 29, 2010); online at http://www.wlox.com/Global/story.asp?S=13414338; Walker, Doug. "Taylor, Palazzo Square Off in First and Only Debate," *WLOX*. October 29, 2010. www.wlox.com/Global/story.asp?S=13414338.

3. Gene Taylor, Interview, quoted in Maria Recio, "Mississippi Democrat's Vote for McCain Starts Internet Furor," McClatchy Newspapers (October 26, 2010); www.mcclatchydc.com/2010/10/26/102628/mississippi-democrats-vote-for.html.

4. *The Washington Post,* "The U.S. Congress: Votes Database—Gene Taylor," online at www.govtrack.us/congress/person.xpd?id=400399.

5. *CBS News,* "Democratic Rep. Gene Taylor: I Voted For McCain," (October 25, 2010); online at www.cbsnews.com/8301–503544_162–20020654–503544.html.; Recio, Maria. "Mississippi Democrat's Vote for McCain Starts Internet Furor." McClatchy Newspapers. October 26, 2010. www.mcclatchydc.com/2010/10/26/102628/mississippi-democrats-vote-for.html.

Chapter 6

New York District 20 Race (Gibson v. Murphy)

The Red Tide Returns to the Upper Hudson Valley

Jeffrey Kraus

Christopher P. Gibson
Party: Republican/Conservative
Age: 46
Sex: Male
Race: White
Religion: Roman Catholic
Education: B.A., Siena College; M.P.A., Ph.D., Cornell University
Occupation: Colonel, U.S. Army (retired)
Political Experience: No prior political experience

Matthew Scott Murphy
Party: Democrat/Working Families/Independence
Age: 40
Sex: Male
Race: White
Religion: Roman Catholic
Education: A.B., Harvard University
Occupation: Entrepreneur
Political Experience: U.S. Representative, April 29, 2009–present

On January 23, 2009, Governor David Paterson ended what had become a seven-week-long comedy of errors by selecting Kirstin Gillibrand, a Democrat who had just been elected to a second term in Congress, to replace Hillary Rodham Clinton as New York's junior Senator after Clinton assumed the office of Secretary of State in the Obama administration.

In the special election to replace Gillibrand, the candidates were Matthew Scott Murphy (Democrat), an entrepreneur who had briefly served as an aide to Missouri governors Mel Carnahan (1992) and Roger Wilson (2000–2001), making his first run for elective office, and Jim Tedisco, (Republican), the Minority Leader of the New York State Assembly.

Tedisco, who was not registered to vote in the congressional district (he was registered to vote in Schenectady County, which was located in his Assembly District but not within the 20th Congressional District), was selected by the Republican county committee chairs, defeating State Senator Betty Little and John Faso, the party's 2006 gubernatorial candidate.

The Democrats originally courted Mike Richter, who had been the New York Rangers' Goalie (1989–2003), leading the National Hockey League team to their 1994 Stanley Cup.[1] When Richter decided not to run, the Democrats nominated Murphy (who moved to the area in 2006) because he committed to self-financing his race.

Murphy defeated Tedisco, by 726 votes out of more than 160,000 cast.[2] The election was seen as an early referendum on President Barack Obama's policies, and both parties made a significant effort to win. The Republican National Committee (RNC), the Republican Congressional Campaign Committee (RCCC) and other allied groups spent more than $1.7 million on the race.[3] On Murphy's behalf, the Democratic Congressional Campaign Committee (DCCC) spent $150,000[4] and the Democratic National Committee (DNC), $10,000.[5] The Service Employees International Union (SEIU) expended $315,000 for Murphy.[6]

The count took more than three weeks to complete as Murphy held a 59-vote lead on election night, pending an official re-canvass and the counting of absentee and valid affidavit ballots.[7] After Tedisco conceded, Murphy said, "I look forward to rolling up my sleeves in Washington to bring jobs, opportunity, and prosperity back to Upstate New York."[8] Murphy took his seat on April 29, 2009.

CHARACTERISTICS OF THE 20TH DISTRICT

The 20th District includes all or parts of Columbia, Delaware, Dutchess, Essex, Greene, Otsego, Rensselaer, Saratoga, Warren and Washington counties. The district takes in about 7,200 square miles of upstate New York, stretching from Poughkeepsie in the south to Lake Placid (site of the 1932 and 1980 Winter Olympics) in the north and west out beyond Cooperstown (home of the Baseball Hall of Fame). The cities of Glens Falls and Saratoga Springs are among the 137 cities and towns located within the district. In 2007, the district's population was 677,533, with 44.9 percent of the district's residents living in urban areas and 56.1 percent residing in rural areas.[9]

Figure 6.1 New York Congressional District 20

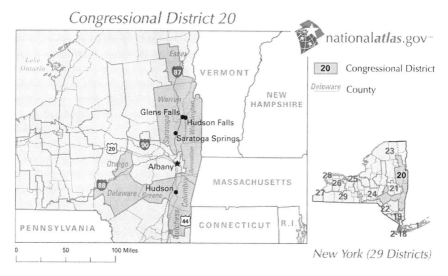

Congressional District 20

New York (29 Districts)

Historically, the area has been represented by Republicans in Congress. John E. Sweeney had served four terms in the House (1999–2007). His predecessor, Gerald B.H. Solomon, had represented the area for 20 years (1979–1999).

Gillibrand defeated Sweeney by a 53 to 47 percent margin in 2006. Gillibrand benefited from newspaper accounts of a December 2005 domestic violence incident involving the congressman and his wife that appeared shortly before the election.[10]

She also was helped by the statewide landslide victories of Eliot Spitzer (Governor) and Hillary Rodham Clinton (Senate), as the two candidates carried all the counties in the 20th District. Gillibrand lost only sparsely populated Delaware and Greene Counties to Sweeney.

In Congress Gillibrand was a member of the Blue Dog Coalition, a group of moderate and conservative Democrats in the House of Representatives. The Blue Dogs assert that Americans have become increasingly conservative and that Democrats should present an agenda that protects the interests of the vulnerable, respects traditional cultural values and keeps taxes low. Gillibrand also had a 100 percent rating from the National Rifle Association (NRA), which helped her attract support from conservative voters in her district. In 2008, she defeated Alexander (Sandy) Treadwell, the former Chair of the New York State Republican Committee (2001–2004), by 62 to 38 percent, despite an overwhelming Republican registration edge and being outspent, $7,038,557 to $4,489,397.[11]

Party Balance

While the Democratic candidate had prevailed in three consecutive elections, party enrollment favored the Republicans. According to the New York State Board of Elections, enrolled Republicans outnumbered Democrats by a substantial margin.

However, while Republicans constitute a plurality of the electorate within the District, more than 152,000 of the 467,392 registered voters (32.5 percent) are enrolled in third parties or not registered in any political party, making it possible for a moderate or conservative Democrat to be competitive in the district.

Voting and Electoral History

Notwithstanding the three consecutive Democratic victories, this district had sent Republicans to Congress for a number of years. Sweeney, prior to his loss to Gillibrand in 2006, had first won office in 1998 with 55 percent of the vote (when most of the present district was part of the 22nd District) and was subsequently re-elected (in the re drawn 20th District) with 68 percent (2000); 73 percent (2002), and 66 percent (2004).

His Republican predecessor, Solomon, was first elected in 1978 (when many of the communities that are part of the present 20th District were part of the 29th District, and were then redistricted, in 1980, to the 24th District, and finally, in 1990, to the 22nd District), and served 10 terms in the U.S. House of Representatives before retiring in 1998.

In presidential politics the 20th has, with the exception of 2008, been a red spot in one of the more reliably blue states in the union. Democrat Barack Obama carried the district in 2008, 50.7 percent to 47.7 percent for Republican John McCain.[12] In 2004, President George W. Bush defeated his Democratic challenger, Senator John Kerry, by a 54-to-46 percent margin.[13] The 20th was one of the nine (out of 29) Congressional Districts carried by Bush in New York in 2004 and one of the six (of 32) carried by Bush in his 2000 race against Vice President Al Gore.

Demographic Character of the Electorate

In 2007, the District's population was estimated to be 677, 533, an increase of 3.5 percent from the 2000 Census.[14] The district is overwhelmingly White (92.1 percent), with Blacks (2.5 percent), Hispanics (2.7 percent), Asians (1.4 percent), Native-Americans (0.1 percent) accounting for less than eight percent of the population. Only one New York district, the 23rd, had a larger proportion of white residents (92.4 percent).

Table 6.1.   Voter Enrollment by Party Affiliation and Status

County	Status	Democrats	Republicans	Third Parties	Blanks	Total Voters
Columbia	Active	12,669	12,368	4,030	10,695	39,762
Columbia	Inactive	1,247	805	457	1,077	3,586
Columbia	*Total*	*13,916*	*13,173*	*4,487*	*11,772*	*43,348*
Delaware	Active	6,604	10,626	1,725	4,291	23,246
Delaware	Inactive	808	811	234	645	2,498
Delaware	*Total*	*7,412*	*11,437*	*1,959*	*4,936*	*25,744*
Dutchess	Active	18,950	20,650	4,766	17,220	61,586
Dutchess	Inactive	2,101	1,755	542	1,927	6,325
Dutchess	*Total*	*21,051*	*22,405*	*5,308*	*19,147*	*67,911*
Essex	Active	2,173	4,093	706	1,542	8,514
Essex	Inactive	253	399	98	235	985
Essex	*Total*	*2,426*	*4,492*	*804*	*1,777*	*9,499*
Greene	Active	7.020	12,175	2,511	7,189	28,895
Greene	Inactive	895	1,100	309	930	3,234
Greene	*Total*	*7,915*	*13,275*	*2,820*	*8,119*	*32,129*
Otsego	Active	2,055	3,139	564	1,326	7,084
Otsego	Inactive	211	228	81	191	711
Otsego	*Total*	*2,266*	*3,367*	*645*	*1,517*	*7.795*
Rensselaer	Active	9,750	13,497	5,063	12,652	40,962
Rensselaer	Inactive	874	1,036	440	1,200	3,550
Rensselaer	*Total*	*10,624*	*14,533*	*5,503*	*13,852*	*44,512*
Saratoga	Active	37,144	62,868	10,409	32,761	143,182
Saratoga	Inactive	2,609	3,141	709	2,452	8,911
Saratoga	*Total*	*39,753*	*66,009*	*11,118*	*35,213*	*152,093*
Warren	Active	10,479	20,573	3,026	7,943	42,021
Warren	Inactive	984	1,358	370	922	3,634
Warren	*Total*	*11,463*	*21,931*	*3,396*	*8,865*	*45,655*
Washington	Active	8,769	15,735	2,850	7,116	34,470
Washington	Inactive	1,179	1,423	463	1,171	4,236
Washington	*Total*	*9,948*	*17,158*	*3,313*	*8,287*	*38,706*
District	Active	115,613	175,724	35,650	102,735	429,722
District	Inactive	11,161	12,056	3,703	10,750	37,670
20th Congressional District	Total	126,744	187,780	39,353	113,485	467,392

Source: New York State Board of Elections, NYS Voter Enrollment by Congressional District, Party Affiliation and Status; Voters Registered as of November 1, 2010.

The median age of the district's population was 40.0 years, with 14.1 percent of the population over the age of 65 and 21.8 percent of the population under the age of 18. 88.5 percent of those 18 and older were high school graduates; 27.9 percent had college degrees and 12.0 percent held graduate degrees.

The median family income was $54,941, and the median home value was $186,600. The percentage of households living in the District living below the poverty line was 8.5 percent and 12 percent of the residents of New York-20 were veterans, an important constituency given the challenger's background.

Employment/Occupational Characteristics

Notwithstanding the district's geographic proximity to the state capitol, 72.6 percent of the employed population in the district worked for private employers; 18.9 percent in the public sector, and 8.5 percent were self-employed. Blue collar employees constituted 21.7 percent of the workforce; white collar, 60.3 percent; 0.2 percent held khaki collar (civilian employees with the military) jobs, and 17.8 percent were classified as others.

Major in-district employers include Glens Falls Hospital (3,000), the largest hospital between Albany, New York and Montreal, Canada, the largest employer in the region that includes Warren, Washington, northern Saratoga, Essex, Hamilton and northern Rensselaer counties; Stewart's Ice Cream (1,550) of Greenfield, Saratoga County; and a Target Stores Distribution Center (1,000) located in Wilton, Saratoga County.

THE CANDIDATES

Scott Murphy

Murphy, the Democratic incumbent, voted against the Affordable Health Care Act in November 2009. He opposed the Stupak Amendment, which restricted federal funding and subsidies for health plans that covered elective abortion procedures. Murphy voted for the Patient Protection and Affordable Care Act in March 2010. Murphy, acknowledged his change in position, noting that, "This bill is fundamentally different than the bill we voted on last November. . . . This legislation will not only make coverage more affordable for New York families, but it will also reduce the federal deficit. . . . This is the most important piece of deficit reduction work that's been done here in a decade."[15]

In the House, Murphy served on the same committees as his predecessor: Agriculture and Armed Services. During his term in the House, Murphy sponsored 12 bills; three resolutions, and four amendments to bills. Murphy's legislation included proposals to extend, by one year, a jobs tax credit (H.R. 3118); a bill to reduce the number of dairy cows in production in order to stabilize milk prices (H.R. 3322): and a bill that would have permitted veterans to use educational benefits at institutions other than colleges and universities (H.R. 4320). None of Murphy's bills became law.

Chris Gibson

On the Republican side, the field was a bit more crowded at the beginning of the race, and the Republican county leaders from the district agreed on a framework for selecting a candidate, setting a March 7 deadline for hopefuls to inform them of their interest in the party's nomination, with an endorsement coming at the end of March.

On February 19, Queensbury Town Supervisor Dan Stec became the first announced candidate, stating he was "going to pursue the endorsement process."[16] On February 16, David Harper, Saratoga County's First Assistant District Attorney, resigned his position and announced his candidacy five days later, declaring that he was "running for Congress to put an end to the out of control spending and fiscal irresponsibility that dominates Washington and is ruining our economy."[17] He created a campaign committee with $50,000 of his own money.

On March 3, Tea Party activist Patrick Ziegler, 37, an insurance salesman and member of the Ballston town (Saratoga) Republican Committee, a volunteer state coordinator for former presidential candidate Mike Huckabee's political action committee, HuckPac, and a founder of the NY Liberty Council, "a coalition of grassroots organizations committed to Constitutionally-limited government, fiscal conservatism and local control over issues."[18]

John Faso, a former assemblyman and gubernatorial candidate, considered entering the race: "I have had many people throughout the district encouraging me to get in this race. I have had a number of the chairs calling me up to get in the race," he said. "While I have always said that I am interested in it, I at the same time have a pretty full plate of other obligations. I don't know if it's possible, but I'm seriously looking at it."[19] In the end, Faso would decide not to run, and back the final candidate to enter the race, Chris Gibson.

Gibson announced his candidacy on March 6, just days after retiring as a Colonel from the United States Army. During his 24-year Army career, Gibson completed four tours in Iraq, one during Desert Storm and three during Operation Iraqi Freedom. He was also deployed in Kosovo, a counter-drug operation with the 82nd Airborne in New Mexico and his final posting was as commander of the 82nd Airborne's Second Division combat team, in the opening month of the Haiti earthquake relief effort. During this time, he also was a Hoover National Security Affairs Fellow, a Congressional Fellow in the office of Representative Jerry Lewis, and taught American politics at the United States Military Academy at West Point.[20]

At a "homecoming" event hosted by Faso, Gibson established the rationale for his candidacy:

> Today our way of life is being threatened. . . . Terrorist groups led by al-Qaida want to end Western Civilization and remake the world in their diabolical vision. . . . Domestically we are taxing, spending and borrowing at an unsustainable pace. We are accumulating a mountain of debt. . . . Today I announce that I am running for Congress to reverse these troubling trends and to help get our country back on track again.[21]

By the end of March, as it became clear that Gibson had won the support of enough county organizations to secure the Republican endorsement, the other candidates withdrew, leaving the way clear for Gibson. Ziegler, the Tea Party activist, became Gibson's campaign manager.[22] On March 31, in an Albany meeting, the 10 county chairs endorsed Gibson. Accepting the support, Gibson sounded the themes of the campaign: "Their nomination of my candidacy is proof that a message of reducing taxes, curbing government spending, eliminating onerous regulations and reducing health care costs resonates with the citizens of the 20th District."[23] In August, the National Republican Congressional Committee (NRCC) designated Gibson a "Young Gun," and targeted the race.

Gibson was cross-endorsed by the New York Conservative Party while Murphy received the backing of the Independence and Working Families parties.

Campaign Issues

The campaign, like elsewhere in America, came to be dominated by the economy, health care reform, and the Democratic Party's control of Congress.

As the general election campaign began, Gibson linked Murphy to Speaker of the House Nancy Pelosi and President Obama. On the stump, in debates, and in paid media, the Gibson campaign attacked Murphy for supporting what they termed the "failed stimulus plan," "Obamacare," and for voting with Nancy Pelosi 91 percent of the time.

The incumbent responded to the attacks by emphasizing his efforts to cut taxes, create and save jobs, and his willingness to advocate on behalf of the values of his district in Washington. He also attacked Gibson for supporting tax credits for sending American jobs overseas and for backing a continuation of the Bush-era tax cuts for the wealthy.

At their October 21 debate, Murphy declared that, "I want to close loopholes on companies that are shipping jobs overseas."[24] Gibson rejected this approach, responding that "Now is not the time to raise taxes."[25] Instead, Gibson rebutted, the way to keep jobs in the United States was to repeal the health care legislation and replace it with a law that would not hurt small business.

CAMPAIGN STRATEGY

Paid Media

Each candidate aired a series of television spots. The Murphy campaign's introductory spot ("Our Kids") highlighted his extended family, and the 58 family members whom he had dinner with each Sunday. The lighthearted spot suggests that Murphy takes the upstate values with him to Washington where he works to cut spending, create jobs and make the federal government listen.

In subsequent spots, Murphy highlighted his support (in two spots) for legislation ending tax breaks to companies that sent jobs overseas, tax breaks he asserts his opponent supported ("Stop Sending Jobs Overseas" and "Time to Stop Shipping Jobs Overseas"); and the 1,000 jobs he created as a businessman and how he was fighting to save and create jobs in upstate New York ("Businessman" and "Saved"). One surprising spot aired by Murphy highlighted his support for the Health Care Reform law. In the spot ("Reality"), a narrator warns that:

> Chris Gibson would let insurance companies go back to denying coverage for pre-existing conditions. He would let them restore lifetime limits on coverage. Chris Gibson would eliminate mandatory coverage for preventive care like mammograms and colon screenings, and seniors would pay more for prescription drugs. Chris Gibson: He's for the insurance industry, not you.

Embracing health care reform was an unusual and risky strategy in this election cycle. Most Democrats in tough races avoided the subject, Murphy was an exception.

The Gibson campaign went on the air after a number of Murphy's commercials had aired. The campaign spent $120,000 to run an introductory ad for two weeks in early September district wide on broadcast and cable TV. The "meet the candidate" spot featured footage of Gibson with his family and his hometown, Kinderhook ("New Leadership"). It started with images of Gibson in the military and a female narrator who says, "From Kinderhook to Kosovo, Iraq, Haiti." A male narrator steps in, "wherever America faced serious challenges, Chris Gibson answered the call." The message is: Gibson will use his leadership skills learned on the job in the military to represent you in Congress. The scenes then changed to images of Gibson with "voters." Several shots featured his wife. Unlike Murphy's first spot, which was light-hearted, Gibson's was serious.

Later spots featured Gibson speaking about creating jobs and stimulating the economy by cutting taxes and regulation ("Jobs and the economy"); and a number of ads attacking Murphy's support of the Health Care bill, the stimulus package and Speaker Pelosi ("Scott Murphy is a voice for Nancy Pelosi," "Disappointed," "Our Jobs,"). Other spots featured Gibson calling to repeal and replace the Health Care Bill ("Hard Choices") and to extend the Bush era tax cuts for everyone. "Especially the middle class" ("Common Sense").

Gibson's spots appear to have been more effective. By the end of the campaign, Murphy's "unfavorables" increased among independents and Republicans, while Gibson's name recognition and "favorables" increased.[26]

Murphy's charge that Gibson supported sending jobs overseas appears not to have been effective. The Gibson campaign claimed that the Murphy spots misrepresented the candidate's position. Daniel Odescalchi, a Gibson spokesman rebutted the ads:

> To imply that Chris Gibson, who grew up in a middle-class Kinderhook family and whose father was a union worker for Otis Elevator, is for shipping jobs to China is absurd and disingenuous. Chris Gibson is for strengthening American businesses to ensure they can create good paying jobs for American workers. It is Scott Murphy who has weakened American business and made it less competitive by voting for the government takeover of healthcare, cap and trade and card check.[27]

Media Endorsements

A number of media outlets serving the District endorsed the Democrat. The *Albany Times-Union*, in its endorsement, said that Murphy "has demonstrated the ability to weigh issues on their merits and make difficult choices. Here is a representative, for example, who supported one of his fellow Democrats' most important bills—health care reform—yet earns top marks from the National Rifle Association."[28]

The *Poughkeepsie Journal, The New York Times, The Daily Star* of Oneonta, *The Lake George Mirror News, The Columbia Paper, The Whitehall Times and Granville Sentinel, The Glens Falls Post-Star* and *The Millbrook Independent* also endorsed the Democrat.

Gibson was endorsed by *The Saratogian, The Glens Falls Chronicle,* and *The Register-Star.*

Campaign Finance

Both candidates were well financed; Gibson demonstrated his viability by out-raising the incumbent during the first full quarter (April 1–June 30, 2010) of his candidacy. During that period, Gibson raised $426,411, compared to Murphy's $348,023.

Table 6.2. Candidate Financial Summaries, 20th Congressional District, 2008–2010 Cycle (through November 22, 2010)

Candidate Name	Net Receipts	Net Disbursements	Cash	Debt	Through
Chris P. Gibson	1,693,788	1,692,654	1,134	$50,000	11/22/10
David A. Harper*	52,960	52,960	0	0	3/31/10
Scott M. Murphy	3,567,922	3,531,147	69,557	1,000	11/22/10
Eric Sundwall*	8,747	8,338	0	0	12/31/09
Patrick Ziegler*	4,734	4,734	0	0	6/30/10

*Not a candidate in the 2010 general election.
Source: Federal Election Commission, FEC Campaign Committee Reports.

As might be expected, the lion's share of PAC support went to the incumbent. Murphy received $1,337,660 through PACs and Gibson, $194,712.

One interesting development was that as the tide of the race turned in Gibson's favor some local donors who had contributed early in the cycle to Murphy made contributions to the Republican.[29]

According to data gathered by OpenSecrets.org, the five largest "industries" that contributed to Murphy were securities and investments ($495,820); Democratic/Liberal ($481,742); Leadership PACs ($274,300); Candidate Committees ($207,950), and Lawyers/Law Firms ($205,753). Murphy was the top recipient of contributions from candidate committees, Democratic Leadership PACs and teachers' unions.[30]

Table 6.3. Sources of Receipts, 20th Congressional District, 2008–2010 Election Cycle (through November 22, 2010)

Candidate Name	Total Receipts	Individual	PAC	Party	Candidate	Other
Chris P. Gibson	1,693,788	1,274,745	207,013	26,850	59,900	125,380
David A. Harper*	52,960	2,960	0	0	50,000	0
Scott M. Murphy	5,615,898	3,016,234	1,909,950	12,484	250,000	427,230
Eric Sundwall*	8,747	8,547	200	0	0	0
James Tedisco*	1,711,192	848,354	484,338	62,427	200,000	116,073
Patrick Ziegler	4,734	4,734	0	0	0	0

*Not a candidate in the general election.
Source: Federal Election Commission

Table 6.4.   Independent Expenditures, 20th Congressional District (through November 22, 2010)

	Murphy	Gibson
For	$61,336	$6,860
Against	$1,726,022	$674,537

Source: Federal Election Commission

Gibson's five largest sources of contributions were retirees ($110,052); general contractors ($89,349); securities and investments ($84,957); Leadership PACs ($62,500), and what OpenSecrets described as miscellaneous finance ($39,856).[31]

There were a significant number of independent expenditures in this contest, with Gibson receiving far more help than Murphy.

The more than $1.7 million spent against Murphy certainly helped Gibson overcome any fundraising advantage enjoyed by the incumbent. Among the groups making the largest independent expenditures (according to FEC data) against Murphy were American Crossroads ($447,366), National Republican Congressional Committee ($398,031), and the 60 Plus Association ($516,436). The Democratic Congressional Campaign Committee spent $696,418 opposing Gibson.

Bases of Support

Murphy's prominent supporters included the National Rifle Association (NRA) Political Victory Fund; the Veterans of Foreign Wars (VFW) PAC; the National Farmers Union; the Alliance for Retired Americans; the New York League of Conservation Voters; the Sierra Club; NARAL Pro Choice America; the Planned Parenthood Action Fund, and the Human Rights Campaign. The incumbent received labor backing from the New York State AFL-CIO; the New York State Public Employees Federation (PEF); the Civil Service Employees Association (CSEA) of New York State; the Communications Workers of America, and the New York State United Teachers (NYSUT)

A number of prominent Democrats campaigned for Murphy. His predecessor, Senator Gillibrand appeared with Murphy the Sunday before the election as she campaigned for election to the remaining two-years of Hillary Clinton's term.[32] State Attorney General Andrew Cuomo (the Democratic Party's successful candidate for Governor) and former President Bill Clinton also campaigned in the District for Murphy the weekend before the election.

Richter, the former hockey player who had considered a run for the seat in 2009, recorded a "robo call" for Murphy.[33]

Gibson had the support of the National Federation of Independent Businesses (NFIB), Move America Forward[34] and Americans for Prosperity, the group founded by billionaire David Koch and Richard Fink (a member of the Board of Koch Industries). Former New York City Mayor Rudy Giuliani appeared with Gibson on September 22 at a campaign stop at a local business, Total Tool, in Schodack, before attending an Albany fundraiser for the candidate. House Minority Leader John Boehner also came into the district to campaign for Gibson.

ELECTION RESULTS

Early polls showed Murphy leading. A poll released by the conservative American Action Forum released in late August showed Murphy holding a 45 percent to 40 percent lead.[35] However, the poll also found that Gibson has

Table 6.5.   20th Congressional District Vote Tally

County	Scott Murphy Dem	Christopher P. Gibson Rep	Scott Murphy Ind	Christopher P. Gibson Con	Scott Murphy Wor
Columbia	9,548	10,432	858	1,947	950
Greene	5,314	8,099	639	1,581	496
Warren	9,237	11,087	897	1,464	450
Washington	7,054	8,785	657	1,407	437
Part of Delaware	4,548	5,754	487	744	468
Part of Dutchess	13,704	13,780	1,143	2,845	1,086
Part of Essex	1,978	1,754	216	208	125
Part of Otsego	1,484	1,756	169	258	157
Part of Rensselaer	8,428	11,373	1,094	2,761	753
Part of Saratoga	30,282	37,993	2,696	6,150	1,720
Total	91,577	110,813	8,856	19,365	6,642
Recap	107,075	130,178			

Source: New York State Board of Elections. General Election Results. Certified December 13, 2010.

37 percent name recognition, compared to 91 percent for Murphy, encouraging Republicans.[36] A poll conducted by the Siena Research Institute between September 12–14, 2010, had Murphy ahead by 17 points, 54 to 37 percent.[37] However, as the Siena pollster Steven Greenberg observed:

> This campaign has a long way to go. The vast majority of voters have seen or heard Murphy commercials. That is not yet true for Gibson, although it is likely to change as the campaign heats up. As voters learn more about Gibson, will their views about who would better serve them in Congress change? Will they change enough to close the gap or put Gibson in front? It's going to be fun to watch.[38]

During the next six weeks the tide turned. A Siena poll conducted October 23–25, 2010 found that Gibson had taken a nine-point lead, 51 to 42 percent.[39] He was able to solidify his support among Republicans and win over the independents.

The final tally was not even close. Gibson defeated Murphy by more than 23,000 votes out of slightly more than 237,000 cast.

Gibson carried every county and part of a county in the congressional district, with the exception of the part of Essex County in the district.

NOTES

1. Richter, who retired from hockey after a series of concussions in 2003, briefly considered running against Republican Christopher Shays in Connecticut's 4th District in 2008, before announcing he would not run in March 2007. While Richter resided in Connecticut, he maintained a second home in Essex County, New York.

2. New York State Board of Elections. 2009. Statement of Canvass, 20th Congressional District. New York State Board of Elections. May 2009.

3. Kane, Paul. 2009. "Murphy Ekes Out Win in NY-20 Special Election," The Washington Post.com. voices.washingtonpost.com/capitol-briefing/2009/04/murphy_eeks_out_win_in_ny-20_s.html?hpid=moreheadlines. Retrieved 21 November 2010.

4. The Hill Staff, "SEIU spends $90K in NY-20." The Hill's Blog Briefing Room. Posted 12 March 2009. thehill.com/blogs/blog-briefing-room/news/campaigns/37945-seiu-spends-90k-in-ny-20. Retrieved 16 November 2009.

5. Kane, Paul. 2009. "Murphy Ekes Out Win in NY-20 Special Election," The Washington Post.com. voices.washingtonpost.com/capitol-briefing/2009/04/murphy_eeks_out_win_in_ny-20_s.html?hpid=moreheadlines. Retrieved 21 November 2010.

6. Fund, John, New York Has a Referendum on Obama. *Wall Street Journal* 28 March 2009, A9.

7. Liu, Irene Jay, and Leigh Hornbeck. 2009. "Murphy Going To Congress." *Albany Times–Union*, 25 April 2009, A1.

8. Liu, Irene Jay, and Leigh Hornbeck. 2009. "Murphy Going To Congress."

9. Barone, Michael and Richard E. Cohen. 2009. *The Almanac of American Politics 2010*. Washington, DC: National Journal Group: 1081.

10. On October 31, 2006, the *Albany Times–Union* reported that Sweeney's wife had called the State Police on December 2, 2005, claiming that the Congressman was "knocking her around" during an argument at their home: Lyons, Brendan J, "Congressman's Wife Called Police." Times-Union.com. web.archive.org/web/20061213205513/timesunion.com/AspStories/storyprint.asp?StoryID=530664, retrieved 9 November 2010.

11. Federal Elections Commission. 2009. *2008 House and Senate Campaign Finance for New York: 20th Congressional District. www.fec.gov/DisclosureSearch/HSRefreshCandList.do?category=disH&stateName=NY&congressId=20&electio n_yr=2008, retrieved 10 November 2010.*

12. Swing State Project. 2009. NY-20: Traditionally Red District Turned Blue in 2008. Posted 23 January 2009. www.swingstateproject.com/showDiary. do?diaryId=4324, Retrieved 16 November 2010.

13. Barone, Michael. 2009. *Political Bloodlines of Kirsten Gillibrand, Senator From New York*. Thomas Jefferson Street Blog. *U.S. News and World Report*. Posted 26 January 2009. politics.usnews.com/opinion/blogs/barone/2009/1/26/political-bloodlines-of-kirsten-gillibrand-senator-from-new-york.html. Retrieved 16 November 2010.

14. Barone, Michael and Richard E. Cohen. 2009. *The Almanac of American Politics 2010*. Washington, DC: National Journal Group: 1081.

15. Dlouhy, Jennifer. 2010. "Updated: Murphy to Vote for Health Care Overhaul" New York on the Potomac. Posted 19 March 2010. blog.timesunion.com/nypotomac/breaking-murphy-to-vote-for-health-care-overhaul/2069/. Retrieved 21 February 2011.

16. Thompson, Maury. 2010. "Stec Confirms Candidacy for Congressional Seat," PostStar.com. poststar.com/news/local/article_c2f3334e-1da1-11df-a420-001-cc4c002e0.html. Retrieved 28 December 2010.

17. Vielkind, Jimmy. 2010. "Officially, Harper in Against Murphy," *Capital Confidential,* Posted 21 February 2010. blog.timesunion.com/capitol/archives/22776/officially-harper-in-against-murphy/. Retrieved 28 December 2010.

18. New York Liberty Council. 2010. *Website Home Page*. www.nylibertycouncil. com/. Retrieved 21 February 2011.

19. All Politics is Local. 2010. "Congressional Candidate Hopes Geography Works in His Favor." PostStar.com. poststar.com/app/blogs/?p=40982&cat=259. Retrieved 28 December 2010.

20. Gibson holds a Ph.D. in government from Cornell University and wrote *Securing the State* (Ashgate Publishing, 2008)

21. Lachman, Robert. 2010. "Kinderhook Republican to Challenge Murphy for House Seat." The Register Star Online, 7 March 2010. www.registerstar.com/

articles/2010/03/07/news/doc4b9334038da60507063369.txt. Retrieved, 28 December 2010.

22. Ziegler would resign as campaign manager in early September, becoming a coordinator for the Republican National Committee's regional victory committee in the Hudson Valley.

23. Lachman, Robert, "Gibson Tapped to Challenge Murphy in the 20th." *The Daily Mail*, 1 April 2010.

24. Thompson, Maury, "Gibson, Murphy Spar Over Jobs in Third Debate." PostStar.com, posted 21 October 2010. mail.google.com/a/wagner. edu/?AuthEventSource=SSO#inbox. Retrieved 2 January 2011.

25. Thompson, Maury, "Gibson, Murphy Spar Over Jobs in Third Debate.*"*

26. Siena Research Institute, "Siena College 20th Congressional District Poll: Gibson Takes 9-Point Lead over Murphy into Final Week." Press release, 26 October 2010.

27. Chris Gibson for Congress, "Murphy Again Makes False Claims in New Television Commercial." Press release, 27 September 2010.

28. Albany Times-Union, Editorial: Scott Murphy in the 20th. *Albany Times-Union,* 24 October 2010. www.scottmurphyforcongress.com/release_details.asp?id=201. Retrieved 21 November 2010.

29. Among the local donors who contributed to Murphy early in the election cycle and to Gibson later were: Daniel Burke, a regional president of NBT Bank, contributed $500 to Murphy on June 30, 2009, and another $500 on June 10, 2010. He contributed $500 to Gibson on August 25, 2010. William Dake, chairman of Stewart's Shops, contributed $1,000 to Murphy on March 22, 2010, and another $1,000 on July 9, 2010. He contributed $2,000 to Gibson on August 17, 2010. Eamonn Hobbs, CEO of Delcath Systems, a contributed $2,400 to Murphy on Dec. 31, 2009, and another $2,400 on August 24, 2010. He contributed $1,000 to Gibson on August 24, 2010. Thomas Hoy, president and CEO of Arrow Financial Services, contributed $500 to Murphy on June 30, 2009, and $1,000 to Gibson on August 25, 2010. David Kruczlnicki, president and CEO of Glens Falls Hospital, contributed $500 to Murphy on June 10, 2010, and $500 to Gibson on August 25, 2010. John Nigro, a developer, contributed $1,000 to Murphy on July 26, 2010, and $1,000 to Gibson on August 16, 2010. Source of Data: All Politics is Local. "Updated: Some Donors Supporting Both Sides in the Congressional Race." PostStar.com, posted 9 September 2010. Retrieved 29 December 2010.

30. OpenSecrets.org. 2010. "Top Industries: Representative Scott Murphy 2009–2010." www.opensecrets.org/politicians/industries.php?cycle=2010&cid=N0003068 2&type=I. Retrieved 2 January 2011.

31. OpenSecrets.org, "Top Industries: Chris Gibson 2009–2010." www.opensecrets.org/politicians/industries.php?cycle=2010&cid=N00031998&type=I. Retrieved 2 January 2011.

32. Gillibrand was successful in her race, defeating former U.S. House member Joseph DioGuardi (better known these days as the father of former *American Idol* Judge Kara DioGuardi) by a margin of 62.0 percent to 35.8 percent.

33. Haberman, Maggie, "Ex-Ranger Richter robos for Murphy in NY-20 " Maggie Haberman on New York. Politico.com., posted 31 October 2010. www.politico.com/blogs/maggiehaberman/1010/ExRanger_Richter_robos_for_Murphy_in_NY20_.html#. Retrieved 2 January 201.

34. Move America Forward is a California-based conservative group that was founded in 2004 by political operatives who had organized the 2003 effort to recall Governor Gray Davis, Howard Kaloogian and Sal Russo. Russo and Kaloogian founded, in 2009, the Tea Party Express.

35. Jacobs, Jeremy P., "*NRCC Names Six New Young Guns.*" Hotline On Call, posted 31 August 2010. hotlineoncall.nationaljournal.com/archives/2010/08/nrcc_names_6_ne.php. Retrieved, 29 December 2010.

36. Geraghty, Jim, "Good Signs for GOP in New Batch of Polls from Key House Districts." National Review Online. www.nationalreview.com/campaign-spot/243889/good-signs-gop-new-batch-polls-key-house-districts, Retrieved 1 January 2011.

37. Siena Research Institute, "Siena College 20th Congressional District Poll: Scott Murphy Has Early 17-Point Lead Over Chris Gibson." Press release, 17 September 2010.

38. Siena Research Institute, "Siena College 20th Congressional District Poll: Scott Murphy Has Early 17-Point Lead."

39. Siena Research Institute, "Siena College 20th Congressional District Poll: Gibson Takes 9-Point Lead over Murphy into Final Week." Press release, 26 October 2010.

Chapter 7

Ohio District 6 Race (Johnson v. Wilson)

Ripe for Independent Spenders

William Binning and Sunil Ahuja

Bill Johnson
Party: Republican
Age: 56
Sex: Male
Race: Caucasian
Religion: Protestant
Education: B.A., Troy University; M.A., Georgia Tech
Occupation: U.S. Air Force, (Retired, Lt. Col.); Corporate executive
Political Experience: None

Charlie Wilson
Party: Democrat
Age: 67
Sex: Male
Race: Caucasian
Religion: Roman Catholic
Education: B.A., Ohio University
Occupation: Mortician
Political Experience: Ohio House of Representatives (1997–2005); Ohio Senate (2005–2007); U.S. House of Representatives (2007–2011)

The race for the 6th District was a surprising upset of Democratic Representative Charlie Wilson (D-OH), who did not think he was going to lose to novice Republican Bill Johnson. The next Speaker of the House, John Boehner, on a campaign visit on behalf of Johnson, said on October 31, 2010, "I tell you the race (6th District) wasn't on anyone's chart."[1] Spending by independent groups arguably made the difference in this race in the ever important battle-ground state of Ohio.

CHARACTERISTICS OF THE DISTRICT

The 6th District of Ohio is a long meandering district that runs for over 300 miles along the Ohio River and then goes north to the southern suburbs of Youngstown in the Mahoning Valley. The district lines were drawn after the 2000 census to accommodate Ohio's loss of one congressional seat. The Republican mapmakers in Columbus carved up the district of the then indicted Congressman James Traficant. His district was cut in half. In the redistricting, the 6th was made more Democratic because it added Democratic voting areas from Representative Bob Nye's (R-OH) district to shore up the Republican vote in 18th District then held by Nye. The Democrats retained the redrawn 6th District with the reelection of Representative Ted Strickland (D-OH).

The 6th District has no center core. *The Vindicator,* Youngstown's newspaper, covers the southern suburbs of Mahoning County, which has the largest vote in the district. The rest of the newspapers are relatively small town dailies and weeklies. The TV market is also fragmented. Television ads have to be run in the Youngstown market, the Steubenville, Ohio, station, and on stations in Wheeling and Huntington, West Virginia. There is not even a good highway connecting the district from one end to the other, making campaigning very challenging, which is one of the reasons the Republicans ceded the district to

Figure 7.1   Ohio Congressional District 6

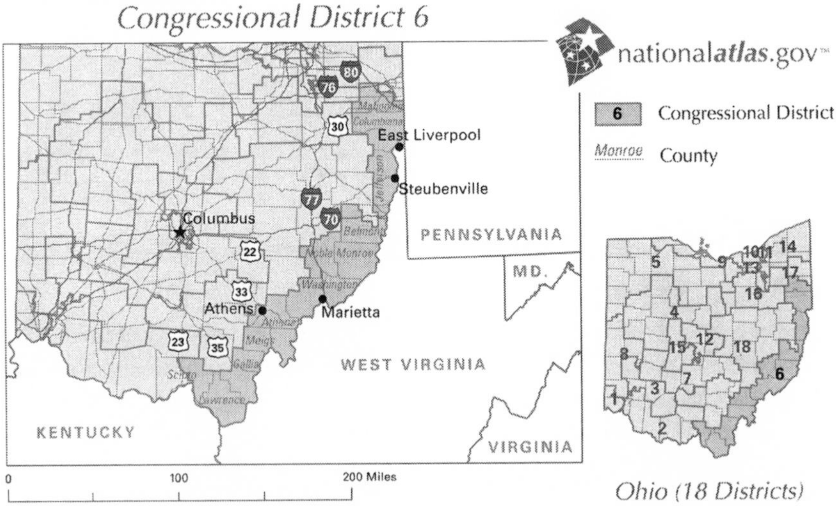

Wilson after his successful write-in campaign in 2006, where he collected more write-in votes in the Democratic primary than the entire Republican field.

Like the media market, the economy and the voters of the 6th District are also fragmented and diverse. It ranges from the middle class suburbs of Youngstown to part of Ohio's poorest Appalachian regions; most of the counties in the district are on the Ohio River and meet the federal government's definition of Appalachia. The district consists of twelve Ohio counties. There is very little interaction between these areas that share a congressional district. George W. Bush carried the district by 51 percent to 49 percent over John Kerry and John McCain bested Barack Obama 50 percent to 48 percent.

THE CANDIDATES

Charlie Wilson

Charlie Wilson, the incumbent, appeared to be pretty secure at the beginning of 2010. He was a long-time successful politician from St. Clairsville, Ohio, which is in the southwestern part of the district. Wilson was born in Martins Ferry, which is across the river from Wheeling, West Virginia. He started the Wilson Funeral and furniture company in 1966 and the Wilson Realty Company in 1978. Also in 1978, as a 37-year-old businessman, he earned his Bachelor's degree from Ohio University.[2] In 1996, Wilson won the first of four two-year terms to the Ohio House. He was term limited out of the Ohio House and was elected to the Ohio Senate in 2004 to a four year term. It was from that post that he launched his 2006 bid for the 6th Congressional District in Ohio. The congressional seat was open because the incumbent Ted Strickland successfully sought the office of Ohio governor that year. Wilson's first victory was noted by the fact that Wilson had filed faulty petitions and had to run as a write-in candidate for the Democratic nomination.[3] Wilson, who spent a lot of his own money on the write-in nomination in 2006, collected more write-in votes than the total vote in the Republican primary that year. He went on to defeat Republican Ohio House leader Chuck Blaisdel by 63 percent to 38 percent. After that beating, the Republicans ceded the district to Wilson. He was not seriously challenged in 2008.

Bill Johnson

Bill Johnson, who won the Republican nomination by less than 2,000 votes, was a political unknown from Poland, Ohio, which is in the southern part of Mahoning County. Born in Roseboro, North Carolina, Johnson and his wife LeeAnn reside in Poland with their son Nathan. He is also the father of three other children and has four grandchildren. Johnson entered the U.S. Air Force in 1973. After serving 26 years, he retired as a Lieutenant Colonel. He graduated from Troy University in 1979 and received a Master's degree from Georgia Tech in 1984. Since 2006, he has served as a chief information officer for a global manufacturer of electronic components in northeast Ohio.

Initially, Johnson announced he was going to run in the heavily Democratic 17th District represented by Tim Ryan (D-OH). He later changed his mind and announced he was going to run in the neighboring 6th Congressional District, which is more favorable to Republicans, but still he was not seen as a winning candidate and the National Republican Congressional Committee (NRCC) did not get actively involved in the race until long after the primary. Among others in the race, he faced Donald Allen, a well-known Veterinarian in Mahoning County. Johnson also upset some of the local Mahoning Republican party officials who were putting their support behind Allen. Unfazed, Johnson moved ahead. He hired a professional consultant and put some of his own money in the race and won the primary by 2,000 votes. Johnson was known to frequent and speak at Tea Party rallies around the district. It was also rumored that former Representative James Traficant (D-OH), recently released from federal prison, was considering running as an independent in the 6th District. Traficant's possible candidacy was seen as a liability for Wilson. In fact, Traficant announced he was running as an independent in both the 6th and 17th congressional districts. Traficant did not file in the 6th and ran only in the 17th Congressional District, and although he drew more than 16 percent of the vote, Democrat Ryan won easily with over 50 percent of the vote.

There were other candidates running for the 6th District in the general election besides Republican Bill Johnson and Democrat Charlie Wilson. They included Libertarian candidate Martin Elsass and Constitution Party candidate Richard Cadle.

PRIMARY ELECTION

Both political parties held primaries to nominate the respective party candidates for the 6th District in Ohio. The outcome of the Democratic primary was known before the race started. A look back at the Democratic primary results suggests some weakness for Charlie Wilson. The incumbent was challenged by a virtually unknown Jim Renner of North Benton, Ohio. Renner, who owned a construction company, did not spend any money in the primary. He indicated that the reason he was running was because of his opposition to the health care bill. When asked what he would do to improve the bill, Renner said

"I can't tell you what I want in a health care bill. I don't know. They could have done a better job."[4] Wilson defended his vote on the health care bill, saying it was a "vote for my district." "The bill is on par with the votes to establish Social Security and Medicare." He said it was the biggest vote he ever cast.[5] He also defended his vote for the $787 billion federal stimulus bill and said he sees the light at the end of the tunnel and the end to the recession. Wilson was treated as the incumbent who was not in a competitive race. He was invited to be the speaker at a number to local Chamber of Commerce events where none of the other candidates were invited and Wilson was treated with the respect of a sure winner even by business groups during the primary season.

During the primary, the Catholic Bishop of the Youngstown Diocese asked Wilson not to vote for the health care bill in its present form. Bishop Murray said the bill in its current form "fails to meet the minimum moral criteria of protecting and freedom of conscience of all citizens." Murray urged Wilson, who is Catholic, to oppose the bill "in its current form due to expansion of abortion funding. What we need is just health care reform that protects the life and dignity of all."[6] Wilson responded to the Bishop by stating that he is opposed to abortion and that the Senate version of the health care reform bill ensures that there will be no federal funding of abortions. Wilson described himself as a pro-life Catholic.

There was an ethical issue raised about Wilson during the campaign. In June 2009, *The Cleveland Plain Dealer* did an analysis of various office holders' financial disclosure reports, including Charlie Wilson's. Wilson's primary opponent, James Renner, got a hold of the *Plain Dealer* report which showed that Wilson sold Huntington Bank stocks valued between $15,001 and $50,000 in November 2008 the day the bank received Troubled Assets Relief Program (TARP). The story also reported other bank stocks traded by Wilson who were receiving TARP money. Wilson's interest was questioned because he served on the House Financial Services Committee which had oversight of TARP. The essence of the ethics questions were raised again by the *Salem News* during the primary. Wilson's office denied any wrongdoing, claiming Wilson took no active role in his investments. His opponent did not accept that response.[7]

The May 4, 2010, primary results in the 6th District arguably do show some voter discontent with Wilson. He prevailed with a total vote of 34,772 to 15,674. It was not a resounding endorsement for Wilson, who was running against an unfunded and unknown candidate.

The outcome of the Republican primary was far more unpredictable. There are a number of points worth noting about the Republican primary field of candidates for the Ohio 6th district. It was quite apparent that there was no recruitment effort by the NRCC. With the exception of Richard Stobbs of Dillonvalle, a former Sheriff from one of the smaller counties, who had few campaign resources, the other two candidates had almost no campaign experience unless you count Donald Allen's write-in campaign for President in 2008, which indicates his quixotic views but led to doubt about his ability to mount a campaign. And finally there was Johnson, who had no roots in the district and switched at the last minute from the 17th District to run in the 6th District. Johnson did not live in the 6th District but in justifying switching to the 6th he said, "The 6th is a much more conservative district."[8] Any role of savvy party operatives or national interest in recruiting a credible candidate is not evident from this field of candidates. The general consensus was that none of these candidates had much of a chance to defeat the well-financed incumbent. Wilson had spent $29,473 between April 15 and June 30, 2010. He had a balance in his account of $610,182 for the general election.

The Republican candidates included Richard D. Stobbs from Dillonvalle, who was a deputy recorder with the Franklin County Recorder's office. Wilson had easily beat Stobbs in the 2008 general election for the 6th District by 62 percent to 33 percent. Previously, Stobbs had run for Belmont County sheriff four times, winning once in 1980. In the 2010 Republican primary, he received the endorsement of *The Vindicator* because the editorial board was unimpressed with the other two candidates: Bill Johnson and Donald Allen, both from Mahoning County.

Allen from Mahoning County, which has the largest number of votes in the district, is a well-known veterinarian, and had run as a write-in for president of the United States in the November 2008 election in Ohio. He finished in ninth place with 212 votes. Allen said he would fight to stop the federal government from allowing others to dictate policy, such as environmental groups from shaping energy policy. He objected to Wall Street running economic policy and teacher unions controlling education. In his statement to *The Vindicator*, he said he would oppose all bills that further socialism and entitlements, and work to reduce taxes and government. Allen was pretty well known in the southern part of Mahoning County and he benefited from that, as shown in Table 1 (see the primary results). His campaign committee was made up mostly of college students from Youngstown State University, who worked tirelessly knocking on doors. He had a campaign manager of very limited experience, who was no match for the professional consultant hired by Bill Johnson.

Johnson was a self-recruited candidate. As indicated above, he first declared that he was running in the very Democratic 17th Congressional District against Tim Ryan and then later switched to run in the 6th District in which he was not a resident. Johnson had almost no roots in the district. In explaining his switch to the 6th District, he said, "The 6th is a much more conservative district" compared to the 17th.[9] He was neither born nor raised in this part of Ohio and he was a relatively new resident. Johnson was chief information officer for Stoneridge, Inc., a $475 million publicly traded company. The company makes electrical components for the automotive industry. It has 250 employees in its Warren, Ohio, headquarters where Johnson works and 5,200 people in its manufacturing and design centers and 14 sales and engineering support offices in Brazil, China, Estonia, France, Germany, India, Japan, Mexico, Spain, Sweden, and the United States.[10] His employer's overseas operations would become an issue in the general election. Few local notables knew him and those who did knew very little about him. He had appeared at many Tea Party events and was an occasional speaker at those events. Although he got his name in the paper for attending and speaking, he was not the headline speaker at the Tea Party rallies; former Representative Traficant, recently released from federal prison, was usually the main figure at these rallies.

The candidates traveled to the far reaches of the district to Athens, Ohio, where the League of Women Voters sponsored a candidates' forum. The candidates spelled out some of their positions and had frequent disagreements. The first question was their support for the Tea Party and did they side with the Tea Party over the Republican Party? Johnson was forthright on his support of the Tea Party. He said, "I believe strongly in the Tea Party's movement's ideals, and I'm proud to have the support of many members. The movement has moved the discussion about wasteful spending and conservative values back into the mainstream and for that the members should be proud."[11] In reference to the Republican Party, he said he would not side with ANY party on matters that are first not good for America, second not constitutional, and third not good for the district. The other candidates also indicated support for the Tea Party.

On health care, Johnson said, "I've signed a pledge to seek a repeal of government-run health care."[12] He said he supported solutions like HSAs (health savings accounts). He also supported portability of health insurance between jobs and across state lines.

There was little disagreement from the other Republican candidates on most of the outstanding issues, and all offered some supporting remarks for the Tea Party but none of them were as strong as Johnson's remarks in support of the positions of the Tea Party.

The NRCC played no role in the recruitment of candidates for the Ohio 6th District and none of the many county GOP parties endorsed any of the candidates seeking that party's nomination. Many in the local Mahoning County party favored Allen. The most significant Republican Party leader in the 6th District, David Johnson of Salem and chair of the Columbiana County Republican Party, said he thought Johnson was by far the best candidate but he did not lead his party to endorse Johnson.[13] He said the NRCC did not take an interest in the race until well into the summer of 2010, when polls began to show that Johnson had a chance to win.

There were two reasons why Johnson was able to overcome the problems of being perhaps the least well known of the candidates at the start of the primary and the lack of support from the local Mahoning County Republican potentates. First, his consultant was crafting a professional primary campaign. Allen's campaign was run by amateurs, only some of whom were getting paid. Second, and most importantly, Johnson raised significant amounts of money compared to the other candidates. Between April 15 and June 30, 2010, he raised $161,831, more than what Wilson collected in that period. In addition, Johnson already had raised over $100,000 for his exploratory committee for the 17th Ohio Congressional District before the race started. He also donated over $40,000 of his own money to his campaign. He spent $76,542 in this reporting period and had a balance of $147,612 on June 30, 2010. He focused on mailers and radio ads in the primary. His TV buys were very limited. Johnson's campaign was quite impressive for a candidate whose opportunity looked very bleak when the race started. His major opponent for the nomination, Allen, raised a paltry $12,277, which included $5,067 of his own money. Table 7.1 shows the county breakdown of the primary vote.

Although Johnson narrowly defeated Allen due to his spending of significant sums of campaign money and also due to the quality of his campaign, there

Table 7.1. Primary Results in Ohio 6th District (May 2010)

County	Allen	Johnson	Stobbs
Athens	340	522	365
Belmont	358	808	921
Columbiana	2,872	2,837	914
Gallia	766	986	508
Jefferson	1,359	1,207	726
Lawrence	721	977	509
Mahoning	3,075	2,152	637
Meigs	543	462	678
Monroe	134	283	163
Noble	434	585	353
Scioto	335	697	225
Washington	1,469	2,577	638
Total	12,406	14,103	6,637

Source: Ohio Secretary of State Web site

were clearly challenges for his upcoming general election. In the primary, he was defeated in Mahoning County, the area he claimed to be his home county, to Allen by almost a thousand votes and he lost in Columbiana County, the next largest county and a county close to his newly-claimed home, by a narrow margin. He won the primary with his margins in a number of smaller counties along the Ohio River.

At the time, Johnson's victory seemed pyrrhic. There was no sense of momentum generated from his win, and his major GOP opponent continued throughout the campaign to undermine Johnson's candidacy. Allen was not a gracious loser. He posted on his website on July 4, 2010, that in January 2010 *The Cook Political Report* "showed a 12-point Democratic advantage in the 17th district just north of the 6th district and a 2-point Republican advantage in the 6th for the upcoming 2010 general election." He went on to say that while he was traveling up and down the 6th District. Republican candidate Johnson had been building a warchest from contributors in the 17th district to defeat Ryan. He said since he had first met Johnson, they both sat down with the Mahoning County leadership to request backing for their respective races and agreed to support one another. The bitter Allen went on to point out that after seeing *The Cook Political Report,* Johnson jumped down to the 6th District to take on what appeared to be a more winnable race. Allen pointed out that Johnson burned many bridges by doing that.[14] The Johnson campaign wisely never publicly responded to Allen and his supporters' whining and bitter grapes. During the campaign, Allen took a swipe at Johnson's military record, saying "He's using his military experience for his campaign and no one knows what he did except he did (information technology)." Johnson defended his military record. Johnson said he was extremely offended that anyone would question the "validity of my military service." The third GOP candidate said he was not questioning Johnson's service. Bitter to the end, Allen wrote letters to the editor in various newspapers criticizing Johnson during the general election.

CAMPAIGN ISSUES

Health Care

Health care reform was a recurring issue in this congressional race. Wilson voted for health care reform. He indicated that he was proud of his vote for health care and said it rose to the stature of the vote for creating Social Security and Medicare. The issue of health care had been raised by his primary opponent. As noted earlier, the Bishop of the Youngstown Catholic

Diocese had asked Wilson not to vote for the health care bill because of the implications for funding of abortions. Wilson, although he is a Catholic, was not endorsed by the National Right to Life Political Action Committee; Johnson was endorsed.

Johnson was critical of the new health care reform act, the hallmark of the recent Democratic-controlled Congress. On his campaign website, he wrote "We must move towards the goal of making health care affordable and available to all Americans."[15] He said patients and doctors—not bureaucrats—should make health decisions. He said the federal government, instead of "controlling and providing healthcare," should enact policies that will stimulate competition and innovation through free enterprise. Johnson expressed support for health insurance portability. However, his major initiative focused on tax incentives to encourage the creation of "robust health savings accounts." The idea of health savings account is the hallmark of conservative think tanks as the way to create competition and market behavior in health markets. It was a key part of the health reforms under George W. Bush and was trimmed under the Affordability Care Act of the Obama Administration and the Democratic Congress. Johnson was an unabashed conservative on health care reform. He was not talking about tinkering with the recently-enacted law; he pledged to scrap it. His attack on the law Wilson voted for was a frontal assault. Johnson was also critical of recent Medicare policies that are tied to this Congress to finance the reform. He maintained that this will contribute to a shortage of physicians for seniors. Johnson had signed a pledge during the primary to repeal the Affordability Care Act.

Congressman Wilson voted for the Affordable Care Act and was proud of it. He did not run from it during the campaign, the way many of his Democratic colleagues had. He was sensitive to the political ramifications of the ACA law especially with seniors, who in national polls were supporting Republicans. One of Wilson's official press releases was entitled "Health care reform is helping thousands of seniors at home in Ohio."[16] In the release, Wilson offered data from the Centers for Medicare and Medicaid Services that showed that Medicare enrollees in Ohio's 6th District were getting help with their prescriptions. Wilson's press release claimed the seniors in the district received $1.2 million to help pay for their prescription drugs. Wilson said, "That's what we said reform should do and that's what it's doing. I know that the cost of prescription drug medication is a source of extreme worry for seniors on fixed incomes and I'm pleased that we're on a path that will wipe that worry away."[17] Wilson argued that this direct benefit to seniors is a result of the Affordability Care Act, which Congress passed in March 2010 and President Obama signed into "law [this] historic health care reform legislation." One of the immediate benefits of the new law was assistance to seniors with high drug expenses.

The release went on to report that an additional 4,480 seniors from the district are expected to enter the Part D "donut hole" before the end of the year. (The donut hole is based on an annual calculation.) Each of those seniors who reach the donut hole will get a $250 rebate to help cover the burden of the donut hole. That will be a total of 9,200 seniors in the 6th District that will receive this assistance. That additional money will total $2.3 million for seniors in the 6th District. Wilson's release went on to point out that "This year, all seniors who have drug expenses of $2,830 or more—and thereby enter the Medicare Part D 'donut hole'—will receive a $250 rebate to help with their high drug costs."[18] In January 2011, all seniors who hit the donut hole will receive a 50 percent discount on brand name drugs. This was expected to save seniors in the 6th District $4.8 million. The discount will be 52.5 percent in 2013 and 55 percent in 2015. The savings will continue to grow until 2019 when the donut hole will be closed.

Wilson defended his vote for the Affordability Care Act on the campaign trail. In a debate in late October, sponsored by a local newspaper and a TV station, Wilson rebutted the attacks of Johnson against the health care plan and Medicare cuts. Wilson, while admitting the plan was not perfect, maintained that it would sustain Medicare for another 12 years. He said it would help small businesses provide health insurance to their employees and prevented denial of children with preexisting conditions. The bill would help seniors with tests such as mammograms and colonoscopies. The bill would also keep children on plans until they were 26 years old. It should be noted that most of Wilson's focus was on the impact of the Affordability Care Act on Medicare, although the central elements of the bill did not address Medicare. The impact of the bill on Medicare was to trim its costs to finance the rest of the program. Wilson tried to mitigate that by talking about its benefit to Medicare enrollees, especially the closing of the donut hole. He often visited senior centers to make his pitch for the bill. In June, he visited seven senior health centers to discuss the law and its impact on Medicare.

Johnson was unimpressed with Wilson's defense of the Affordability Care Act and continued to press for repeal of the health care reform law. He said health care premiums were skyrocketing and taxes would rise because of the reform. He continued to promote health savings accounts.

Jobs and Taxes

A second issue where the candidates differed was on jobs, the economy, and taxes. Johnson was very critical of the growing national debt. He called for a balanced budget. The way to do that, he argued, was to hold down spending. He maintained a strong supply-side position on tax policy. On his webpage he said, "Today's Federal tax code penalizes the wealthy and incentivizes the poor to subsist on entitlement programs. Reducing taxes at all levels of income will stimulate the economy both from the top down (allowing more investment in business and job creation) and from the bottom up (giving people more purchasing power)."[19] He went on the record for renewing the Bush tax cuts for all income levels.

Wilson was more of a Keynesian and defended his vote for the $787 billion stimulus bill. He said he saw the light at the end of the tunnel and we would soon be getting out of the recession. He was sensitive about the debt issue and said he offered a number of bills to reduce the debt. He did not take an open position on the expiration of the Bush tax cuts and what income levels they should cap out at. After the election, Wilson did say he would vote for the Obama deal with the Republicans to continue the Bush tax cuts for two years with an extension of unemployment benefits.

Johnson was not willing to let Wilson present himself as a fiscal conservative Blue Dog Democrat. Johnson pounded away with one of his major negative advertising themes asserting that "My opponent has characterized himself as a fiscal conservative." Said Johnson, "But every time that Nancy Pelosi has asked for a vote for her liberal job-killing policy, he has."[20]

Late in the campaign, Wilson pressed what became his major negative theme against Johnson. Wilson said it was time to review U.S. trade policies and stop shipping jobs overseas. He went on to say "That's what Bill Johnson does for living. Here we work for our living. All we want is a fair day's work for a fair day's dollar."[21] Johnson's company, Stoneridge, Inc., in which he claimed to be a member of the "executive leadership team," closed a plant in Sarasota, Florida, while it expanded its presence in Mexico, China, and Estonia. The Democrats made hay out of this research, finding "Corporate Executive Bill Johnson personally profited from his company shipping jobs to Mexico, China, and Estonia while 300 American workers were fired," said Ryan Rudominer, spokesperson for the Democratic Congressional Campaign Committee (DCCC). He went on and said, "Bill Johnson puts his profits from outsourcing ahead of American jobs and that's wrong for Ohio."[22] Wilson chimed in: "I've watched my Republican colleagues vote over and over against closing loopholes that ship good American jobs overseas." He went on saying that same party is spending money "to support an outsourcer like Bill Johnson."[23] Johnson attempted to refute those charges about shipping jobs overseas. He said he was not involved in those decisions by the company he works for. Wilson finally found a theme that resonated with the voters and he could go on the attack rather than play defense. He said, "As someone who has spent my whole life here, I have seen the devastation that outsourcing has caused in this area, and that is why I have voted to close loopholes that reward companies for shipping jobs overseas." He said that is why he is working to repeal NAFTA (North American Free Trade Agreement). Wilson went on: "These issues are key to Ohio's economic future, and it's pretty obvious that Bill Johnson doesn't understand that." He said he was against NAFTA, CAFTA (Central American Free Trade Agreement), and any other "afta." The job outsourcing issue was a potential game-changer, evidently discovered by the DCCC about Johnson's employer. Protectionism has long been a strong sentiment in the Mahoning Valley and along the Ohio River. Free trade has never been popular, starting at least from the days of President William McKinley, who was from the area, and whose political boss in that era was the famous Marcus Hannah, who hailed from Lisbon, Ohio, the county seat of Columbiana County, which is in the center of the Ohio 6th District. Kristina Paolina said Wilson would start airing "a negative ad next week" about Johnson. It was the closing theme of Wilson's campaign and it likely turned out to be too little too late. The Wilson campaign made the same mistake George W. Bush made when he suffered his first defeat for a Texas state legislative seat in 1978. Bush, in his book *Decision Points* wrote, "I learned that allowing your opponent to define you is one of the biggest mistakes you can make in a campaign."[24] In this upset in Ohio, Wilson had allowed Johnson to define him, and it was too late to change the narrative.

GENERAL ELECTION CAMPAIGN

In late May and early June, the race did not appear to be competitive especially to the local political notables. Johnson continued to push ahead and the race gradually gained notice by national pundits and influential national Republicans like Sarah Palin.

Despite a lack of political buzz and encouragement by local notables for the primary win, Johnson continued to do what is most important for a challenger to someone of Wilson's stature; he continued to raise impressive amounts of money. It is likely that his growing warchest began to draw notice of this race in Washington.

One of the first signs that national figures were taking notice of the Johnson candidacy was a contribution in July from Palin's PAC to Johnson for $3,500. There was no comment from Palin or her SarahPAC specifically about Johnson's candidacy. Johnson put out the press release on the donation and quoted from SarahPAC's goals. In the middle of summer, the NRCC recognized the race in Ohio's 6th District and Johnson's candidacy. The NRCC announced in July that Johnson made "on the radar" status, the first of three levels of the committee's "Young Guns" programs that identifies those campaigns that are viable. Viability is based on raising money and building "a successful campaign structure."[25] Johnson certainly showed he could raise money and that obviously contributed to the rising status of his campaign in national circles. However, he was still viewed with skepticism by the local political establishment. In early October 2010, the NRCC moved candidate Johnson to the top level of the three-tiered "Young Guns" program. Only two weeks before that he was elevated to the "contender" status. To be designated as "Young Guns," the candidates must prove they "have built a winning campaign and achieve substantial fundraising goals."[26] On October 14, 2010, the NRCC made Ohio's 6th District the "Race of the Day."

Campaign Strategies

During the summer and into early fall, Wilson and his supporters were not convinced that he was in any serious danger despite the fact that well respected national handicapper Charlie Cook moved the race from "safe Democrat" to "likely Democrat." Wilson took the high road campaigning as an incumbent officeholder by making announcements and visiting new plants. He did not mention his opponent's name, despite the fact that Johnson would give a negative response to anything Wilson said, if he was given a chance. In March, Wilson pointed out that a review of his voting record by the *National Journal* demonstrated that he was in the middle of the liberal-conservative spectrum and that this reaffirms his argument that he is a moderate "Blue Dog" Democrat. He was a member of the Blue Dog caucus in Congress. During the summer, Wilson gave out medals to veterans, and he visited a Habitat for Humanity project in Salem, Ohio. With Governor Strickland, he visited a plant expansion in Salem. Wilson had a "Build in America" tour and visited Lawrence County's The Point, a large industrial park, for which he had secured $3.6 million and had another $700,000 in a transportation bill. He announced that workers at a plastics plant in Mingo Junction would get Trade Adjustment Assistance. He announced a federal grant to the Scioto County Airport Authority. He walked the streets of Ironton and talked to merchants. He frequently spoke at local Chamber of Commerce functions, and his opponents were not invited. Late in the campaign, the U.S. Chamber of Commerce endorsed Johnson. He campaigned on local concerns and expressed few positions on national issues. He did defend the health care bill and tried to explain its benefits. He also expressed support for stimulus bill to support teachers. At the Steel Trolley diner in Salem, he announced that he was serious about reducing the national debt and that he has introduced ten bills that will chip away at the national debt. However, in most instances, he acted as if he was not actually in a competitive election, and he often did not respond to various issues and charges brought up by Johnson. Energy, a key issue in the district because of the use of coal, did not develop as an issue because Wilson had voted against the cap and trade bill.

Johnson used various campaign gimmicks to draw attention to his candidacy and to criticize Wilson. Johnson rented an RV and toured the entire district stopping in various communities along the Ohio River. He scheduled town hall meetings and invited the other candidates to join him. In July, Johnson wrote Wilson a letter letting him know that many people in the district wanted to hear from him, so Johnson invited Wilson to 12 debates, one in each county.[27] He was frequently able to get attention from the local paper or get an interview on a local radio station. He talked about his religious faith and creating jobs. He was not shy about his involvement with the Tea Party; he told the conservative *Human Events* that: "This is Tea Party country out here—and Tea Parties are big in the tri-county area, I know because I've been to most of them."[28] Johnson worked to establish as his major theme that Wilson was tied to the Washington establishment. He said, "I believe that we've got smart people in our country, and we've never needed Obama, Nancy Pelosi or Charlie Wilson to tell us how to run it." Johnson's effort to tie Wilson to Pelosi became the hallmark of his campaign and also that of the ads by the independent groups that made expenditures on behalf of his campaign.

Wilson tried to run as the local candidate, who recognized those who had done good things for their communities and went around the district announcing various grant projects. He tried to localize the campaign, which is a good strategy if you can make it work. Tip O'Neil, the former Democratic Speaker of the House, was famous for the old adage "all politics is local." Johnson made every effort to nationalize the race by hammering away at the national debt, the weak jobs market, and the health care reform act. He also tried to generate other national issues that Wilson would not take the bait on and/or did not resonate with the voters. Johnson brought up the Supreme Court repealing the Arizona immigration search law, the alleged ethics violations by Congressman Charlie Rangel (D-NY), and New York City's proposed mosque near ground zero. Johnson used every opportunity to tie Wilson to Pelosi and that was the major theme of his campaign in his public remarks and in his advertising.

There were a number of national political figures who made visits to the district to drum up support for their respective candidates. Dick Morris, former Clinton political consultant and current pundit, made an appearance for three Republican congressional candidates, one of whom was Johnson. The August 15th event was put on by the chair of Columbiana County, Dave Johnson, at the Spread Eagle Tavern, a must stop for every Republican visiting Ohio. On October 31st, House minority leader John Boehner (R-OH) held a rally outside the Spread Eagle Tavern for Johnson. At the rally, Boehner told the crowd: "I tell you the race (6th District) wasn't on anyone's charts."[29] It was at a Johnson rally where the soon-to-be Speaker made one of his last campaign appearances.

There were no notable Democrats traveling to the 6th District in support of Wilson for two reasons: (1) Wilson was not seen to be in a competitive race until early October and (2) there were not many Democratic leaders who were very popular in this corner of Ohio. On occasion, Governor Strickland would appear with Wilson and, of course, Strickland had been quite popular when he served in Congress from the 6th District. One Democratic figure who was very popular in Ohio, who came to the Mahoning Valley to drum up support for the Democrats, was former President Bill Clinton. His visited Youngstown for a breakfast rally in Mahoning County the last Saturday before Election Day and it was a packed house. Wilson was in the center of the hoopla to generate turnout for all Democratic candidates in this reliable bastion of Ohio Democratic voters. After the event, Wilson went to a Youngstown State University football game to press the flesh. Clinton had left town.

Advertising War

The nature of the district, the lack of any central population group or media market, and the relatively low cost of TV ads turned this race into a highly-charged and eventually a very negative media campaign. TV advertising was the major expenditure of the 6th District race.

The Wilson campaign started quite civil with the candidate talking about what he had done and what his accomplishments had been. He started his campaign on the high road. It was obvious in the early stages of the race that the Wilson campaign did not see Johnson as a threat but felt they had to counter Johnson's advertising. When it became obvious that Johnson's negative media campaign was gaining traction, the Wilson campaign turned negative and attacked Johnson on the job outsourcing issue, which is described above.

The Johnson campaign started with ads funded by his own campaign, the NRCC, and later by American Action Network, a 501(c)4 organization, which will be discussed below. The campaign of the candidate and the independent spending groups focused on making the case that Wilson was tied to Pelosi and did her bidding. *The Washington Post* showed Wilson voting with Pelosi 98 percent of the time. That made it difficult for Wilson to identify himself as a rogue. A campaign Ad Watch by Jonathan Riskind of *The Columbus Dispatch* captured one the NRCC television ads in a newspaper report. He describes the TV ad he viewed on YouTube: "The spot opens with an image of U.S. Rep. Charlie Wilson, D, St. Clairsville, on a podium next to a blank outline of a person on the wall, which is filled in with photo of House Speaker Nancy Pelosi (D-Calif). The spot employs a 'rubber stamp' to place 'Wilson-Yes in red ink over his image as the ad says'" that Wilson has become a rubber stamp for Pelosi on health care bill, the lifting of the debt limit, and the bailout of the financial system. Wilson works for Pelosi. Since Pelosi took over, Wilson has become a rubber stamp for her agenda.[30] Other ads put up by the NRCC depicted Wilson towing the line for Pelosi. Later, the American Action Network, an independent group, tied Wilson to Pelosi and depicted him voting for all sorts of ludicrous pork barrel projects. The media campaign was endless and it was a continuing attack on Wilson. Seldom was Johnson even mentioned in the attack ads that tied Wilson to Pelosi.

The Columbus Dispatch's Riskind, who did another story on this race, pointed out anecdotally what he discovered in his trip to the district. Wilson was in a difficult race. Riskind found a "Pam Shaffer, a floral designer in East Liverpool, who said the television ads lumping Wilson with Obama and Pelosi kind of scare her. She worries that the health-care overhaul sounds good but will mean higher premiums for her own health care coverage." She said, "I always thought Charlie Wilson was doing OK until I saw these ads," said Shaffer. Riskind goes on in the story and points out that Shaffer, who was a past Wilson voter and who remained undecided, was also disturbed by TV ads charging that the global company Johnson works for closed a plant in Florida and moved jobs abroad.[31] The barrage of negative ads was not the only challenge facing Wilson. Riskind found another voter, Josh Martin, age 33, of Negley, a former Wilson voter who was now supporting Johnson. He said Wilson is hurt by the stigma a lot of Democrats have. After the 2008 election, "People were hoping for a big spike and we haven't seen it. People are looking for a change."[32]

There was more than anecdotal evidence that this race was getting tight. In September, the Johnson campaign released polling results that showed Johnson in a statistical dead heat with Wilson. Wilson held a narrow 3-point lead of 47 percent to 44 percent over Johnson. The Johnson camp spun the results with Johnson reiterating his theme that "the environment does not bode well for Wilson and his 98.1 percent voting record with Nancy Pelosi and President Obama."[33] A later Johnson poll, released in early October by Neil Newhouse of Public Opinion Strategies with a sample of 400, found Johnson had taken the lead by 46 percent to 44 percent margin. Other findings of that survey showed Johnson led by 47 percent to 33 percent with independents. Obama's job approval in the district was 38 percent to 56 percent (with 46 percent strongly disapproving). The Wilson camp had its own confidential internal poll showing Wilson at 42 percent, Johnson at 37 percent, Caddie 3 percent, and Elsass 2 percent. The internal polling memo also said, "We're being outspent on TV 4–1 in Y-Town. We'll increase our buy there but we won't be able to match because of the outside money." The outside spending was the most significant and the most interesting characteristic of this race.

Campaign Finance

There was a considerable amount of money spent in this race. A significant amount of that spending was by independent committees. Wilson's fundraising and spending was not out of the ordinary for an incumbent. What was unusual was the amount of money Johnson was able to raise as a first time candidate challenging an incumbent.

The amounts reported are from the Federal Election Commission (FEC) required reports as of November 22, 2010, for the period 01/01/2009 to 11/22/2010. Wilson reportedly raised a total of $1,057,441, some of that brought forward from 2009. Of those contributions, $247,774 was reported as itemized individual contributions. The bulk of his campaign funds came from other committee donations. The largest donors in that group included the Blue Dog Coalition with $5,000, United Steelworkers Political Action Fund with $5,000, International Brotherhood of Electrical Workers with $5,000, KKQ Corporation Good Government Fund of Fort Lauderdale, Florida, with $5,000, UAW-V-CAP with $5,000, American Crystal Sugar Co. PAC of Moorhead, Minnesota with $5,000, New Democratic Coalition PAC with $5,000, SEIU COPE with $5,000, United Mine Workers of America with $5,000, United Steelworkers PAC Pittsburgh with $5,000, Sheet Metal Workers' with $5,000, U.S. Plumbing and Pipefitting Industry, Washington D.C., with $5,000, Machinists Non-partisan Political Action League of Upper Marlboro, Maryland, with $5,000, Communication Workers Association of America with $5,000, National Beer Wholesalers donated $5,000, a 2nd contribution of $5,000 from LKQ Corporation Good Government Fund, Americans Work PAC with $5,000, American Postal Workers Union with $5,000, and $5,000 from the NEA Fund for Children and Public Education.[34] There were numerous other large donors; the above are presented to give a sampling of the largest donors to Wilson's campaign. These are reportable hard money contributions allowed under federal campaign finance law. It does demonstrate the power of incumbency that approximately two-thirds of Wilson's campaign funds came from PACs that generally support Democratic congressional candidates. Wilson received $2,048 as direct party contributions and he loaned his campaign $80,000, which was apparently done late in the campaign since it does not show up in earlier reports. The reports show a positive balance of $82,498, with debts of $271,650.

The Johnson FEC report for 01/01/2009 to 11/22/2010 showed that he raised a total of $662,855 and spent and total disbursements of $616,932. It shows a personal loan of $45,050, which appears to be for the primary since it was an earlier report. It also showed another loan of $14,000, which showed repayment in this report. The loan was not from Johnson.

What is most impressive about Johnson's FEC report is that he raised $346,591 as itemized individual contributions. A review of those contributors shows that these were area contributors, many of whom were people involved in business throughout or near the 6th district. He showed un-itemized individual contributions of $117,695. Johnson, for being virtually a political unknown and a candidate without prior experience, had the capacity to raise a lot of money on his own. This is an ability that many challengers do not possess. He spent his campaign money early in the election cycle and that is one of the factors that drew the attention of national independent expenditure groups.

Johnson's report showed that he raised only $127,280 from other committee contributions. That is not surprising since PACs are reluctant to back challengers to entrenched incumbents. Some of those groups include the Murray Energy PAC with $5,000, the Freedom Project with $5,000, the Liberty Committee with a total of $1,650, the Mike R. Fund Springfield VA with 2,500, which has ties to the NRCC, and of course SarahPAC with $3,500. The reports showed debts owed at $70,000.

The most interesting part of the race for the Ohio 6th District was the independent expenditures. The Democratic Congressional Campaign Committee (DCCC) came to the aid of Wilson with outside spending of $704,662, much of that on attack ads against Johnson for being tied to a company that shipped jobs overseas. The NRCC came to the aid of Johnson with $337,662 with ads that maintained that Wilson toed the line for Pelosi. The new campaign finance actor that entered the race late was a group called the American Action Network, which spent $1,010,000 with negative ads against Wilson for supporting Pelosi and in the ads gave all sorts of examples of reckless and foolish pork barrel spending.

The American Action Network is a 501(c)4, Washington-based "action tank" created in February 2010 after the U.S. Supreme Court's *Citizens United v. F.E.C.* decision permitting corporations to spend unlimited money influencing elections. It was formed by Norm Coleman, a former Republican senator from Minnesota, who serves as chief executive officer and Rob Collins, a former chief-of-staff of House Minority Whip Eric Cantor, who serves as the president. A prominent member of the board of American Action Network is Fred Malek, who goes back to the Nixon political campaigns. Haley Barbour, governor of Mississippi, Ed Gillespie, former chair of the Republican National Committee, and Jeb Bush, former governor of Florida, were also part of this group. American Action Network won 14 races and lost 10. Although Karl Rove was not directly involved in this group, American Action Network shared offices with similar groups created by Rove. Crossroads was the Rove group that received the most national press attention but Crossroads did not spend money in the 6th District. It is also apparent that these various 501(c)4s that supported GOP congressional campaigns coordinated their spending among some 56 House districts around the country and moved their funds around to the most competitive races. The 6th District fit the profile of the races targeted by these groups since they focused on congressional districts where Obama had lost in his presidential election.

The American Action Network entered the 6th District late with very significant spending. The FEC-50227 filing for American Action Network covering 10/12/2010–10/14/2010 for $505,000.00 named Wilson and a second filing FEC-510439 covering 10/12/2010–10/22/2010 for $505,000.00 named Wilson.[35] The group was naming the candidate they were opposing. Donors do not have to be disclosed for this type of corporate group under the federal tax code. There were other outside groups spending money in this race, all of them for Johnson or against Wilson, including Americans for Prosperity with $1,170, FreedomWorks with $5,359, National Right to Life with $4,501, and Revere America with $1,602.[36]

ELECTION RESULTS

In October, national prognosticators from RealClearPolitics.com, Charlie Cook, and the *New York Times* FiveThirtyEight blog started to forecast the Ohio 6th district race as very close. The result of the election, although surprising to many, was not particularly close. Johnson collected 103,170 votes to Wilson's total of 92,823. Wilson carried four of the twelve counties in the district. He lost many of the counties on the Ohio River which were considered his base. He carried the largest county, Mahoning, but only by 478 votes. Columbiana and Washington counties gave Johnson significant pluralities. County results are offered in Table 7.2.

Johnson's upset of incumbent Wilson was a significant win for the national Republicans. This seat was not on anyone's radar on the filing date in February 2010. At that time, it was seen as a relatively easy win for Wilson. The NRCC took no role in the recruitment of a candidate for this race. Johnson was self-recruited and in fact he was not welcomed by a number of local party notables in his home county of Mahoning. He took two very important steps that contributed ultimately to his win: he hired a professional political consultant, and he spent a great deal of his time successfully raising money early in the election

Table 7.2. General Election Results Ohio 6th District (November 2, 2010)

County	Charlie Wilson Democrat	Bill Johnson Republican	Richard Cadle Constitution	Martin Elsass Libertarian
Athens	7,761	4,141	227	278
Belmont	8,657	8,139	439	398
Columbiana	13,081	18,081	1,195	1,100
Gallia	3,735	5,259	166	171
Jefferson	11,257	11,987	653	553
Lawrence	7,706	9,501	308	265
Mahoning	19,845	19,367	1,138	971
Meigs	2,978	3,699	167	114
Monroe	2,981	2,190	112	101
Noble	2,343	2,590	132	92
Scioto	4,760	5,502	137	132
Washington	7,719	12,714	403	330
Totals	92,823	103,170	5,077	4,505

Source: Columbiana County Board of Elections

cycle. That money surprisingly put him in the race. What arguably contributed significantly to his win was the independent spending by the American Action Network, formed as a result of recent Supreme Court's decision in *Citizens United v. F.E.C.*, which spent more than $1 million attacking Wilson in the closing weeks of the general election.

NOTES

1. Tom Giambroni. "Boehner appears at rally for Johnson," *Salem News*, October 31, 2010.

2. Michael Barone and Richard E. Cohen, *The Almanac of American Politics: 2010.* Washington, D.C.: National Journal Group, 2009, pp. 1178–1179.

3. William C. Binning and Sunil Ahuja, "The Sixth District of Ohio: The Race with the Write-in Campaign," in *The Roads to Congress 2006*, ed. Sunil Ahuja and Robert E. Dewhirst. New York: Nova Science Publishers, 2007.

4. www.vindy.com/news/2010/apr/23/4-candidates-vie-to-unseat-us-rep-wilson/? print.

5 "Candidates vie."

6. Tom Giambroni, "Bishop opponent keep after Wilson," *Salem News*, March 20, 2010.

7. Tom Giambroni, "Wilson rival raps share sale during bailout," *Salem News,* April 28, 2010.

8. www.vindy.com/news/2010/feb/12/johnson-to-seek-gop-nomination.

9. David Skolnick, "Johnson to Seek GOP Nomination," *Vindicator,* February 12, 2010.

10. "As Race Tightens, Johnson Dials for Dollar," *Business Journal Daily,* October 18, 2010.

11. David DeWitt, "GOP 6th District candidates agree on taxes, tea parties," *The Athens News* www.athensnews.com/ohio/print-article-30990-print.html.

12. DeWitt, "GOP 6th District candidates."

13. Interview with David Johnson, December 6, 2010.

14. drallenforcongress.com/pages.

15. www.billjohnsonleads.com/issues.html.

16. www.charliewilson.house.gov/index.php?view=39&id=845%3Aoctob. ...

17. Wilson web site.

18. Wilson web site.

19. www.billjohnsonleads.com.

20. www.irontontribune.com/2010/10/06/candidates-tout-reasons-why-they-should-get-job/.

21. "4 Congressional candidates get final shots in as election nears," *Salem News,* October 18, 2010.

22. www.vindy.com/news/2010/oct/09/candidates-differ-on-views-about-free-tr/?print.

23. "As Race Tightens, Johnson Dials for Dollars," *Business Journal Daily,* October 18, 2010.

24. George W. Bush, *Decision Points* (New York: Crown Publishers, 2010), p. 41.

25. www.vindy.com?new/2010/jul/23/johnson-gets-gop-attention/?print.

26. billjohnsonleads.com/blog/bill-johnson-named-a-young-gun.

27. www.scribd.com/doc/34908940/Johnson-Debate-Letter.

28. wwwhumanevents.com/article.php?print=yes&id=36890.

29. Giambroni. "Boehner appears at rally."

30. www.dispatch.com/live/content/local_news/stories/2010/10/25nrccwilsonwatch-gp.

31. dispatch.com/live/content/editorials/stories/2010/10/31/blue-dog-wilson-finds . . .

32. Blue dog Wilson.

33. billJohnsonleads.com/blog/bill-johnson-in-a-statistical-dead-heat-withdemocratic-inc.

34. This is from the Federal Election Commission website.

35. See query.nictusa.com/egi-bin/dedev/form/C30001648/502227/f93, query.nictusa.com/cgi-bin/dcdev/forms/C30001648/501439.

36. www.opensecrets.org/races/indesp.php?cycle=2010&id=OH06.

Chapter 8

Virginia District 5 Race (Hurt v. Perriello)

A Congressman Falls to a Republican Tsunami

Bob N. Roberts

Robert Hurt
Party: Republican
Age: 41
Sex: Male
Race: Caucasian
Religion: Presbyterian
Education: B.S. from Hampden-Sydney College (1991), J.D. from Mississippi College School of Law (1995)
Occupation: Attorney, H. Victor Millner, Jr., Professional Corporation, (1999–present)
Political Experience: Member, Chatham Town Council, (2000–2001); Delegate, Virginia State House of Delegates, (2002–2008); Senator, Virginia State Senate, (2008–2010)

Thomas S. P. Perriello
Party: Democrat
Age: 36
Sex: Male
Race: Caucasian
Religion: Catholic
Education: B.A. from Yale University (1996), J.D. from Yale University (2001)
Occupation: National security consultant; Founder of faith based organizations.
Political Experience: United States House of Representatives, (2009–2011)

CHARACTERISTICS OF VIRGINIA DISTRICT 5

The 5th District is Virginia's largest congressional district. Prior to the reapportionment of the district in 2011, it included all or parts of the counties of Albermarle, Bedford, Brunswick, Campbell, Charlotte, Fluvanna, Franklin, Greene, Halifax, Henry, Lunenburg, Mecklenberg, Pittsylvania, Nelson and Prince Edward Counties. It also included the independent cities of Bedford, Charlottesville, Danville, and Martinsville. The central Virginia county of Albermarle and the city of Charlottesville anchored the northern part of district. Albermarle County and Charlottesville is the home of the University of Virginia. Largely due to the economic impact of the University of Virginia, the northern part of the district historically has had a low unemployment rate.

The southern part of the district borders North Carolina. Through the 1960s, the textile and tobacco industries provided the economic foundation of this part of the district. By the late 1970s, however, the economic condition of the southern part of the district began to deteriorate. The region lost thousands of manufacturing jobs due to the closure of textile plants. Many of the well paying jobs left the country. Even during the economic booms of the 1980s and 1990s, unemployment would remain high.

The 2001 session of the Virginia General Assembly saw the Republican party control the Senate, House of Delegates and Governorship for the first time since the end of Reconstruction. Republican legislators drew the boundaries of the 5th District to off set the heavily Democratic city of

Figure 8.1   Virginia Congressional District 5

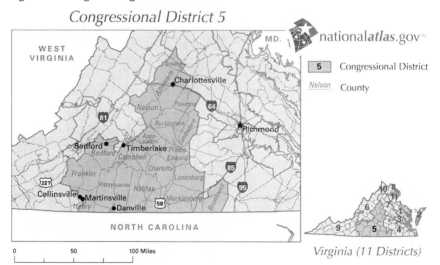

Charlottesville and competitive county of Albermarle counties with the heavily Republican southern part of the district. Beginning in the 1970s, voters in the southern part of the district gradually shifted their political support from conservative Democratic candidates to conservative Republican candidates. The realignment in the southern part of the 5th District was similar to the realignment that took place with respect to rural white voters in many areas of the South. By the end of the 1990s, the southern part of the 5th District had become one of the most reliable Republican areas in Virginia.

Party Balance

Virginia does not permit voters to declare themselves as a member of a political party. As a result, all voters may cast ballots in any party primary. From the 1880s through the 1960s, Virginia effectively operated under the control of the Democratic party. From the mid-1920s through much of the 1960s, the political machine of Harry Byrd Sr. controlled all aspects of political life in Virginia.[1] Through this period, Virginia voters consistently cast ballots for Democratic candidates in statewide races for Governor, Lieutenant Governor and Attorney General as well as for candidates for the Virginia House of Delegates and Senate. A Republican candidate for the United States Senate did not win election until the 1972 upset victory of William Scott over incumbent Democratic U.S. Senator William B. Spong Jr. Yet, beginning with the presidential election of 1952, Virginia voters began to shift their allegiance to Republican presidential candidates. Republican presidential candidate Dwight David Eisenhower carried Virginia in 1952 and 1956, and Republican Richard M. Nixon carried the state in 1960. Even though President Lyndon Johnson succeeded in winning Virginia in the 1964 presidential election, from 1968 through 2004, Republican presidential candidates would carry Virginia. This string of victories ended with Barack Obama winning Virginia in the 2008 presidential campaign.

The party balance in the 5th District reflected the largely conservative and rural nature of the district. The 2004 presidential race saw Republican presidential candidate President George W. Bush defeat Democratic presidential nominee John Kerry by 55.91 percent to 43 percent. While Obama carried Virginia in the 2008 presidential election, U. S. Senator John M. McCain defeated Obama by a margin of 50.59 percent to 48.29 percent in the 5th District. Despite the fact that Democratic U.S. Senate candidate James Webb narrowly defeated incumbent Republican U.S. Senator George Allen in the 2006 contest, Allen defeated Webb by a margin of 53.79 percent to 45.15 percent in the 5th District.

In the 2001 race for Virginia Governor, Democratic nominee Mark Warner won the 5th District, defeating Republican nominee Mark Early, by a margin of 52.39 percent to 46.20 percent. Warner also beat Early statewide to win the Virginia governorship. The 2005 race for governor saw Democratic nominee for Governor Tim Kaine, narrowly win the 5th District by defeating Jerry Kilgore, the Republican nominee, by a margin of 49.59 percent to 48.42 percent. Tim Kaine also won the statewide race for the governorship. And the 2009 race for Virginia governor saw Republican gubernatorial candidate Bob McDonnell win the 5th District by defeating Democratic candidate Creigh Deeds by 61.34 percent to 38.56 percent. McDonnell went on defeat Deeds for the governorship.[2]

Voting and Electoral History: U.S. House Races

From the 1888 through 1996 congressional elections, voters elected Democrats to the 5th District. From the late 1920s through the 1960s, the Democratic political machine of Harry Byrd Sr., controlled the 5th District. The Virginia Constitution of 1902 shaped the political landscape of Virginia through the mid-1960s by disfranchising many Virginia voters. To avoid violating the 14th and 15th Amendments of the U.S. Constitution, the new Virginia Constitution required voters to pass a literacy test and to pay a poll tax. Within a decade of the adoption of the 1902 Constitution, the number of Virginia voters fell sharply. Not surprisingly, the largely rural 5th District proved exceptionally loyal to the Byrd machine.

During the late 1950s and early 1960s, the southern part of the 5th District strongly supported the "Massive Resistance" policy of the Byrd machine that sought to block the integration of Virginia schools. Of particular significance, after the Virginia Supreme Court ordered the end to Massive Resistance, on May 1, 1959, Prince Edward County, located in the southern part of the 5th District, closed its entire public school system.[3] The Prince Edward School Foundation then established a series of private schools to educate the county's white students. It would take a 1964 Supreme Court decision banning Virginia's tuition grants for students attending private schools to force Prince Edward County to open an integrated school system.[4]

Conservative Democrat William M. Tuck served as the 5th District congressman from April of 1953 through his decision not to run for reelection in 1968. Danville, native and conservative Democrat "Dan" Daniel held the 5th District seat from his 1968 congressional election victory until his death late in January of 1988. In a departure from tradition, a June 14, 1988 special election saw real estate developer and moderate Democrat L.F. Payne Jr. win the 5th District seat and hold it until 1996. Payne then made a decision not to run for reelection to Congress in order to run for Virginia Lieutenant Governor. Payne narrowly lost the race to Republican John H. Hager. The

1996 5th District congressional race saw conservative Democrat Virgil H. Goode, Jr. defeat Republican G. C. Landrith III by a margin of 120,323 to 70,869 votes.

Goode would take much more conservative positions than former Congressman L. F. Payne, Jr. on a wide range of issues. Angry with a perceived movement of the national Democratic party to the left, Goode left the Democratic party to run as an independent in his 2000 reelection bid. Significantly, the Republican party did not run a candidate against Goode. Not surprisingly, Goode went on to easily defeat his Democratic challenger J. W. Boyd Jr. by a margin of 67.4 percent to 30.7 percent. Early in August of 2002, Goode announced his decision to run in November of 2002 as a Republican. Goode easily won reelection as a Republican in 2002, 2004 and 2006.

The campaign of 2008 saw the Democratic party nominate political new-comer Thomas S. P. Perriello. Prior to receiving the nomination, Perriello had not run for elective office. Perriello put together an effective grass roots campaign that focused on the impact of the recession on residents of the 5th District. By a margin of 50.8 percent to 49.85 percent or 158,810 to 158,083 votes, Perriello narrowly defeated Goode. A recount confirmed Perriello's narrow victory. Political experts credited Goode's unexpected victory to the effectiveness of the Obama campaign to turn out college students attending the University of Virginia and African American voters, along with anger over high levels of unemployment in Southside Virginia. Instead of conceding Virginia to U.S. Senator John McCain, the Obama campaign decided to poor millions of dollars into an effort to take Virginia. Key to the strategy to take Virginia was the registration of new voters including college students and minorities.

Demographic Characteristics of the Electorate

According to the Census Bureau's 2006–2008 Community Survey, the 5th District had a population of 664,324. Ninety-six percent of district residents were born in the United States and 68 percent were born in Virginia.[5] The survey estimated that whites made up 70.7 percent, African Americans 19.5 percent, and Hispanics or Latinos 6.6 percent of the district. The survey estimated the median household income of the district in 2008 to be $43,125. Significantly, the survey found a notably higher median income in the northern part of the district. Albemarle County had an estimated medium family income of $84,581 and Charlottesville's estimated median family income of $61,089. In contrast, the Southside Virginia city of Danville had an estimated median family income of $42,845 and Martinsville $35,321. Southside Halifax County had an estimated median family income of $43,932.[6] The survey also found that the 5th District had an overall 14 percent poverty rate. People age 65 and over had a 13 percent poverty rate. Families headed by females had an estimated poverty rate of 28 percent.

Key Voting Blocks

Virginia is the only state in the United States with independent cities. Residents of the 39 independent cities in Virginia are not residents of the counties that surround them. The city of Charlottesville, for instance, is surrounded by Albemarle County. The 5th District contains four independent cities, Bedford, Charlottesville, Danville, and Martinsville. The 2010 contest saw Democrat Thomas Perriello receive 42.62 percent of the vote in Bedford, 79.91 percent of the vote in Charlottesville, 57.56 percent of the vote in Danville and 60.20 percent of the vote in Martinsville. Of the eighteen counties that make-up at least part of the 5th District, Perriello only managed to receive the majority of votes in Albemarle (57.23 percent), Brunswick (61.22 percent), Buckingham (51.47 percent), Nelson (54.11 percent), and Prince Edward (53.18 percent). Of the Southside counties, Brunswick had an African American population of 56.9 percent in 2000, Buckingham a 39.1 percent African American population in 2000 and Prince Edward County an estimated 38.5 percent in 2008.

A number of factors explain why residents of independent cities in Virginia vote more heavily for Democratic than Republican candidates. First, Virginia independent cities historically have had more diverse populations. Second, a number of Virginia independent cities have colleges or universities located within their boundaries.

Like the nationwide trend, African Americans in the 5th District vote heavily for Democratic candidates. With African Americans in 2008 making up an estimated 22.9 percent of the population of the district, a moderate leaning Democratic candidate for Congress must receive a significant percentage of the white votes to be able to carry the District. With the exception of the northern part of the 5th District, since the early 1970s moderate Democratic candidates have experienced considerable difficulty winning the majority of white votes in the District.

Employment/Occupational Characteristics

The 2006–2008 American Community Survey estimated that 79 percent of the 5th District residents over the age of 25 had graduated from high school. Twenty-two percent of district residents over the age of 25 had a bachelor's degree or higher. The survey estimated that for employed individuals over the age of 16, 25 percent worked in the educational, health care and social assistance fields. The importance of the University of Virginia as an employer helps to explain the large number of district employees employed in the areas of education and health care. Fourteen percent held manufacturing positions. Eleven percent provided retail services. Nine percent worked in construction related occupations. Eight percent provided professional, scientific, management, administrative and waste management services. Five percent provided finance, insurance, real estate and rental leasing services. Five percent worked in the field of public administration.[7] For a district that once saw a significant number of individuals working in agriculture, the survey estimated that only two percent of residents worked in the area of agriculture.

THE CANDIDATES

Barely six months after Tom Perriello was sworn in as a U.S. Representative the Republican Party targeted Perriello as one of the most vulnerable freshman Democrats.[8] Party officials believed Perriello's victory was a fluke driven by a heavy turnout of University of Virginia college students who voted for Perriello after casting their vote for Barack Obama and by the anger of independent voters blamed on the administration of President George W. Bush for the recession and high levels of unemployment.

During early 2009, a number of Republicans expressed interest in running against Perriello. Fifth District Republicans faced one major problem. Would six-term Congressman, Virgil H. Goode, seek to regain his House seat challenging Perriello to a rematch? Late in July of 2009, Goode ended speculation over this plans by announcing that he would not seek a rematch against Perriello.[9] Not surprisingly, Goode's decision not to seek the 5th District Republican nomination opened the door for a number of candidates to enter the race for the Republican nomination.

By October of 2009, six candidates had declared their intention to seek the Republican nomination. These included Kenneth Boyd, a member of the Albemarle County Board of Supervisors, Bradly Rees, a Bedford County factory worker and flat tax advocate, Laurence Verga, a Charlottesville businessman, Mike McPadden, an airline pilot, and Feda Kidd Morton, a high school biology teacher from Fluvanna County. State Senator Robert Hurt became the sixth Republican to declare for the race.[10] During early November 2009, Rees announced his decision to drop out of the contest for the Republican nomination and launch a bid on the Virginia Conservative party. Ron Ferrin, a Campbell County resident and owner of an Internet firm and Jim McKelvey of Franklin County subsequently entered the race.

National and Virginia Republican party officials, however, saw Robert Hurt as having the best opportunity to take back the 5th District seat. Hurt had the major advantage of representing a significant part of the 5th District in the Virginia Senate. Equally important, many political observers viewed Hurt as a pragmatic Senator who had been willing to make compromises. During the 2004 stalemate over the Virginia budget, for instance, Hurt broke ranks with the majority of Senate Republicans, and voted for Governor Mark Warner's budget that included a $1.4 billion tax increase. Hurt subsequently defended his vote as necessary to prevent the shutdown of Virginia government. Hurt, however, had one major problem. He was not well known in the populous northern part of the district.

Early in November of 2009, Perriello cast a key vote in support of the Democratic health care reform bill. Defending his vote, Perrielo stressed that his "vote on health care legislation came down to a simple choice for me: do we sit back and let premiums skyrocket for middle-class families and small businesses, and watch the cost of prescription drugs bankrupt seniors and the cost of health care bankrupt the federal government?"[11] To the surprise of no one, Hurt took the lead in attacking Perrielo's vote. "Make no mistake: this bill is a devastating blow to our economy at just the wrong time. With job losses continuing to mount, Congressman Perriello voted to raise taxes on small business," stressed Hurt.[12] Hurt's decision to take the lead in attacking Perriello's health care reform vote reflected an effort by Hurt to establish himself as the best candidate to take on Perriello.

By late November of 2009, political pundits began to speculate whether Hurt could win a district convention or have a better chance of winning the nomination in a primary. The fact that Bill Hay, chairman of the Jefferson Area Tea Party, indorsed real estate investor Laurence Verga further fueled speculation that Tea Party activists might try to deny Hurt the nomination. On December 12, 2009, the 5th District Republican Committee voted 19–13 to hold a June 8, 2010 primary instead of a District convention. Significantly, all of the candidates seeking the nomination, with the exception of Hurt, signed a letter to the committee supporting a convention over a primary.[13] In writing the letter arguing for a convention, the other candidates argued that because Virginia law permitted any voter to cast a ballot in a primary, independents and Democrats might try to influence the outcome of the primary. Equally important, Virginia law required that any candidate filing for a primary to sign an agreement not to run as an independent if they lost the primary. By the end of January of 2010, it became apparent that Hurt was the frontrunner.

The struggle within the Republican Party gave the Perriello campaign hope that the Republican nomination battle would so weaken the eventual nominee that Perriello would have a much easier time winning reelection. Equally important, by the end of 2009, Perriello had raised $1.14 million worth of campaign contributions.[14] While Perriello could continue to raise contributions for the general election campaign, the Republican candidates for the Republican nomination would be using campaign contributions to fight the primary campaign.[15]

The decision of Jeffrey Clark, a strong supporter of the Tea Party, to run as an independent, also created uncertainty regarding the ability of a Republican nominee to unify conservatives to defeat Perriello. Republican leaders feared that an independent Clark campaign might draw enough conservative votes from Hurt to help Perriello prevail in a close contest. The owner of American Water Testing and a residential and commercial inspection business in Danville, Clark initially considered running for the Republican nomination but decided not to enter the crowded Republican field. Instead he decided to run an independent campaign focusing on limited government, low taxes, traditional marriage and sharply limiting abortion.[16]

From February through early June of 2010, the Republican candidates fought it out for the nomination. A series of debates between the Republican candidates revealed few substantive differences. All of the candidates expressed their strong opposition to the policies of President Obama. All called for lower taxes, the repeal of health care reform, and sharply reducing government spending. An early February 2010 poll of 400 likely 5th District Republican voters found 22 percent of those surveyed supporting Hurt. Albemarle County Supervisor Kenneth C. Boyd came in second with 12 percent of those surveyed. The survey, however, found 51 percent of respondents undecided. [17]

On June 8, 2010, 5th District voters chose State Sen. Robert Hurt to take on Rep. Tom Perriello. Hurt received 48 percent of the vote, Jim McKelvey received 26 percent of the vote and Michael McPadden received 10 percent of the vote.[18] Only 8.2 percent of active voters participated in the Republican primary. Hurt's strong showing surprised many political pundits and dashed Democratic party hopes that Republicans would nominate a candidate too far to the right to win a general election campaign. Subsequently, Jeff Clark, a self-described Tea Party supporter would file petitions with a sufficient number of signatures to get on the 5th District congressional election ballot.[19]

Not surprisingly, 5th District Democrats selected Perriello to run for reelection. By the beginning of 2010, Perriello faced growing anger over the policies of President Obama and the Democratic Congress. Perriello's support for the stimulus package, health care reform and cap-in-trade legislation were most damaging with conservative 5th District voters. Despite the criticism, the Perriello campaign believed they had the ability to reassemble the coalition that had permitted Perriello to defeat Goode in 2008.

CAMPAIGN ISSUES

The Debate over Debates

It is highly unusual to find an incumbent member of Congress the underdog in a congressional race. The fact that almost all political experts viewed Perriello's 2008 victory over Congressman Goode as an upset helps to explain why many pundits viewed Perrielo as the underdog in his 2010 reelection bid. Consequently, it was not surprising that Hurt would set a number of conditions to agreeing to debates with Perriello. The most important condition was Hurt's insistence of not permitting independent Jeff Clark to participate in the debates. The Hurt camp feared that permitting Clark to participate in the debate would provide Clark the ability to attack Hurt for supporting tax and fee increases while serving in the Virginia Senate. Although Hurt initially had given some indication of being willing to permit Clark to participate in the debates,[20] by the end of June Hurt made clear that he had no intention to provide Clark a forum. In sharp contrast, the Perriello campaign made clear it had no problem permitting Clark to participate in three-way debates. The Perriello campaign recognized that if Clark could draw a few thousand conservative votes from Hurt it could mean victory for Perriello. Specifically, the Perriello campaign hoped that Clark might attract conservative voters unhappy with Hurt's decision to support fee and tax increases to end the 2004 Virginia General Assembly budget impasse.

Through July of 2010, the debate over debates raged. The Perriello campaign agreed to a three-way debate proposed by a Roanoke, television station.[21]

Holding to its guns, the Hurt campaign refused. In an attempt to counter criticism of his campaign's refusal to participate in three-way debates, Hurt announced his willingness to participate in televised debate in Charlottesville, with both Perriello and Clark if Clark received at least 10 percent support in a poll conducted by NBC 29 in Charlottesville, the proposed sponsor of the debate. The Hurt campaign fully understood it was highly unlikely that Clark would receive 10 percent support in any poll. The Hurt campaign also attempted to deflect criticism of his debate stance by attacking Perriello for declining to participate in a two candidate debate sponsored by the Lynchburg and Danville Pittsylvania Chamber of Commerce proposed for early October

2009.[22] By the end of July a number of polls gave Hurt a substantial lead over Perriello.[23] On August 13, 2010, faced with this situation, the Perriello campaign gave up its demands for three-way-debates and agreed to participate in a series of one-on-one debates with Hurt.[24]

Health Care Reform

Not surprisingly, Perriello's November 2009 vote in support of health care reform legislation made health care reform a major issue in this race.[25] Recognizing that a significant number of 5th District voters had concerns about the health care reform package, Perriello devoted considerable time and energy defending his vote by arguing that the legislation would protect consumers from insurance companies that routinely denied coverage to individuals with pre-existing conditions and imposed lifetime coverage caps.[26] And not surprisingly, throughout the campaign Hurt would pound Perriello for voting for health care reform even though many voters in the 5th District, according to Hurt, opposed the legislation.[27]

Tax Issues

Also not surprisingly, Perriello and Hurt fought it out over tax issues. With Bush era tax cuts expiring at the end of 2010, the debate raged across the country and in the 5th District over whether tax cuts should be extended for all tax payers or just for lower income and middle class tax payers. Perriello supported Obama's plan to extend only tax cuts for the low income and middle class tax payers and allowing the tax cuts to expire for high income tax payers. Perriello argued that the extension of the tax cuts to all taxpayers would add another $700 billion to the national debt. Hurt strongly supported extending the Bush era tax cuts to all taxpayers arguing that it was bad economic policy to raise taxes on anyone with the country trying to recover from the most serious recession since the Great Depression.[28] Hurt also argued that the new health reform law would drive up health insurance premiums for small employers due to new health coverage mandates or force them to pay new taxes if they choose not to provide health coverage to their employees. In addition to the Bush era tax cut issue, Perriello touted his support for the passage of the Small Business Jobs Act that would give $12 billion in tax cuts to small businesses.[29]

Free Trade Agreements

Throughout the campaign, Perriello pounded Hurt for not flatly opposing NAFTA-style free trade agreements. Many Southside residents blamed free trade agreements on the loss of large numbers of manufacturing jobs; particularly in the textile industry.[30] The free trade issue also provided Perrielo the opportunity to argue that he did not support President Obama on all issues. Much like prior Republican and Democratic administrations, the Obama administration believed the advantages of free trade outweighed the impact of such agreements on manufacturing jobs.

Card Check

Late in the campaign, the Hurt campaign attempted to tie Perriello to the controversial card check issue. Under legislation proposed by Congressional Democrats, unions would be able to become the bargaining agents for a bargaining unit by collecting a significant number of cards from members of units expressing support for a union serving as their bargaining unit. Existing provisions of the National Labor Relations Act (NLRA) required the NLRA to conduct secret ballot elections. The Hurt campaign would quote a 2008 article in the *Martinsville Bulletin* that quoted Perriello as supporting card check. During the 2010 campaign, however, Perriello maintained that he did not support card check legislation.[31]

Cap and Trade

Perriello also faced strong attacks from the Hurt campaign for his House vote for the so-called Cap-And-Trade legislation strongly supported by the Obama administration. Hurt argued that if the Senate followed the lead of the House, it would force electric utilities to significantly increase power rates to pay for new technology to reduce pollution or to purchase pollution credits on the open market. The Obama administration viewed the legislation as an important tool for reducing greenhouse gasses going into the atmosphere. Passed by the House of Representatives but not the Senate, the legislation capped the amount of pollutants from fixed sources such as power plants. If the owners of these sources of pollution wanted to place more pollutants into the atmosphere the law required them to purchase pollution credits or allowances from pollution producers who had not used up their pollution allowances or credits. The Obama administration strongly supported the legislation as necessary to provide polluters a financial incentive to invest in equipment to reduce pollution. Critics of cap and trade argued that it would sharply drive up the cost of electric power and other products that required the burning of fossil fuels.

CAMPAIGN STRATEGY

Media

The 5th District includes the Charlottesville media market at the northern part of the district. Two commercial television stations, WVIR-TV 29 and WCAV-TV 19 and one public television station, WHTJ-TV cover the northern part of the district. Although both the cities of Lynchburg and Roanoke lie outside the 5th District, the two cities are the home of a number of commercial television stations that cover political races in the southern part of the 5th District. WSET-TV 13 is a commercial station located in Lynchburg. A number of Roanoke, Va. commercial television stations also provide coverage of the 5th District including WSLS-TV 10. Two daily newspapers cover the district. The *Daily Progress* of Charlottesville provides extensive coverage of 5th District congressional campaigns in the northern part of the district and the *Danville Register & Bee* provides extensive coverage of 5th District campaigns in the southern part of the District. In addition, the Lynchburg *Advance* and the *Roanoke Times* also have a history of covering 5th District races. Not surprisingly, televisions stations in and outside of the 5th District would broadcast hundreds of ads paid for by the Perriello and Hurt campaigns as well as by independent groups supporting either Perriello or Hurt.

Significantly, on October 12, 2010, Perriello and Hurt made their first joint appearance on WSLS-TV 10 in Roanoke on the station's 6 p.m. newscast.[32] The 30 minute one-on-one forum saw Hurt and Perriello stake out their positions on a range of issues. Hurt took a flat no new tax stand. Perriello restated his support for health care reform legislation. Although Hurt stressed the need to make major cuts in federal spending, he did not specify programs he would cut. Hurt also expressed his support for a constitutional amendment to require a balanced federal budget. Perriello alleged that Republicans planned to cut benefits to seniors and to increase Medicare co-pays.[33] On October 19, 2010, Perriello and Hurt appeared in a second televised debate at Piedmont Valley Community College hosted by the Charlottesville-Albemarle League of Women Voters and broadcast on Charlottesville television station by WCAV-TV 19.[34] Neither Hurt nor Perrielo broke new ground in the debate.

On October 21, 2010, Hurt and Perriello fought it out in an hour-long debate sponsored by the University of Virginia's Sorensen Institute for Political Leadership, the *Danville Register & Bee* and WSET-13. Attended by 500 people, Hurt used the debate again to attack Perriello for his support for cap-and-trade legislation that Hurt argued would cost Virginia 50,000 jobs. Perriello promised to defend Social Security and attacked Hurt for refusing to support an extension of unemployment insurance benefits for the long-term unemployed.[35]

Image and Advertising

Early in July 2010, the Perriello campaign began to run its first TV ad in the Charlottesville and Roanoke media markets.[36] The ad showed Perriello working and getting dirty to demonstrate how hard he worked to bring jobs to Southside Virginia. During mid-August the Perriello campaign launched its second ad of the campaign again in the Charlottesville and Roanoke media market. In contrast, the second ad attacked Hurt for failing to show up at a forum. The ad also attacked Hurt for a vote in the Virginia Senate rejecting the acceptance of federal funds to extend unemployment benefits and for supporting a tax loophole that allegedly led to jobs being sent overseas.[37] Political observers credited Perriello's decision to go negative to the fact that some public opinion polls showed Perriello trailing Hurt by double digits.[38] Significantly, through mid-August the Hurt campaign had not run any TV ads.

The decision of the Perriello campaign to go negative did not end with the August TV ad. During late September and October, the Perriello campaign launched a series of so-called "World of Hurt" ads. In one ad titled Seniors Can't Afford a World of Hurt, a senior citizen rebutted attacks against health care reform that alleged it would lead to major cuts in Medicare benefits.[39] Another Perriello ad attacked Hurt for allegedly voting for legislation permitting utility companies to sharply raise electric rates.[40]

On August 20, Hurt released his first campaign ad. The ad introduced Hurt to 5th District voters by stressing that Hurt pledged to fight tax increases, stop Washington's spending, and create new jobs.[41] The ad sought to depict Hurt as a Washington outsider. Throughout the campaign, Hurt ads pounded Perriello for supporting Obama's agenda that included health care reform and cap-in-trade legislation.

Finance

The 5th District campaign saw Rep. Tom Perriello raise $3,383,054 through October in comparison to the $1,899,261 raised by the Hurt campaign. The ability of Perriello to raise such a large amount permitted the Perriello campaign to spend heavily on campaign ads and get-out-the vote activities. Yet, the direct expenditures by the Perriello and Hurt campaigns only told half the story. Twenty-five outside groups would spend $5 million in an

Table 8.1. Outside Spending in Support of Tom Perriello

Committee	All 2010 Total	Supported	Opposed
America's Family First Action Fund	$444,984	$194,000	$250,984
Democratic Congressional Campaign Cmte	$689,608	$82,947	$606,661
League of Conservation Voters	$404,445	$404,445	
League of Conservation Voters Victory Fund	$203,825	$203,825	
Matthew 25 Network	$20,586	$20,586	
Mid-Atlantic Laborers' Political League	$10,224	$10,224	
Mid-Atlantic Progressive Leadership Cmte	$100	$100	
Moveon.org	$150,008	$150,008	
National Education Assn	$284,962		$284,962
Service Employees International Union	$32,500	$32,500	
Service Employees International Union	$565,287	$246,947	$318,340
Sierra Club	$20	$20	
United Food & Commercial Workers Union	$436	$436	
VoteVets.org Action Fund	$241,495		$241,495
Total	$3048472		

Source: Center for Responsive Politics. http://www.opensecrets.org/races/indexp.php?cycle = 2010&id = VA05

effort to influence the outcome of the campaign. These groups ran ads either supporting or opposing the election of Perriello (Table 8.1) or Hurt (Table 8.2).

The Perriello campaign and outside groups supporting Perriello outspent direct expenditures by the Hurt campaign and independent groups supporting Hurt.

Table 8.2. Outside Spending in Support of Senator Robert Hurt

Committee	All 2010Total	Supported	Opposed
American Action Network	$234,000		
Americans For Responsible Health Care	$11,330		$11,330
Americans United 4 Life Action	$30,279	$1,719	$28,560
Faith & Freedom Coalition	$209,988		
Family Research Council	$15,746		$15,746
Foundation For a Secure & Prosperous America	$37,907	$37,907	
National Fedn of Independent Business	$19,164	$19,164	
National Republican Congressional Committee	$1,091,200	$85,000	$1,006,200
National Right to Life	$9,950	$9,950	
Revere America	$5,038		$5,038
US Chamber of Commerce	$442,765		
Total	$2107367		

Source: Center for Responsive Politics. http://www.opensecrets.org/races/indexp php?cycle=2010&id=VA05

ELECTION RESULTS

Through much of the 5th District campaign conflicting poll resulted made it difficult for the media and pundits to handicap the race. A July 20 poll conduct by SurveyUSA for Roanoke's WDBJ-TV gave Hurt a 58 percent to 38 percent lead over Perriello.[42] A September 29 SurveyUSA poll also gave Hurt a 23-point lead.[43] In sharp contrast, an October 18 poll by Roanoke College's Institute for Policy and Opinion Research found Hurt with a six-point lead over Perriello. The poll found that the economy was the dominant issue in the race.[44]

In the end, State Senator Robert Hurt defeated U.S. Rep. Tom S. Perriello by a margin of 50.81 percent to 46.98 percent. Independent Jeffrey Clark only managed to attract 2.12 percent of the votes. In raw numbers, Hurt received 119,560 votes to Perriello's 110,561 votes. Hurt's margin of victory was

Table 8.3. U.S. Representative Tom Perriello Comparison of 2008 and 2010 Results

County/City	2008	2010	Vote Drop Off
Albemarle County	31,827 (63.30 percent)	22,874 (57.23 percent)	8,953 (28.13 percent)
Appomattox County	2,758 (36.43 percent)	1,968 (33.44 percent)	790 (28.64 percent)
Bedford County	7,124 (38.25 percent)	4,086 (30.71 percent)	3,038 (42.64 percent)
Brunswick County	3,720 (62.31 percent)	2,596 (61.22 percent)	1,124 (30.21 percent)
Buckingham County	3,446 (50.15 percent)	2,545 (51.47 percent)	901 (26.14 percent)
Campbell County	8,837 (35.59 percent)	5,770 (31.12 percent)	3,067 (34.70 percent)
Charlotte County	2,596 (44.08 percent)	1,877 (42.90 percent)	719 (27.69)
Cumberland County	2,195 (48.36 percent)	1,561 (47.06 percent)	634 (28 percent)
Fluvanna County	6,564 (52.27 percent)	4,857 (50.68 percent)	1,707 (26.00 percent)
Franklin County	9,475 (37.69 percent)	6,629 (35.77 percent)	2 846 (30.03 percent)
Greene County	3,733 (46.02 percent)	2,292 (37.47 percent)	1,441 (38.60 percent)
Halifax County	7,528 (46.80 percent)	5,454 (45.60 percent)	2,074 (27.55 percent)
Henry County	6,846 (42.94 percent)	4,511 (40.64 percent)	2,335 (34.10 percent)
Lunenburg County	2,737 (49.54 percent)	1,889 (45.05 percent)	848 (30.98 percent)
Mecklenburg County	6,454 (44.59 percent)	4,345 (43.22 percent)	2,109 (32.67 percent)
Nelson County	4,562 (56.29 percent)	3,339 (54.11 percent)	1,223 (26.80 percent)
Pittsylvania County	11,025 (37.73 percent)	8,032 (36.48 percent)	2,993 (27.14 percent)
Prince Edward County	4,697 (53.82 percent)	3,199(53.18 percent)	1,498 (31.89)
Bedford City	1,316 (49.67 percent)	821 (42.62 percent)	495 (37.61 percent)
Charlottesville City	15,909 (80.83 percent)	11,036 (79.91 percent)	4,873 (30.63 percent)
Danville City	11,487 (57.97 percent)	8,552 (57.56 percent)	2,935 (25.55 percent)
Matinsville City	3,974 (61.18 percent)	2,655 (60.20 percent)	1,319 (33.19 percent)

8,999 votes out of a total of 235,298 votes cast. Two years earlier, Perrielo defeated U.S. Rep. Virgil Goode, Jr. by a margin of 50.08 percent to 49.85 percent. Perrielo received 158,810 to Goode's 158,083 votes. The 2008 5th District congressional race saw a total of 317,076 votes cast in contrast to 235,298 votes cast in the 2010 5th District congressional race or 81,778 fewer votes cast than in 2008.

At the beginning of the race, the Perriello campaign recognized that they needed to build up significant margins in the northern part of the district to offset expected loses in the southern part of the district. To prevail, Perriello needed to avoid the traditional decline in voter turnout in mid-term congressional election in Albemarle County, Charlottesville City, Danville City and Martinsville City. Of the twenty-three jurisdiction in the 5th District, Perriello only managed to win majorities in the counties of Albemarle, Brunswick, Buckingham, Nelson and Prince Edward as well as the independent cities of Charlottesville, Danville and Martinsville. Despite having raised hundreds of thousands of dollars more than the Hurt campaign and having the additional advantage of millions of more in independent expenditures, the Perriello campaign failed to reduce Hurt's strong advantage in the southern part of the District. Equally important, Perriello failed to maintain his 2008 margin of victory in Albemarle County (Table 8.3).

A remarkable feature of the contest between Perriello and Hurt was the lack of attention paid to local issues and the focus of the race almost entirely on national issues. The primary strategy of the Hurt campaign was to turn the race into a referendum on the Obama administration. The strategy barely worked. The Hurt campaign underestimated the impact of Perriello's constituent service work on voters and the growing role of the northern part of the district in determining the outcome of 5th District races. Yet, Perriello proved unable to hold back the Republican tide.

NOTES

1. Harvie J. Wilkinson III. *Harry Byrd and the Changing Face of Virginia Politics* (Charlottesville, University of Virginia Press, 1968).

2. Electoral results for the elections discussed in this section is available at the web site of the Virginia Board of Elections. Available at www.sbe.virginia.gov/cms/Election_Information/Election_Results/Index.html

3. The Civil Rights Movement In Virginia: The Closing of Prince Edward County's Schools. Available at www.vahistorical.org/civilrights/pec.htm

4. Civil Rights Movement in Virginia.

5. U.S. Census. *Fast Facts for Congress*. 2006–2008 American Community Survey, Congressional District 5, Virginia. Available at fastfacts.census.gov/home/cws/main.html

6. U.S. Census.

7. U.S. Census.

8. Brian McNeill, "GOP Hopefuls Weigh Challenge to Perriello in '10," *The Daily Progress,* June 14, 2009.

9. Brian McNeill, "With Goode Out, Who Will Run Next?" *The Daily Progress,* July 28, 2009.

10. Janelle Rucker, "Another Perriello Challenger Emerges," *The Roanoke Times,* October 8, 2009.

11. Brian McNeill, "Perriello Votes In Favor of Health Care Bill," *The Daily Progress,* November 8, 2009.

12. McNeill, "Perriello Votes."

13. Janelle Rucker, "Primary Will Decide GOP Candidate in 5th District," *The Roanoke Times,* December 13, 2009.

14. Brian McNeill, "Perriello Coffers Outstrip Opponents," *The Daily Progress,* January 31, 2010.

15. Ken Boyd-$7,610 in addition to $11,000 loaned by the candidate; Robert Hurt-$293,458; Jim McKelvey-$1,200 in addition to $500,000 loaned by the candidate; Mike McPadden-$9,227 in addition to $7,000 loaned by the candidate; Laurence Verga-$73,715 in addition to $213,889 loaned by the candidate. Janelle Rucker, "Crowd of Candidates Jostle For Chance to Unseat Perriello," *Roanoke Times,* February 22, 2010.

16. Catherine Amos, "Danville Business Owner Challenging Perriello," *Danville Register & Bee,* February 2, 2010.

17. Brian McNeill, "GOP Voters Favor Hurt; But Most Undecided," *The Daily Progress,* February 12, 2010.

18. Janelle Rucker, "Hurt Picked To Challenge Perriello in 5th District," *The Roanoke Times,* June 9, 2010.

19. Michael Sluss, "Independent Gets Added in 5th Race," *The Roanoke Times,* June 17, 2010.

20. Brian McNeill, "Hurt, Perriello Differ On 3-Way Debate," *The Daily Progress,* June 18, 2010.

21. Catherine Amos, "Perriello Agrees to Three-Way Debate; Hurt Says No," *Danville Register & Bee,* July 14, 2010.

22. Catherine Amos, "Hurt Attacks Perriello For Declining One-On-One Debate," *Danville Register & Bee,* July 15, 2010.

23. Media General News Service, "Poll in 5th District Race Show Hurt With Comfortable Lead Over Perriello," *Richmond Times-Dispatch,* July 22, 2010.

24. Brian McNeill, "Hurt Agrees To Debate Perriello On TV," *Richmond-Times Dispatch,* August 14, 2010.

25. Brian McNeill, "Perriello Votes In Favor of Health Care Bill," *The Daily Progress,* November 8, 2009.

26. Brian McNeill, "Perriello Touts Health Care Reform," *The Daily Progress,* September 22, 2010.

27. Brian McNeill, "Hurt, Perriello Square Off On Direction of U.S." *Danville Register & Bee,* October 19, 2010.

28. Brian McNeill, "Hurt Pushes Lower Taxes In Visit to Area," *The Daily Progress,* September 29, 2010.

29. Catherine Amos, "Perriello Wants To End Tax Cuts For Wealthy," *The Daily Progress,* September 25, 2010.

30. Catherine Amos, "Perriello, Hurt Spar Over China, Overseas Jobs," *Danville Register & Bee,* October 23, 2010.

31. Ray Reed, "Perriello, Hurt Focus On Business In Debate," *Richmond Times-Dispatch,* October 28, 2010.

32. Ray Reed, "Hurt, Perriello Stake Out Positions In First Joint Appearance," *Danville Register & Bee,* October 13, 2010.

33. Olympia Meola, "Hurt, Perriello Square Off In First TV Debate," *Richmond Times-Dispatch,* October 14, 2010.

34. Janelle Rucker, "Debate Draws Overflow Crowd," *The Roanoke Times,* October 20, 2010.

35. John Crane, "Hurt, Perriello Duke It Out In Danville," *Danville Register & Bee,* October 21, 2010.

36. Tyler Whitley, "Perriello Airs First TV ad," *Richmond Times Dispatch,* July 1, 2010.

37. Catherine Amos, "Perriello Calls Out Hurt In A New Ad," *Danville Register & Bee,* August 18, 2010.

38. Ibid.

39. TV Ad: Seniors Can't Afford a World of Hurt. perrielloforcongress.com/node/382.

40. TV Ad: "Shocking," perrielloforcongress.com/node/391.

41. Catherine Amos, "5th District Campaigns Taking Shape," *The Daily Progress,* August 22, 2010.

42. Daily Progress Staff Reports, Poll: Hurt Enjoys a 23-Point Lead Over Perriello," *The Daily Progress,* July 20, 2010.

43. GoDanRiver Staff, "SurveyUSA Poll Has Hurt Up 23 Point," *Danville Register & Bee,* September 23, 2010.

44. WSLS-TV Staff Reports, "Roanoke College Poll Shows Close Race in 5th District," *The Daily Progress,* October 18, 2010.

Part III

U.S. Senate Elections

Chapter 9

Alaska Senate Race (McAdams v. Miller v. Murkowski)

Alaska's Three-Way Senate Race and Lisa Murkowski's Write-In Victory

Jerry McBeath and Carl Shepro

Scott McAdams
Party: Democrat
Age: 41
Sex: Male
Race: Caucasian
Religion: United Methodist
Education: B.A. in secondary education, Sheldon Jackson College, Sitka
Occupation: Director of Sitka Community Schools
Political Experience: Elected member of Sitka School Board, (2002–2008); President, Alaska Association of School Boards; Mayor of Sitka, (2008–2010); member, Board of Directors, Alaska Municipal League; Chairman, Southeast Alaska Conference of Mayors

Joe Miller
Party: Republican
Age: 43
Sex: Male
Race: Caucasian
Religion: nondenominational Christian
Education: B.A., United States Military Academy, West Point, 1987; J.D., Yale Law School, 1995; M.A., University of Alaska, Fairbanks (economics), 2008.
Occupation: Attorney
Political Experience: Candidate (unsuccessful) for the Alaska House of Representatives, District 8, 2004

Lisa Murkowski
Party: Republican/Write-in candidate
Age: 53
Sex: Female
Race: Caucasian
Religion: Roman Catholic
Occupation: U.S. Senator
Political Experience: Alaska State House of Representatives, (1998–2002); United States Senate, (2002–present), Committee on Energy and Natural Resources, ranking member; Appropriations Committee; Committee on Health, Education, Labor & Pensions; Select Committee on Indian Affairs

In the late August Republican primary, upstart candidate Joe Miller, endorsed by former Alaska Governor Sarah Palin and the Tea Party Express, narrowly defeated incumbent senator Lisa Murkowski. Within two weeks, Murkowski announced that she would "make history" by staging a write-in campaign; and indeed, make history she did by narrowly defeating Miller and Democratic candidate Scott McAdams in the general election. In this chapter we analyze the characteristics of Alaska, the three candidates, campaign issues, campaign strategy, and election results, which together explain one of the most unusual senate elections in recent American history.

CHARACTERISTICS OF ALASKA

Party Balance

Nominally, Alaska is a Republican state; it has voted Republican in every presidential election since 1964. In state politics, however, Democrats are competitive. For the 27th Alaska Legislature (elected in 2010), the state senate is evenly divided between the political parties; it is managed by a bipartisan coalition with a Democratic majority. The state house, on the other hand, has had a Republican majority since the 1994 election, but the size of this majority has varied over time.

   To register to vote in Alaska, no identification with a political party is required. In fact, providing information about political affiliation is optional. Table 9.1 indicates that Republicans have a sizable edge over Democrats in the state, but nonpartisan and undeclared voters are a majority of registrants—52.7 percent.

Voting and Electoral History

At statehood in 1959, Alaska was a Democratic state. The first governor, Bill Egan, was a Democrat, as were members of the congressional

Table 9.1. Alaska Statewide Voter Registration

Affiliation	Number	Percentage
Alaska Independence Party	14,206	2.9
Democratic	74,719	15.0
Libertarian	8,886	1.8
Republican	130,585	26.3
Nonpartisan	80,498	16.2
Undeclared	181,699	36.5
Green	2,320	0.5
Republican Moderate	2,672	0.5
Veterans	1,661	0.3
Total	497,246	100.0

Source: Alaska Division of Elections, December 16, 2010.

delegation. Democrats also controlled the state senate, but control of the house alternated between parties. In the 1966 election, Wally Hickel defeated Egan, and this election marked the decline in electoral power of the Alaska Democratic Party. Republican presidential issues—typically including stronger emphases on economic development, less concern for environmental issues, and greater protection of gun ownership—are more attractive to Alaskans than Democratic ones. Also, after oil began flowing through the pipeline in 1977, Alaskans became wealthier. Modernization and nationalization of the state attracted professionals who were more likely to vote Republican. Finally, Alaska's large military population tends to support Republicans too.

The state's congressional delegation appeared to follow this trend line in partisanship, but fate intruded at several points. The U.S. Senate seat first held by Ernest Gruening remained under Democratic control until 1980, when Frank Murkowski narrowly won the race against Clark Gruening (the elder Gruening's grandson, who had defeated Democrat Mike Gravel in the primary). The seat held by Democrat Bob Bartlett until his death in 1968 became Republican when Governor Hickel appointed Ted Stevens to fill the vacancy. Alaska's lone U.S. House seat was held by both Democrats and Republicans until Don Young won a special election in 1973 to replace Democrat Nick Begich (declared missing, later presumed dead, in a plane crash). Young has held the seat since then; in 2008 he became the senior member of the delegation. From the 1980 election to 2008, when Mark Begich defeated Ted Stevens, the state's delegation had only Republicans, reflecting the increased power of incumbency in congressional seats nationally.

In Alaska's 52 years of statehood, it has had Democratic governors for 28 years and Republican governors for 24 (including Wally Hickel's second term from 1990 to 1994, when formally he had run for office as a candidate of the Alaska Independence party). Alaska's constitution limits governors to two four-year terms, and the primary reason Bill Egan lost the 1966 race to Hickel was the perception that he had served two terms already and thus was ineligible. However, Egan was hospitalized in Seattle at the start of his first term, and the secretary of state substituted for him, thereby making him eligible constitutionally for another term. Only two governors served two consecutive terms after Egan—moderate Republican Jay Hammond (1974–1982) and moderate Democrat Tony Knowles (1994–2002). Two governors lost primary elections while seeking reelection (Democrat Bill Sheffield and Republican Frank Murkowski). Two governors—Democrat Steve Cowper and Republican Wally Hickel—declined to seek reelection to a further term. And two governors, Hickel in1968 and Sarah Palin in 2009, resigned their posts before completing a full term. Recent gubernatorial elections display a Republican bias in voting, but Alaska political parties are weak, and attractive candidates and campaigns on issues and personality keep the office competitive.

For one period of Alaska statehood, a single party exercised relatively long-term dominance of the state legislature. In the 1994 election, Republicans gained control of both the House and Senate. With the support of the "bush (rural) Democrats," they held nearly veto-proof majorities until the 2006 election. For most of the earlier period, bipartisan coalitions ran one or both houses, a pattern reappearing in the senate after 2006. In sum, both Republicans and Democrats are competitive at the state level, where election contests tend to emphasize what legislators can do to help constituents. There is a relatively high turnover rate in the legislature, which facilitates party competition too. For many politicians, attending the legislative sessions in Juneau (the only state capital not accessible by road) is inconvenient. Compensation for legislative work (the part-time salary was just $24,000 until it doubled in 2009) provides little incentive for long service.[1]

Demographic Character of the Electorate

Alaska's population in 2010 stood at 710,231. It is the fourth most sparsely populated state, but growing at the rate of 11.4 percent in the first decade of the twenty-first century, above the national average. Natural increase in population explains most of this growth. Alaska does have the highest population turnover of the American states, but the rate of transiency has declined substantially since statehood.

The oil industry is the most important pivot of the Alaska economy, and taxes on oil and gas production, royalties, and oil industry corporate income taxes supply 85–89 percent of the general purpose, unrestricted revenue of the state.[2] The oil industry employed just 12,200 oil/gas workers in 2010, but an additional 52,000 work for support contractors; the indirect effects of spending by oil employees create an additional 30,000 jobs. The second pivot of the Alaska economy is the Alaska Permanent Fund, valued at $37 billion in late 2010. It influences the economy through the distribution of earnings to residents in the form of annual Permanent Fund Dividends. Because Alaskans spend most of their dividends in-state (the amount in 2009 was $1,305), the dividend has a multiplier effect estimated to be 1.6. The third pivot of the economy is "everything else"—mining, fisheries and seafood processing, trade, utilities, professional and health services, and tourism. Of greatest concern in the political context are government employees.

Both state and local governments distribute oil revenues to communities in the form of services and government positions (such as school teachers), and they comprise another 20 percent of the workforce. Also, Alaska is highly dependent on federal expenditures for the four large military installations in the state, for the management of federal lands covering more than 60 percent of the state, for off-shore fisheries management, and for distribution of federal payments and services to Alaska Natives, seniors, and disabled veterans.[3] Civilian and military federal employees and their dependents made up nearly 20 percent of the state's population.

The per capita income of Alaskans in 2009 was $43,209, making it the eighth highest in the U.S. Still, the state has large pockets of rural poverty, and one in ten Alaskans lives below the poverty line. Notwithstanding special efforts to develop rural areas where one-quarter of Alaskans live, in 2006 some 34 percent of Alaska villages lacked running water and waste disposal.

The state's largest minority is the Alaska Native population, numbering around 108,000 or 15.3 percent. Most Natives continue to live near areas settled thousands of years ago, but rural migration to the cities has increased recently. The numbers of other ethnic/racial minorities—African Americans, Latinos, Asians—collectively approach those of Alaska Natives. Non-Hispanic Caucasians comprise 66 percent of the state's population. Education levels resemble those of other states, with 60 percent having graduated from high school and taken some post-baccalaureate work, graduated from college, or gained a graduate degree. Last, the median age of the state is rising (nearly 7 percent are 65 or older) and the sex ratio (52 percent male) is narrowing.

In these two respects, the Alaska population increasingly resembles that of other states.[4]

Key Voting Blocs

Alaska is America's largest state in land area, and it has diverse biogeographical regions: rural areas of the frigid north and west have a mostly Alaska Native population; the Interior, centering on Fairbanks, the state's second largest city, also includes many road system towns and Native villages; Southcentral focuses on Anchorage, the state's largest city, and extends north to the expanding bedroom areas of Matanuska-Susitna Borough (Mat-Su) and south to the Kenai Peninsula; and the Southeast, the panhandle, has the capital city Juneau and both terrain and climate resembling the Pacific Northwest.

Regional differences explain much of the conflict in the state legislature, and because they are overlaid with distinctions of ethnicity and income, they influence elections to state and federal office. Southeast Alaska is a distinct voting bloc, and Juneau, the region's largest city, is a government town and historically has voted Democratic. Rural Alaska with a majority Native population and small numbers of school teachers, health, social, and government administrators, also historically has voted Democratic.

Anchorage is the most economically diverse city in the state and has been competitive politically, yet with a Republican tilt. Although home to the state's flagship university campus, Fairbanks remains a blue-collar town, and typically leans Republican. The fastest growing region in the state is Mat-Su, and it also is the most conservative. (Wasilla in Mat-Su is the home town of former governor Sarah Palin.) Additional Republican strongholds are the Kenai Peninsula and North Pole (south of Fairbanks).

Alaska is a strong union state, and unions represent construction trades and most public sector jobs. Approximately one-fourth of the voting population is union-affiliated; union members and their families are spread throughout the state, and they usually vote Democratic. Nearly 10 percent of registered voters are military personnel, who tend to vote more for Republican than Democratic candidates, but most are transients and they have low turnout rates.

Major Urban Areas and Employment/Occupational Characteristics

Anchorage has about two-fifths of the state's population. It is the state's commercial center and offers more job opportunities than elsewhere. The population of the Fairbanks borough (county-type local government unit) is nearly 100,000. It has a narrower range of job opportunities than Anchorage, but has two large military installations (Fort Wainwright and Eielson Air

Force Base), the university, and a large nonprofit sector (including the hospital). Juneau is the state's third largest city with a population of about 35,000. In contrast, rural/bush Alaska has relatively few full-time jobs. A majority of Alaska Natives lack full-time employment; they are dependent on government transfer payments and subsistence hunting/fishing/gathering for sustenance.

THE CANDIDATES

The Alaska Primary System

For most of the statehood era, Alaska had a blanket primary system. Although candidates were listed by party on the ballot, voters could elect candidates of any party for each office up for election. This seemed to satisfy most voters and fit into the independent and individualist nature of state politics then. As Alaska politics nationalized by the late 1980s, Republican partisans (who were mostly social conservatives) sought greater control over nominations and focused on the primary system. In the 1990s, Republican legislators changed electoral law to establish a "classic open" primary system. Each registered party (Republicans, Democrats and the two minor parties—Alaska Independence and Libertarians) could limit entrance into its primary to party registrants while allowing the majority of voters (registered as nonpartisan or undeclared) entry. Only the Alaska Republican party consistently has had its own primary; Democrats and the minor parties in most elections have been on the same ballot designed as "all other." Thus the Republican primary resembles a "closed" system, and as in other states with closed primaries gives advantages to candidates appealing to the party's social conservative base. Although the incumbent U.S. Senator, Lisa Murkowski, was favored to win the Republican primary, she did not appeal sufficiently to the party's hardcore, explaining why in the general election there were two Republican candidates—Joe Miller and Lisa Murkowski (running as a write-in candidate)—and the Democrat Scott McAdams.

Scott McAdams

McAdams was born in California and arrived in Petersburg, Alaska when he was 7. His first jobs were as a deckhand on commercial fishing vessels in Southeast Alaska. He attended public schools in Southeast Alaska and graduated with a degree in elementary education from Sheldon Jackson, a private college in Sitka. He taught school for one year in Riverdale, California, and then returned to Alaska, assuming positions in the education and nonprofit sectors: program coordinator for Big Brothers and Big Sisters, supervisor of museum protection and visitor services, and (currently) director of community schools for the Sitka School District.

McAdams' first electoral position was as member of the Sitka school board (from 2002 to 2008). He served the board as president and also was for one year president of the Alaska Association of School Boards. In 2008 he was elected to a two-year term as mayor of Sitka; while mayor, he served as a director of the Alaska Municipal League and as chair of the Southeast Conference of Mayors.

When the Democratic State Convention met at Sitka in April, 2010, few party activists thought a Democrat would stand a chance in a race against the eight-year incumbent U.S. Senator, Lisa Murkowski. Party leaders solicited convention host, McAdams, and he volunteered to be the nominee; in the August 24, 2010 primary, McAdams was the leading candidate. He won 18,035 votes in a race with two little-known opponents, or 60 percent of the total Democratic ballots.

Joe Miller

Miller grew up in Kansas and attended college at West Point, majoring in political science. At his graduation, he was commissioned in the U. S. Army. He served three years, and was awarded a Bronze Star for his role as a tank commander in the first Gulf War. After military service, Miller attended Yale Law School, graduating in 1995. Thereupon, he joined a private law firm in Anchorage.

In Miller's early years in Alaska, he served the state and federal court system in several capacities. He was magistrate and superior court master at Tok from 1998 to 2002, briefly an acting District Court judge in 2002, and from 2002 to 2004 was a part-time U.S. magistrate judge. Miller also was a part-time assistant attorney for the Fairbanks North Star Borough, from 2002 to 2009.

In 2004 Miller started his political career in Alaska. He won the Republican primary for the state house seat in District 8. He staged an energetic campaign in this moderately Democratic district, and won 48 percent of the vote in a contest with David Guttenberg, the Democratic incumbent. Although Miller was an active force in the Republican Party of the Interior, he did not run for office again until 2010, when he filed against the incumbent Lisa Murkowski for the U.S. Senate seat. Former Governor Sarah Palin endorsed his bid, as did the Tea Party Express, which promised to spend at least $500,000 to help him defeat the incumbent. In a strongly anti-incumbent and issue-based effort, his campaign gained steady momentum, to which the Murkowski reelection campaign did not sufficiently respond. Miller announced himself as a strong pro-life candidate; fortuitously, measure #2 on the primary ballot (requiring parental notification for minors seeking abortions) gained 56 percent of the vote in this relatively low turnout election, and this aided Miller. Although the race was close, Miller won with 51 percent of the vote, and his upstart victory brought Miller national attention.

Lisa Murkowski

Murkowski was the first member of the congressional delegation to have been born in Alaska, the youngest (45), and the first woman. This is largely explained by the fact that she also was the first member of a political family to ascend to the U.S. Congress. Murkowski spent her youth in Ketchikan and Fairbanks, but her post-secondary work was all outside Alaska: She earned a B.A. in economics at Georgetown University, and a J.D. from Willamette University in 1995.

Murkowski had an internship in Senator Ted Stevens' office as a high school student. Between college and law school, she was a legislative aide in Juneau. After law school, she was a court attorney for the state district court in Anchorage, worked for a commercial law firm and then developed her own private practice. In 1998 she won a seat in the state house (representing an Anchorage district) and was easily re-elected in 2000. In the 2002 election, she was pilloried by conservatives for having joined a bipartisan legislative group supporting tax increases and tapping earnings of the Permanent Fund; she won this campaign with only 57 votes to spare. Her legislative colleagues, however, supported her quest for a House leadership position, electing her to the majority leader position for the legislative session beginning in 2003. Then, her father launched her Senate career.

When Senator Frank Murkowski won the gubernatorial election in November 2002, his senate term had two years remaining. Entering office in December, the senior Murkowski announced a short list of potential nominees for this seat (which the governor then had the power to fill), and said he would appoint a person who was young, electable, experienced and shared his views. He passed over several applicants more experienced than his daughter Lisa, and thus made himself subject to charges of nepotism. This was the first occasion in American history when a governor had appointed his daughter to the U.S. Senate. The nepotism charge dogged Lisa Murkowski in the 2004 election when her Democratic opponent was popular former two-term governor Tony Knowles. She defeated Knowles, but the vote was relatively close: 49 to 46 percent, notwithstanding better financing for her campaign and the active support of Ted Stevens and Don Young.

Murkowski's first full term in the Senate demonstrated both effectiveness and capability, but also increasingly drew opposition from social conservatives.[5] Her positions on national issues tended to be centrist, and this disappointed those who sought conservative judicial appointments, restrictions on abortion, and reduced funding for social welfare, among other issues. She was an advocate for opening the Arctic National Wildlife Refuge for oil/gas development, for saving Alaska military installations from closure (especially, Eielson Air Force Base), for the needs of Alaska Native corporations and interests, and for increased federal support for Alaska's special needs (via earmarks). At the start of the 111th Congress in 2009, and despite her limited seniority, Murkowski became the ranking member of the Energy and Natural Resources Committee, and a member of the powerful Appropriations Committee (and also served on Indian Affairs). Her senate colleagues elected her to be vice chair of the Senate Republican Conference—the fifth highest party leadership position in the senate. Observers noted, however, that to retain this leadership position, her votes in the 111th Congress hued closer to the party line than in her previous six years.

In retrospect, Murkowski did not prepare well for the Republican primary of 2010, nor did most observers think that much preparation was necessary. Insiders thought she would win the primary with at least 60 percent of the vote, even though Miller was a credible opponent. However, the Miller campaign developed steady momentum, clearly visible by the end of the campaign. In addition to factors mentioned above, Murkowski's campaign lost its strongest advocate when former Senator Ted Stevens died in a plane crash two weeks before the primary, and before the mostly "feel good" campaign had run an ad he had prepared to support her reelection.

One week after she lost the primary race, Murkowski conceded. However, a week later she said "I'm no quitter. . . . I'm weighing all my options and seeing what's available. Everywhere I'm going there's a huge outpouring of support."[6] Ten days later, just six weeks before the general election on November 2, she announced her write-in campaign: "OK, I get the message. Let's make history. . . . When he (Miller) swung, I didn't swing. . . . The gloves are off, and I'm fighting for Alaska."[7]

Campaign Issues

Three issues dominated the 2010 general election campaign in Alaska for the U.S. Senate seat: anti-incumbency fervor, Murkowski's seniority, and questions about Miller's integrity.

Anti-Incumbency

In most of the print ads for the Miller campaign, this phrase appeared, "To change Washington, D.C., you have to change who's there," a mark of an insurgent campaign. In this case the focus was national, and it had three dimensions: fiscal responsibility, constitutional originalism, and limited government. Miller said that the United States was nearly bankrupt; without sharp reductions in deficits and the national debt, the U.S. would follow Greece into an economic meltdown. He pointed to profligate actions of Democrats and Republicans, and criticized Murkowski for her votes spending hundreds of billions to bail out banks, General Motors, Fannie Mae, and Freddie Mac, even the IMF; in her eight years in the Senate, she had participated in a doubling of the national debt to $13 trillion. When both McAdams and Murkowski pointed out that Alaska was a developing state and reliant on federal funding, including earmarks, Miller said he would not turn down federal funding but would not seek earmarks, which were "the single most corrupting influence in Congress."[8] Alaska's needs for revenue, he argued, could be met through removal of federal restrictions on the development and export of natural resources and reduction (or elimination) of the federal regulatory burden.

Forgetting the elastic clause and the Supreme Court's power of judicial review, Miller emphasized the U.S. Constitution's assignment of designated and specific powers to the national government and residual powers, through the Tenth Amendment, to the states. Then he called for the elimination of the federal education department and other programs, such as Social Security, Medicare, and the minimum wage—which are not mentioned in the Constitution. In this area as in others, he moderated his positions as the campaign advanced; he noted that his parents were dependent on Social Security and Medicare, and those who had paid into the system were entitled to receive the benefits. Eventually, he argued, the system needed to be privatized. Education, health care, the minimum wage: all were social welfare programs appropriate at the state level, but only if the people wanted them. The federal government needed to be one of limited powers.

The anti-incumbency issue (in a national context) was new in an Alaska senatorial campaign, and a good translation of the Tea Party movement to the Alaska context. For obvious reasons, Murkowski labeled it as "extreme." While Miller contended that government could not "solve problems," McAdams countered that it should, and that the federal government was needed to build Alaska's economy, support seniors, and create jobs.

Murkowski's Seniority

Ted Stevens, who died in a plane crash on August 9, 2010, was the longest-serving Republican in the Senate when he lost the 2008 election to Mark Begich. He was an icon of Alaska politics, and lionized as "Alaskan of the Century" in 1999, largely because of the way he used seniority to benefit the state's development. Stevens was Murkowski's mentor in the Senate, and she shared his sense of the value of seniority and demonstrated this by her quick rise in the institution. During the campaign, she touted her experience, positioning, and ability to accomplish objectives in D.C., saying "If either Scott McAdams or Joe Miller were to be sent to the United States Senate, Alaska would have the least seniority of any state."[9] She was not embarrassed by the earmarks she had collected in her eight years, and in the senate voted against attempts to eliminate them. McAdams said that the state deserved its "fair share," and that challenges to earmarks and the seniority that produced them were a threat to Alaska. Of course, McAdams argued that a Democratic incumbent would be more useful than a Republican.

Miller challenged the institution of seniority and Murkowski's use of it. During the campaign he supported term limits on federal legislators, and specifically he called for the repeal of the Seventeenth Amendment (which provided for direct election of U.S. senators). This would increase states' rights and control over their own resources, lessening dependence on the federal government. Perhaps it was the contradiction between the people's power (which he championed as a candidate for the senate) and state power that prompted him to recant this proposal later in the campaign.

Miller's Integrity

During the primary, Miller won praise for his credentials, the bravery he had demonstrated in combat, and his solid representation of family values. Then, as the general election progressed, his character came under scrutiny. First, Murkowski said he had run a primary race that lacked integrity by distorting her position on national health care reform legislation. Second, opposition research and an active media revealed divergence between his campaign positions and personal actions. He had received USDA subsidies for land owned in Kansas in the 1990s, while during the campaign he called for an end to the welfare state. He and his wife received low income hunting licenses when new to the state. Beginning service as a part-time magistrate judge in Fairbanks in 2002, he hired his wife to work for him as an assistant; only six months later, when the US District Court officer told him that the hiring was inappropriate, did he replace her, whereupon she collected unemployment compensation. During the campaign he stated that unemployment compensation benefits were illegitimate because they were not authorized by the Constitution. When asked whether his family had gained from government assistance, he said they had received Medicaid, and benefited from state health care programs for low-income children and pregnant women. Yet he opposed entitlement programs throughout the campaign. Each case seemed to be minor, and Miller's response was that past benefits were irrelevant: the campaign should be about issues. However, the established pattern was one of hypocrisy.

A more significant flaw in character pertained to an episode during Miller's employment as a part-time assistant attorney for the Fairbanks North Star Borough. In 2008, Miller, as the interior regional chair of seven house districts, sought to oust Randy Ruderich, chair of the Republican party of Alaska. He used several borough computers to engage in proxy voting to influence the convention vote (thus violating the borough's ethics policy, which prohibits use of office computers for personal gain). Rumors of this action reached the media during the campaign, and reporters asked Miller to release employment information (which the borough could not release without his permission). His response was: "You can ask me about my background, you can ask me about personal issues, I'm not going to answer; I'm not."[10]

Then, former borough mayor Jim Whitaker (2003–2009) said he nearly fired Miller after the illegal use of computers was disclosed. In consultation with the head of the legal department, Miller was not terminated because of his involvement in an important taxation case between the borough and the Trans-Alaska Pipeline System; but he was reprimanded and suspended from work for a few days. After this revelation, Miller admitted to an ethics misstep in an interview with CNN but did not release his records until all Alaska's print media filed suit against the borough in superior court, and the judge agreed that it was in the public interest to do so. The files detailed Miller's breach of ethics. In his words: "I lied about accessing all of the computers. I then admitted about accessing the computers, but lied about what I was doing. Finally, I admitted to what I did."[11] This reluctance to tell the truth unless ordered by the court, even when it did not concern a life-and-death matter, cast serious doubts on Miller's integrity.

Campaign Strategy

The Murkowski write-in candidacy was a new element for a statewide U.S. Senate campaign. In a three-candidate race each candidate sought to distinguish her or his issue positions and each sought to define the ideological field. Miller staked out a claim for common sense constitutionalism; McAdams called himself a moderate, picturing Murkowski as nearly as far to the right as Miller; and Murkowski wanted to be right in the middle of the electorate. Second, each candidate's strategy emphasized the write-in process from different angles. McAdams said it was obvious in political science if not politics that a write-in effort was impossible. Miller's campaign said a write-in effort, given Murkowski's earlier pledge to support the winner of the Republican primary, was illegitimate. Murkowski formed a new campaign team and pledged to run an aggressive campaign that would canvass the entire state and remind voters that they would have to write-in her name and mark the oval next to the write-in line on the ballot. Candidates' use of media, management of image through ads, finance, grass roots efforts, and appeals to the base described the race.

Media

The three campaigns spent most of their resources on TV spots and used radio amply as well. They advertised in the state's newspapers and invested in direct mail, yard signs, buttons and bumper stickers. Alaska has just three TV markets—in Anchorage, Fairbanks, and Juneau—and other parts of the state receive relays from these or public TV (which does not carry political messages). The state has three daily newspapers—the *Anchorage Daily News (ADN)*, *Fairbanks Daily News-Miner (FDNM)*, and the *Juneau Empire (JE)*—as well as weekly newspapers serving large regions such as Mat-Su and the Kenai Peninsula. The campaigns developed attractive websites (www.scottmcadams.org, http://joemiller.us, and http://lisamurkowski.com), which introduced the candidates and described their issue positions. A number of bloggers followed and commented on the campaign. Finally, the candidates used Facebook and Twitter to keep in touch with supporters.

The print media played a more aggressive and unified role in this election than in any previous U.S. Senate race in state history. When Miller refused to disclose his employment records at the Fairbanks borough, the FDNM, ADN, *Alaska Dispatch,* Associated Press, Alaska Public Radio Network and both *The Washington Post* and *The New York Times* sued in state court to release records on Miller's employment history. Newspapers from Barrow to Ketchikan endorsed Sen. Murkowski's write-in campaign.

Image and Ads

The candidates spent their media dollars telling their histories in Alaska, defining issue positions, and featuring testimonials; they left most of the attack ads in the care of affiliated and unaffiliated groups. Murkowski's ads showed voters how to "fill it in, write it in," and showed a "Mur-kow-ski" pictogram. Although Murkowski had not used a Stevens' endorsement ad in her primary campaign, in the general election, she did. This ad featured first Stevens' widow, Catherine, explaining that the Stevens family approved the endorsement of Murkowski, followed by a brief clip of Stevens shot shortly before he died in the plane crash, saying "We need Lisa and the seniority she's earned now more than ever."[12] Although all three candidates ran statewide campaigns with little variance in message from region to region, Murkowski placed a special focus on Fairbanks, where her primary votes ran behind Miller's. Her campaign developed special messages for the Interior, and featured full-page ads with endorsements from Republicans, Democrats, and independents.

Alaskans Standing Together (AST), the unaffiliated group representing nearly all of the Alaska Native corporations, ran supportive ads, for example showing the important role that federal spending played in Alaska and warning voters not to "cut off our federal leg." Most AST ads, however, attacked outside groups spending heavily on the Miller campaign and Miller himself for refusing to answer questions about his background. One argued that McAdams was a "nice guy" but not electable.

McAdams's ads featured his background in Southeast Alaska and connection to the state's large fishing industry. His strongest issue position in the campaign concerned K–12 education, and he championed himself as the "education" candidate. McAdams used his weight (nearly 300 lbs.) to advantage in ads, saying "I'm Twice the Man Joe Miller is (literally) and probably three or four Lisas."

Miller's campaign commercials emphasized his military background and conservative credentials. Unaffiliated groups and individuals did the heavy hitting. Senator Jim DeMint (R-SC) attacked Murkowski in a fund-raising letter as a "big tent hypocrite." The Pennsylvania-based group LetFreedomRing aired radio ads in Alaska cities calling Murkowski a spoiled princess trying to hold onto a seat her father deeded to her. A Tea Party Express TV spot castigated Miller's opponent as "Arrogant Lisa Murkowski—You Lost."

Finance

Murkowski had a clear edge, both with respect to direct expenditures and money spent on her behalf by unaffiliated groups, as seen in Table 9.2.

Table 9.2. 2010 Alaska U.S. Senate Race, Campaign Finance

Candidate	Direct Funds	Unaffiliated Spending	Total
Lisa Murkowski	$4,615,936	$1,998,418*	$6,614,354
Joe Miller	$3,252,063	$1,756,568	$5,008,631
Scott McAdams	$1,318,022	$408,354	$1,726,376
Totals	$9,186,021	$4,1633,340	$13,349,361

* Alaskans Standing Together reported that it spent $1.6 million on the Murkowski campaign (FDNM, 12/8/10), which is $340,000 greater than the amount reflected in Open Secrets. We report AST's numbers.
Source: www.opensecrets.org, December 27, 2010.

Murkowski entered the general election race at an advantage, as she carried forward approximately $1.2 million from her failed primary campaign. Still she raised more money than Miller, because during the election cycle she attracted large contributions from PACS, totaling more than $1 million (with large donations from electric utilities, oil/gas, leadership PACs, lawyers/law firms, and lobbyists). Miller initially funded about one third of his primary campaign with credit cards, and proceeded to pay this debt off during the campaign. McAdams entered the race last, and attracted most of his funding in individual contributions of less than $200. The total amount raised by candidates through direct fund raising was greater than raised in the 2008 senate campaign of Mark Begich and Ted Stevens because there were three candidates. It was less than raised in the 2004 senate race between Lisa Murkowski and Tony Knowles ($11 million compared to the $9.2 million in 2010).

It was unaffiliated group contributions that made this the most expensive U.S. Senate race in state history, and showed the clear impact of the recent *Citizens United* Supreme Court decision on Alaska politics. Alaskans Standing Together provided the lion's share of unaffiliated support for Murkowski, because she was a known quantity and had helped Alaska Natives through her work on Native health care, education, housing and job creation. Figuring in the campaign was her bill in support of Sealaska Corporation's attempt to select lands from the Tongass National Forest.

As the Republican Party nominee, Miller benefited from $710,323 in unaffiliated spending from the National Republican Senatorial Campaign Committee and $252,749 from the Senate Conservatives Fund (a leadership PAC of Sen. Jim DeMint). The Club for Growth raised $318,602 in unaffiliated spending to support his campaign, and the Tea Party Express raised $662,787. Approximately 20 to 30 percent of these funds financed attack ads on Miller's opponents, with a focus on Murkowski. McAdams' campaign benefited from unaffiliated spending by the Democratic party of Alaska ($125,034) and the Democratic Senatorial Campaign Committee ($194,050), but 84 percent of the latter amount went to oppose Republicans and specifically Miller.

Grass Roots

Alaska elections for seats in the congressional delegation emphasize a strong grassroots component, because in this sparsely populated state, voters believe they should be able to meet candidates personally during the campaign. Because McAdams had lower name recognition than Miller and Murkowski, he spent much of his time outside his base in Southeast Alaska. All candidates sponsored fund-raisers in Anchorage, Fairbanks, and Juneau and also held open forums at community halls. Murkowski took particular advantage of casual meetings to distribute wristbands bearing a filled-in oval and her name, and she consistently stayed on message. Chambers of Commerce in Anchorage and Fairbanks sponsored candidate debates, and there were two televised debates during the campaign, but these did not appear to change many minds.

Bases of Support

McAdams received endorsements from Democratic legislators and a few local government officials; he was not endorsed by Native organizations, and his home town tribal council, Shee Atika, endorsed Murkowski. This is notable because of the well-established pattern of Native organizations to endorse Democratic candidates for office. Nor did McAdams receive strong support from labor organizations, which typically support Democratic over Republican candidates for office.

As the Republican nominee, Miller collected a number of endorsements from national and state party officials—Senate Majority Leader Mitch McConnell, presidential candidate Mike Huckabee, Tea Party darling Michele Bachmann, Alaska governor Sean Parnell, about eight state legislators, and the head of the state Republican party. In addition to the Republican and Tea Party Express PACs, he received support from the FreedomWorks PAC chaired by former U.S. House Majority Leader Dick Armey, the Minuteman PAC (specifically opposed to illegal immigration), and a small Native organization (Alaska Native Veterans PAC). All of Miller's endorsements came from conservative Republicans.

Murkowski also attracted Republican support. When she returned to the U.S. Senate after losing the Republican primary, opponents sought to remove her from her position as ranking member of the Energy and Natural Resources Committee, but the Republican membership declined to do so. What is noteworthy about her campaign strategy was its inclusiveness, and especially its appeal to Alaska Natives. The board of the state's largest and most consequential Native organization, the Alaska Federation of Natives (AFN), entreated her to pursue a write-in campaign, and Alaskans Standing Together formed from leaders of Alaska Native Corporations (who also played extremely active roles in the AFN). Typically, the October AFN convention during election years invites major candidates to address delegates, but at the 2010 gathering in Fairbanks, only Murkowski addressed the crowd, which gave her a standing ovation. Other endorsements came from diverse groups including labor (NEA-Alaska, the state's largest teachers' union), the Alaska Professional Firefighters Association, the Anchorage Police Department Employees, Anchorage Young Republicans, the Alaska Native Brotherhood and Sisterhood (the state's oldest Native organization), the former president of the University of Alaska, and United Fishermen of Alaska. By Election Day, Murkowski had captured the broadest and most diverse constituency, which one would expect of an incumbent.

Election Results

The day after the election, it was clear that the write-ins had won. These ballots commanded 41 percent of the total, compared to 34 percent for Miller and 24 percent for McAdams. However, the ballots needed to be hand counted, and the process took two weeks. First, the two teams of lawyers quarreled over the counting date and procedure. Then, observers from each side watched as 30 ballot-counters sorted all the ballots. Although the statute on write-in voting could be clearer, Alaska is a state emphasizing "voter intent": Supreme Court rulings have said that voter intent must be valued heavily "to make each citizen's vote as meaningful as every other vote."[13] Director of the Division of Elections Gail Fenumiai made the decision whether to count disputed ballots for Murkowski.

November 17 was the deadline for receipt of absentee ballots. By then, Murkowski had a clear lead. Her unchallenged ballot total was 92,929 as compared to Miller's 90,740. Some 8,159 challenged ballots were counted for Murkowski (but not included in the total above), but an additional 2,016 challenged ballots were not put in her column. This prompted the senator to declare that her write-in campaign was victorious as she clearly had 2,189 undisputed votes more than Miller. (Ironically, this was about the size of her primary loss to Miller.) Table 9.3 compares the candidates' performances by several factors:

Table 9.3. Candidates' Performance in Alaska House Districts

Performance metric	McAdams	Miller	Murkowski
# of districts in which candidate led the list	2/40	13/40	25/40
# of Republican districts* in which candidate led	1/25	12/25	12/25
# of Democratic districts in which candidate led	1/15	1/15	13/15
# of districts in which candidate led by >45%	1/2	9/13	9/25

*The winner of the house seat was the Republican candidate.
Source: Authors' calculation from Alaska Division of Elections Unofficial Results, November 17, 2010.

These data indicate that Murkowski had the most effective statewide campaign. She and Miller divided the Republican districts evenly, but she led the other senate candidates in nearly all the districts electing Democratic house members. Finally, her support was highly dispersed, while Miller's was concentrated.

Murkowski demonstrated greater strength than McAdams in Southeast Alaska (with the exception of Juneau). She outpolled both Miller and McAdams in the primarily Native communities of the Southeast, Southwest, West, Northwest, North, and Interior; in districts 38–40 she gained 65 percent of the vote. Although she had lost all house districts in Fairbanks, North Pole and adjacent communities in the primary, she captured a plurality of the votes in districts 8 and 9 (downtown Fairbanks) in the general election. In Southcentral, she won pluralities in most urban and suburban Anchorage districts, the state's major population concentration. Miller did well in the state's most conservative districts: Mat-Su (especially in Palmer and Wasilla), the Kenai, North Pole and the Richardson highway communities of Delta and Eielson. McAdams did well only in two districts—south Kenai and Juneau.

Declaring her victory on November 17, Murkowski said: "If you want something done, tell an Alaskan that they can't do it. Because by God they'll go out and do it. . . . Whether you are old . . . young . . . a member of a union or are a retired individual, my task is to represent everyone of you. And from this day forward, as Alaskans, that's what we need to be doing, coming together."[14] However, challenges by Miller delayed certification of the election.

Court Challenges

Before and during ballot counting, Miller objected to the state's use of discretion in counting the write-in ballots. His campaign staff also alleged several election irregularities: a federal contractor who illegally campaigned for Murkowski, an unsecured ballot box, felons voting in the election. Miller initially filed suit in federal court, asking for a preliminary injunction to stop officials from certifying the election. His argument was that state law required voters to write in the candidate's name as it appeared on the declaration of candidacy or the correctly spelled last name of the candidate. A federal district court judge sent the suit to state courts; in early December, a Ketchikan superior court judge upheld the election results. Miller then appealed to the state supreme court. With $900,000 remaining in campaign funds (while continuing to collect donations for his appeal), Miller had little to lose and much to gain through continued court action.

On December 22, the Alaska Supreme Court ruled unanimously against Miller on all counts, saying his interpretation of the law would erode the integrity of Alaska's election system.[15] Republican leaders urged Miller to concede so that the election could be certified before the start of the 112th Congress in early January 2011, allowing the seating of Murkowski and the retention of her cumulative seniority. Finally, Miller withdrew his opposition to the certification of the election, saying his decision "would allow Alaskans to focus on bringing fairness and transparency to our election process without distraction of the certification issue."[16] At the close of the year, he gave up his legal challenge, saying "The time has come to accept the practical realities of our current legal circumstances."[17] He told Fox News that there was little chance of success in an appeal to the 9th Circuit because it was a "left of center" bench. While he continued to have grave concerns about the nation's direction, he revealed no plans for his political future.

CONCLUSION

The Alaska U.S. Senate rate in 2010 did not affect the balance of party power in this veritable institution, but it did concern public values and the representation of the interests of Alaskans. Lisa Murkowski was targeted in the Republican primary because she did not represent the conservative wing of the Republican party nationally, which invited a strong challenge from Joe Miller, whose candidacy was endorsed by Sarah Palin and the Tea Party Express. Miller's upstart victory in the primary was a catalyst for the regeneration of Murkowski's political career. Already she had a reputation for capable and effective leadership, but she needed to demonstrate that she could speak for all Alaskans and forge new alliances needed to win a very difficult statewide write-in campaign. In this context, the Alaska Native community provided critical support through formation of an unaffiliated group, Alaskans Standing Together, which provided funds in support of her campaign and hundreds of volunteers to educate voters at the grassroots level. Murkowski emerged as a tougher and more resilient political leader, who is not likely to take her position as Alaska's elected representative for granted in the future.

During the general election, Miller's candidacy degenerated. First, opponents pointed to several contradictions between his personal actions and his stated positions against social welfare and in support of conservative constitutionalism—lending credence to the charge of hypocrisy. Then Miller failed to be forthright and transparent about an ethical lapse during his employment with the Fairbanks borough. Finally, his post-election campaign against the election itself indicated that Miller was concerned primarily about his survival politically and not the interests of Alaskans in fair and transparent elections.

NOTES

1. McBeath and Lovecraft, "Alaska Senate Race (Begich v. Stevens): Scandal, Upset, and the End of an Era," *The Roads to Congress 2008,* 227–30.

2. Alaska Department of Revenue, *Fall 2010 Revenue Sources Book,* 30.

3. Alaska Department of Labor and Workforce Development, *Alaska Economic Trends,* July 2010, 18.

4. Jerry McBeath, "What Recession? Alaska's FY 2011 Budget," *Annual Western States Budget Review,* 2010, AK1–5.

5. See Michael Barone with Richard F. Cohen, *The Almanac of American Politics.* Washington, DC: National Journal Group, 2007, 83.

6. *Fairbanks Daily News-Miner,* September 8, 2010.

7. *Fairbanks Daily News-Miner,* September 18, 2010. No one in Alaska history had won a write-in campaign for a state or federal office, and the last US Senator to do so was Strom Thurmond in 1954.

8. *Fairbanks Daily News-Miner,* October 23, 2010.

9. *Fairbanks Daily News-Miner,* October 26, 2010.

10. *Anchorage Daily News,* October 11, 2010.

11. *Fairbanks Daily News-Miner,* October 24, 2010.

12. *Fairbanks Daily News-Miner,* October 16, 2010.

13. *Anchorage Daily News,* November 7, 2010.

14. *Fairbanks Daily News-Miner,* November 18, 2010.

15. *Anchorage Daily News,* December 23, 2010.

16. *Washington Post,* December 27, 2010.

17. *Anchorage Daily News,* January 1, 2011.

Chapter 10

California Senate Race
(Fiorina v. Boxer)

The Great Democratic Exception
in a Republican Year

Marcia L. Godwin

Carly Fiorina
Party: Republican
Age: 56
Sex: Female
Race: Caucasian
Religion: Christian
Education: B.A., medieval history and philosophy (Stanford University, 1976); M.B.A. (University of Maryland, College Park, 1980); M.S., Business Administration (MIT, 1989)
Occupation: AT & T (1980–1994); Lucent Technologies (1995–1999); Chief Executive Officer, Hewlett-Packard (1999–2005)
Political Experience: Advisor, John McCain presidential campaign and speaker, Republican National Convention (2008)

Barbara Boxer
Party: Democrat
Age: 69
Sex: Female
Race: Caucasian
Religion: Jewish
Education: B.S., economics (Brooklyn College, 1962)
Occupation: Public official; Author
Political Experience: Aide, U.S. Representative John Burton (1974–1976); Marin County Board of Supervisors (1976–1982); U.S. Representative (1982–1992); U.S. Senator (1993–present)

Confrontational. Controversial. Media-Savvy. Ground-breaking female leader. Author. All these labels apply to *both* incumbent Senator Barbara Boxer (D-CA) and her Republican challenger, Carly Fiorina.[1] Political observers had waited through three senatorial campaigns for Boxer to face an energetic challenger. For the first time in memory, the national Republican party and interest groups put significant financial resources into a California Senate race. Yet, the result was the same as in past elections—an overwhelming Boxer victory. California voters also chose to bring Democrat Jerry Brown back as governor over eBay billionaire Meg Whitman, elected Democrats to all other statewide offices, and failed to turn out a single incumbent Congress member.

DISCONTENTED CALIFORNIA

To outsiders, it might appear that in 2010 California had reverted to being the "Great Exception," a label coined in 1949 by author Carey McWilliams.[2] Numerous pundits, major national media sources, and even California's own newspapers proclaimed that the Tea Party movement had stopped at California, as if California was fulfilling its name as a mythical island country separated from the rest of the continent.

California has been a dependable "blue" state, voting for Democratic presidential candidates since 1992 and having strong Democratic majorities in both houses of its state legislature since the mid-1990s. However, both Democrats and Republicans have become more rigidly partisan over time, so districts tend to represent the political extremes.[3] Both parties have seen erosion in their registered membership, but independent voters have tended to lean Democratic. The growing proportion of Latino voters has voted strongly Democratic as well.

The consistency in voting behavior masks deep discontent and frustration by Californians. Journalists and authors have long written about California's ungovernability, citing the 1978 passage of Proposition 13 limiting property taxes, bloated state constitution, inconsistent ballot initiatives limiting revenues while mandating expenditures, special interest lobbying, polarized electorate, immigration issues, and differences between its electorate and population.[4]

California suffered through a lingering recession in the early to mid-1990s, exacerbated by military base closures. With the bursting of the dot. com bubble and California energy crisis, recently re-elected Gray Davis was recalled by a large margin in 2003 and replaced by Republican Arnold Schwarzenegger even as most other statewide offices remained in Democratic hands.[5] Schwarzenegger inherited a structural deficit and repackaged state debt with the approval of voters at a special election. Other reform

Figure 10.1 Approval Ratings, 2010, California Registered Voters

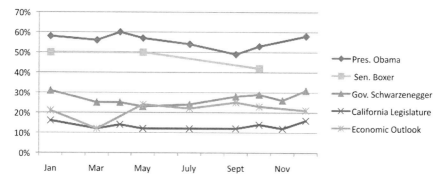

efforts were not as successful, including the defeat of a package of ballot measures at a special election in November 2005 and the defeat of measures to help cut budget deficits in another special election in May 2009.[6]

Since California had already been dealing with major financial problems before the economic downturn in 2007, Californians generally blamed President George W. Bush, Governor Schwarzenegger, and their own political institutions rather than Democratic office holders. While pundits have often cited Senator Boxer's mediocre approval ratings as evidence of her vulnerability, her approval ratings appear much healthier when placed in context.

As shown in Figure 10.1, President Barak Obama has retained relatively high approval ratings, unlike his unpopular predecessor. Sen. Boxer's ratings have trailed by several points, but have fluctuated in roughly the same way. Gov. Schwarzenegger's ratings were in the 20 percent range for most of the year, tracking closely with the percentages of those who had a positive outlook about the economy. With skyrocketing unemployment and home foreclosure rates, these results are hardly surprising. However, the California legislature's ratings were even lower, hovering around 12 percent.

Rather than directing anger towards defeating incumbents, voters have turned to institutional reform. Proposition 11, passed in 2008, transferred redistricting authority from the California legislature to a citizen commission. An initiative to extend the commission's responsibility to Congressional districts qualified for the November 2010 ballot. Voters also passed Proposition 14 in the June 2010 primary election to change from a semi-closed primary system to an open one in which the top two candidates, regardless of party, will advance to the general election. Finally, repeal of the two-thirds supermajority requirement for the legislature to pass a state budget was placed on the November 2010 ballot. Although the supermajority requirement would be left in place for taxes and fees, this requirement moved from being sacrosanct in the eyes of the electorate to being blamed for gridlock.

THE CANDIDATES

Barbara Boxer

Barbara Boxer has been an elected official for decades. After moving to Marin County, north of San Francisco, in the 1960s, she became active with environmental and anti-war issues. She became an aide to legendary California politician John Burton in 1974, the same year that Jerry Brown first was elected Governor of California. On her second try, she was elected to the Marin County Board of Supervisors in 1976 and was elected to the U.S. Congress when Burton stepped down in 1982.

Boxer initially appeared to model her career after Representative Patricia Schroeder (D-CO) by taking on a role as a defense watchdog and pursuing more liberal Democratic issues. After helping to lead protests related to sexual harassment allegations against Supreme Court nominee Clarence Thomas, Boxer ran for an open Senate seat in 1992, the so-called "Year of the Woman." Even with the unusual circumstance of having both California senate seats with competitive races (Diane Feinstein defeated an appointed incumbent for a partial term), the race was the second most expensive in the country.

Republican strategists have long wished for Boxer's defeat and have criticized her voting record as being much more liberal than fellow Democrat Feinstein, but have learned the hard way that Boxer should not be underestimated. Boxer easily defeated State Treasurer Matt Fong in 1998 after compare and contrast TV ads portrayed him as an extremist and Boxer as "fighting for California." The campaign in 2004 turned out to be even less competitive, with Boxer's opponent failing to raise enough funds to run television advertisements in the fall. Even in the 2004 campaign, Boxer maintained a well-run campaign. Long-time aide Rose Kapolczynski has directed Boxer's reelection campaigns, a cadre of consultants has handled media and advertisements, and Boxer has proved to a remarkable fundraiser—she receives high levels of donations from pro-choice EMILY's List, but also from Democratic political action committees, unions, house parties, on-line donations, and high-profile fundraising events with Democratic leaders.[7]

Boxer's campaign strategies have not been particularly imaginative, but have been highly effective at deterring would-be challengers and causing her support to peak at the general election. Her campaigns have been extremely disciplined in holding funds until September and competent in determining the types of ads needed to frame each race. Boxer herself, both as a campaigner and Senator, has had an uncanny ability to mix both substantive, popular policy positions with more symbolic actions on issues such as abortion rights.

Sen. Boxer added novelist to her resume in 2005 with the publication of *A Time to Run*, an account of fictional California liberal senator Ellen Fischer, spanning 1974 to before the September 11, 2001 terrorist attacks.[8] Boxer again teamed up with co-author Mary-Rose Hayes to publish a 2009 sequel, *Blind Trust*, with Fischer fighting right-wing attacks against her character.[9] Now with four grandchildren and co-owner, with her husband, of a retirement home in wealthy Rancho Mirage near Palm Springs and a condo in Oakland near family, Boxer might have been expected to have lost a bit of her passion for "fighting for California."

Yet, at the same time, Boxer's passions have increasingly matched up with serious policymaking. Since Democrats gained a solid majority in the Senate after 2006, Boxer has served as chair of the Environmental and Public Works Committee, giving her real influence related to climate change and energy issues while also allowing her to direct funds for projects to her California constituents. Boxer also simultaneously chaired the Senate Ethics Committee from 2007 to 2008.[10]

Boxer has had a few stumbles in recent years. After being neutral for most of the 2008 presidential primary season, she endorsed Hillary Clinton after Clinton's win in California, joining her colleague Feinstein as a Clinton supporter. Neither Senator suffered politically when Barack Obama won. Feinstein hosted a private meeting between Clinton and Obama to close out Clinton's campaign and Obama hosted a late fundraiser for Boxer in 2010.

More attention was given to Boxer's criticism of Army Corps of Engineers Brig. General Michael Walsh for calling her "Ma'am" instead of "Senator" during a June 2009 committee hearing. The two apparently had a friendly conversation afterward, but critics saw this as a sign that Boxer had become arrogant and unsupportive of the military.[11] The incident seems to have actually served as a red herring for the campaign of Boxer's general election opponent, Carly Fiorina. The Fiorina campaign could not resist the temptation to use it in advertising, long after it ceased to be relevant to voters concerned more about the economy.[12]

Carly Fiorina

Carly Fiorina was born as Cara Carleton Sneed, following a tradition in her father's family of naming daughters after an ancestor who died in the Civil War without leaving any male descendents. Her father became a law professor and federal judge while her mother was an artist, with Fiorina describing them as "rigorous, disciplined, demanding and judgmental"—characteristics that Fiorina's critics have attributed to her as well.[13] Fiorina spent part of her childhood near Stanford University in California and returned as an undergraduate, majoring in medieval history and philosophy. Her first business experiences were as a receptionist for openly gay owners of a beauty salon and for commercial property brokers who asked her to consider training to become a broker. She went to law school for a semester, married her college boyfriend, and followed him to Italy where she taught English. Upon returning to the United States, she was a star MBA student at the University of Maryland, College Park, and was one of the first women accepted into a management training program at AT&T, the result of a court settlement related to past discrimination against women and minorities.[14] She married co-worker Frank Fiorina after the breakup of her first marriage, accepted as "God's plan" the disappointment of being unsuccessful in trying to have children together, but rejoiced in being an active stepmother to two young daughters.[15]

In her autobiography, *Tough Choices,* Fiorina discussed experiencing sexism early in her career, but was able to pursue somewhat non-traditional positions and responsibilities while being rapidly promoted at AT&T. AT&T also sponsored Fiorina for an executive master's degree at MIT; in her autobiography and interviews, she talked about being enamored with a study of the Greek tragedy *Antigone* with its fallen heroine.[16] After moving over to Lucent Technologies, when it spun off into its own company, Fiorina gained national media attention as one of *Fortune*'s 50 most powerful women in business.

Fiorina was hired in 1999 as CEO of Hewlett-Packard, having been approached by a recruiter shortly after her mother, while dying of cancer in California, had wistfully mentioned that it would be nice if Fiorina could become head of a locally headquartered company like HP. Her selection was ground-breaking and Fiorina herself touted the achievement on her web site as being the first female CEO of a Fortune 50 company. In her autobiography, Fiorina described a wildly decentralized company in need of basic management reforms. However, her tenure was controversial, with the HP board of directors firing her in 2005 after a nasty proxy fight led by descendents of the founders over the merger with Compaq Computers, complaints about Fiorina's aggressive management style and excessive cultivation of the media, and declines in the stock price. HP rebounded shortly after the firing, leading to questions about whether Fiorina was evaluated fairly. The authors of a comprehensive history of HP described Fiorina both as catalyst, "saving HP from mediocrity," but also a "reactant, a cathartic sacrifice."[17]

According to Fiorina's personal website, carlyfiorina.com, Fiorina has served on several corporate, educational, and foundation boards since leaving HP, including the Fiorina Foundation and an endowment in support of women. Fiorina has been a featured speaker for corporations and business events, a commentator for the Fox Business Network, and an advisor for various boards, including ones related to defense issues. Fiorina became more directly involved in politics as an energetic campaigner for Senator John McCain (R-AZ) in 2008 and was mentioned as a potential cabinet appointee if McCain won the presidential election.[18] Then, Fiorina had to step down after attracting controversy for commenting that neither McCain nor Palin had the experience to run a corporation. Even though she added Obama and Biden to the list and qualified her comments, her remarks briefly made Fiorina the center of attention and gave credence to critics of the McCain-Palin ticket.[19]

Fiorina underwent treatment for breast cancer in early 2009, but that did not deter her plans to run to the U.S. Senate as she announced that the cancer was gone and that she was "raring to go" against Boxer. Nevertheless, it was startling to see the formerly blond, youthful Fiorina with gray hair that was just beginning to grow back after chemotherapy. Fiorina's openness broke new ground for candidates facing health concerns, and her experience gave her a platform for criticizing proposals to reduce mammogram frequency. Fiorina also often commented that her experience had left her unafraid of a tough campaign against Boxer.[20]

The Primary Campaign: Fiorina Goes After Demon Sheep

The primary campaign season should have been unusually dull, with Boxer having token opposition in the Democratic primary and Fiorina the obvious Republican front-runner. However, Republican gubernatorial candidate and former U.S. Representative Tom Campbell decided to switch to the U.S. Senate race. Suddenly, Fiorina appeared to be facing a competitive race with the moderate Campbell and had to guard against possible criticism from the right from Chuck DeVore, a conservative State Assembly member from Southern California.

The Fiorina campaign's solution was to release an advertisement featuring sheep with red glowing eyes and calling Campbell a Fiscal Conservative In Name Only (FCINO), a variation of the Republican In Name Only (RINO) accusation often used by conservatives against more moderate candidates. While the ad aired sparingly, it went viral on the Internet and garnered national media attention as the "Demon Sheep" ad.[21] The California Democratic party and Democratic Senatorial Campaign Committee reacted with glee at the Republican in-fighting and released its own tongue-in-cheek trailer and web site for a demon sheep movie. "Demon Sheep I" labeled Campbell as "Little Arnold" and repeated Fiorina's criticism of him as "architect of the Schwarzenegger budget nightmare" based on a previous position as California Finance Director; "Demon Sheep II: the Fleecing of California" accused Fiorina of outsourcing 28,000 jobs to other countries and of being a greatly overpaid executive; and "Extreme Sheep III: The Tea Party's Over" effectively dismissed DeVore as a fringe candidate. The piece closed by calling them "a trilogy of mutton we can't afford" and noting that no sheep had been harmed during filming."[22]

In all seriousness, the Campbell campaign forced Fiorina to spend significant campaign funds in the primary, $9.7 million, which included a personal loan of over \$5.5 million. Boxer spent a similar amount, \$9.3 million, but did not run advertisements and had amassed funds for the fall campaign. While Fiorina needed to gain name recognition, the primary campaign may have served more to establish Fiorina's reputation as a maverick Republican than as a candidate with cross-over appeal to Democrats. For example, a late ad criticized Boxer's record on climate change.[23] In hindsight, Fiorina probably could have used a positive approach, as the Campbell campaign never gained traction and Fiorina won the June primary handily with 56 percent of the vote, compared to 22 percent for Campbell and 19 percent for DeVore.[24]

CAMPAIGN ISSUES AND STRATEGY

The Missing Policy Issues

Perhaps one of the most surprising facets of the general election campaign was how little policy issues were covered. It would be expected that both candidates would have claimed to be the most qualified to deal with economic concerns, given that it was by far the most important issue in this election cycle. Past Boxer campaigns also had run compare-and-contrast ads, reminding voters that her views on the environment, education, and abortion were more aligned with Californians than with Republican opponents. Fiorina, as the challenger, had to convince voters that it was time for a change *and* that she would be preferred to Boxer.

In interviews, both Boxer and Fiorina did highlight their policy differences. In an in-depth article with the *Wall Street Journal* early in the campaign, Fiorina knowledgeably discussed trade, energy, and water issues and openly portrayed herself as having conservative values on abortion, same-sex marriage, and taxes.[25] During the general election campaign, there were only two debates—a televised debate a few days before Labor Day weekend and a public radio debate at the end of September with Boxer participating remotely from Washington, DC. Commentators concluded that Fiorina held her own but did not moderate her policy positions. Few voters caught coverage of either debate.[26]

Attack Ads

Instead, Californians were given a steady stream of attack ads. Boxer went straight after Fiorina's record at HP, using the tag line "Carly Fiorina. Outsourcing jobs. Out for herself." in an ad that began airing in mid-September. The number of outsourced jobs was now increased to 30,000, based on Fiorina's own television interview statements. The advertisement also referenced Fiorina's purchase of a yacht, first mentioned in the Democratic demon sheep ad.[27]

A week later Fiorina began running her own attack ads that included a clip of Boxer's "Ma'am" comments.[28] Fiorina focused on the need to remove Boxer from office, but failed to define herself as a competent executive who could use her expertise to help the economy. Instead, Fiorina issued ads critical of Boxer's support of the stimulus bill and calling for an end to "bickering." In another ad issued in mid-October, Fiorina directly spoke to voters to call for an end to partisanship and said she would oppose her own party if needed, without touting her own qualifications. Careful viewers might also have noticed most ads, ironically, were co-sponsored by the National Republican Senatorial Committee.[29]

The *coups de grace* against Fiorina was a final Boxer ad featuring testimonials from former HP employees; each individually faced the camera and angrily blamed Fiorina for being laid off and for outsourcing their jobs. Boxer's campaign manager stated that the series of ads were an "opportunity to define her." Boxer's pollster summed up the corresponding shift in voter opinion as "if there is a mortal sin in this economy, it is exporting jobs."[30]

Money versus Money

Table 10.1 summarizes key aspects of Boxer's reelection campaigns. The escalating amounts of money spent with each campaign are especially notable. Boxer spent more than $26 million in 2010, an increase of more than $10 million from her last reelection campaign. Combined with independent and coordinated expenditures, that total increases by several million dollars. It is estimated that the Boxer campaign spent $14 million directly on television ads, and another $6 million was spent by outside groups, including the Democratic Senatorial Campaign Committee. Abortion rights groups also provided phone banking, Internet, and radio ad support.[31]

The Fiorina campaign spent $22.6 million, according to FEC records. Independent expenditures for television ads included over $4 million spent by the U.S. Chamber of Commerce and $2.8 million by the National Republican Senatorial Campaign Committee, which spent several million more in coordinated expenditures. Overall, it seems that Boxer and her supporters maintained an advantage of several million dollars in campaign spending.[32]

The Whitman Effect

The Boxer-Fiorina race, though, paled in terms of visibility and spending to the governor's race between billionaire Meg Whitman, former CEO of E-Bay, and former Governor Jerry Brown. The governor's race appeared to be much more of a dead heat as Whitman unapologetically self-funded most of her campaign and Brown had to hold funds until the fall campaign. Then, Whitman's support evaporated in spectacular fashion.

Table 10.1. Barbara Boxer's Senatorial Campaigns

Item	1992	1998	2004	2010
Election Cycle	Presidential election; both U.S. Senate seats	Open governor race, all statewide offices	Presidential election	Open governor race, all statewide offices
Primary Competition	Both Democratic and Republican	Republican only	Republican only	Republican only
Boxer Vulnerabilities	Congress check-bouncing scandal	Clinton-Lewinsky scandal; narrow win in 1992	Recall of Democratic governor in 2003	Republican year; aggressive challenger
Boxer TV Ads	Compare and contrast	Compare and contrast	Advocacy, opponent not mentioned	Attack
Spending	Boxer: $10.4 million	Boxer: $13.7 million	Boxer: $16.0 million	Boxer: $26.7 million
	Hershensohn: $7.6 million	Fong: $10.8 million	Jones: $6.7 million	Fiorina: $22.6 million
	Most expensive Senate race	Second-most expensive race	Fourth- or fifth-most expensive race	Second-most expensive race
Late Revelations about Challenger	Frequented adult newsstand and visited strip club	Possible hypocrisy, for accepting Log Cabin Republican and Traditional Values Coalition support	Not running television ads as previously announced	Spillover of negative press from governor race; hospitalized with infection last week of campaign
Election Results	48%–43%	53%–43%	58%–38%	52%–42%

Sources: Compiled by author from media coverage, California Secretary of State *Statement of Vote* reports, Center for Responsive Politics campaign finance reports, www.opensecrets.org, and Federal Elections Commission campaign finance reports, www.fec.gov.

First, Whitman's former housekeeper, Nicky Diaz Santillan, held a press conference with well-known activist attorney Gloria Allred in late September. Diaz Santillan had been fired in June 2009 after Whitman found out that she was an undocumented immigrant. Whitman had to modify her denial that no one knew about her immigration status when Allred was able to show that Whitman's husband had received an inquiry from the Social Security Administration years earlier. (Diaz had been using a relative's social security number.) Although this incident related to an illegal immigrant, Angela Salas from the Coalition for Humane Immigrant Rights noted that most illegal immigrants in California live with a permanent resident or U.S. citizen, so these types of controversies tend to increase Latino interest and turnout.[33]

Near the same time, campaign spending reports indicated that Whitman had spent close to $150 million of her own money on the race.[34] Republican strategist Arnold Steinberg, in an election post-mortem, pulled no punches in concluding that "the vulgarity of Whitman's spending trumped any real connection with voters."[35] Fiorina loaned herself a total of $6.8 million, 30 percent of her total contributions, but voters tended to equate her approach with Whitman's and concluded that both were wealthy corporate leaders out of touch with everyday Californians.[36]

Polls

As shown in Figure 10.2, Boxer led in the polls during all of the three periods when the major California polls concentrated their surveying efforts: after

Figure 10.2 General Election Polls, 2010 California Senate Race

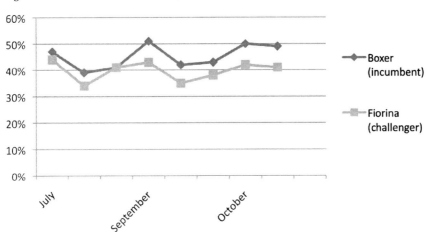

Sources: Public Policy Institute of California, Field, and USC/*Los Angeles Times* polls. Timeline not to scale, includes two July, three September, and three October polls.

the June primary, after Labor Day in September with traditional kick-off of the fall campaign and television ads, and then in October. However, pundits were reluctant to call the race until a few weeks before the election because of uncertainty about spending by interest groups, economic conditions, and Boxer's vulnerability.

Boxer's support ended up closely matching the 1998 campaign—once advertising kicked in, Boxer's support increased while her opponent's plummeted. It appears that the Senate race broke open a bit later in 2010 compared to earlier campaigns. In addition, Fiorina was hospitalized the Tuesday before the election with an infection related to her reconstructive breast surgery. Fiorina was released the next day, apparently after receiving intravenous antibiotics. With many swing voters voting on Election Day, as discussed in the next section, Fiorina probably lost votes in spite of some pundits claiming she could get sympathy support.[37]

ELECTION RESULTS

1998 All Over Again

The results on Election Day had Democrats winning by much wider margins than the polls had indicated. In fact, the results largely mirrored the 1998 election, the last time that there was both an open governor's race and a Senate reelection campaign. In 1998, Democrats swept all statewide offices, with the exception of the narrow reelection of the Republican Secretary of State, Bill Jones. This time, the closest race was for Attorney General, between Democrat Kamala Harris from San Francisco and Republican Steve Cooley. Harris was elected by less than 100,000 votes and won only because of her 300,000 vote margin in Cooley's home county of Los Angeles.[38]

For Boxer, the results were eerily similar to 1998, a race that was much more competitive than her 2004 reelection campaign. As shown in Table 10.2, Boxer again won by 10 percentage points and even won the Bay Area by a wide

Table 10.2. Vote Totals by Region

Region	1998		2004		2010	
	Boxer	Fong	Boxer	Jones	Boxer	Fiorina
Bay Area	63%	33%	70%	26%	67%	29%
Los Angeles County	61%	36%	67%	28%	62%	33%
Rest of California	45%	51%	49%	47%	42%	52%
Total	53%	43%	58%	38%	52%	42%

Source: California Secretary of State, *Statement of Vote* reports, www.sos.ca.gov.

margin, which should have been Fiorina's home base. There is strong evidence that California's electorate remains polarized by geography. Boxer lost the more conservative but less populated counties by a slightly larger margin than in 1998, resulting in winning only 21 counties out of 58 in the state. The only difference in number of counties won was that Boxer narrowly won San Bernardino County in 1998, where she then had a field office. Even in the non-competitive 2004 race, Boxer only picked up 27 counties, less than a majority.[39]

Exit and post-election polls, as shown in Table 10.3, present a similar story. In spite of facing a female candidate, Boxer continued to enjoy higher support from women than her opponent. The support from men fluctuates depending on the exit poll or survey, but appears to have been at least at 1998 levels.

Partisan differences continue to be stark. Voter registration statistics indicate the number of independent voters has increased to 20.3 percent of the electorate, up from 12.7 percent in 1998. However, there now is a larger gap between registered Democrats and Republicans (2008—13.1 percent, 1998—11.2 percent) and independents tend to lean Democratic.[40]

Table 10.3 also indicates that the diversity of California's electorate affects outcomes. With higher margins of error among these subgroups and more discrepancies among the various exit polls and post-election surveys, it cannot be determined whether White/Caucasian voters were split or favored Fiorina.

Table 10.3.   Exit and Post-Election Polls*

	1998		2004		2010		
	Boxer	Fong	Boxer	Jones	Boxer	Fiorina	
Gender							
Men	47%	49%	55%	41%	49%	42%	
Women	57%	39%	62%	34%	54%	42%	
Political Party							
Democrats	86%	12%	93%	4%	85%	11%	
Republicans	13%	85%	16%	81%	10%	83%	
Other	n/a	n/a	n/a	n/a	48%	42%	
Independent/DTS	48%	43%	56%	37%	58%	32%	
Race/Ethnicity							
White	47%	49%	51%	45%	43%	50%	
Asian	48%	51%	66%	29%	60%	34%	*
Black	64%	34%	83%	13%	86%	9%	*
Latino	69%	24%	71%	23%	78%	18%	

Sources: Los Angeles Times, 1998 and 2004, cited in Godwin, "Redefining Barbara Boxer," p. 78; *USC/ Los Angeles Times Poll,* Nov. 2010. May not add to 100% due to rounding and votes for minor party and independent candidates.

*1998 and 2004 represent exit polls while 2010 represent post-election survey results. The margin of error is higher for Asian and Black voters. The Public Policy Institute of California (PPIC) conducted its own post-election survey and excluded both Asian and Black results because of the margin of error. Notable differences in the PPIC results included higher support for Boxer by women (58%), lower support by independents (53%), higher support by white voters (48%), and lower support by Latinos (62%).

However, it is clear that majorities of all other ethnic groups supported Boxer, which is similar to results found for other Democratic candidates.

Misperceptions and Flawed Assumptions

Why, then, did the pollsters and pundits misjudge California? First, there really was a Tea Party effect, but it was restricted to heavily gerrymandered Republican districts. For example, a first-time candidate who had been active with the anti-illegal immigrant Minuteman Project was elected to the State Assembly in a district that included parts of the San Gabriel foothills and high desert east of Los Angeles. Another heavily Republican Assembly district in San Bernardino County went to a candidate who had not held prior elected office—beating out two mayors and a council member in the primary. Republican congressional districts that had narrow victory margins in 2008 returned to being safe seats in 2010.

Pollsters also underestimated voter turnout. The actual turnout of registered voters was a healthy 59.6 percent. Except for the 2003 gubernatorial recall election, this was the highest turnout in a non-presidential election in California since 1982 and far ahead of the 50.6 percent and 50.1 percent turnout rates in the 2002 and 2006 gubernatorial elections. The USC/Los Angeles Times post-election survey showed that much higher percentages of Democrats (61 percent) and Independent/Decline to State voters (64 percent) voted on the day of the election, in contrast to Republicans (49 percent). Latinos (72 percent) were the subgroup most likely to vote on Election Day.[41] Both the USC/Times and Public Policy Institute of California (PPIC) post-election surveys showed high levels of enthusiasm for voting. The PPIC poll also identified strong interest in several ballot measures, including failed initiatives to legalize marijuana and repeal a global warming law.[42]

CONCLUSION

Perhaps the strongest lesson to be learned from the California results is that generic Democratic officeholders will prevail over more memorable Republican candidates in California, especially when those Republicans can be labeled as corporate executives instead of reformers. It may be difficult to think of the liberal Boxer as a generic Democrat, but the Boxer campaign managed that feat in 2010 by making the race about Fiorina's weaknesses. Republicans in statewide races have continued to have difficulties in portraying themselves as moderates in general elections, especially to independent and Latino voters. It remains to be seen whether commission redistricting and new primary rules will lead to more competitive legislative and congressional races and eventually to more competitive races for statewide offices.

NOTES

1. The author would like to thank doctoral student Lisa Henkle for research assistance and undergraduate assistants Jose Arias, Jr. and Velky Richard. Students in the Spring 2010 Gender and Politics course at the University of La Verne provided valuable insights about the candidates and their strategies. The author especially appreciates the contributions made by Jean Reith Schroedel, Claremont Graduate University, who was the lead author of the analysis of Boxer's 1998 campaign that was published in *The Roads to Congress 1998*.

2. Carey McWilliams, *California: The Great Exception.* (Berkeley: University of California Press, 1949).

3. Gary C. Jacobson, "Partisan and Ideological Polarization in the California Electorate," *State Politics and Policy Quarterly* 4 (2): 113–139.

4. Sherry Jeffe, "California: The Not-So-Golden State Legislature," *The Reform of State Legislatures and the Changing Character of Representation*, ed. Eugene W. Hickok, Jr. (Lanham, MD: Commonwealth Foundation/University Press of America, 1992), 101–112.

Peter Schrag, *Paradise Lost: California's Experience, America's Future* (Berkeley: University of California Press, 1998). Peter Schrag, *California: America's High-Stakes Experiment,* (Berkeley: University of California Press, 2006). Joe Mathews and Mark Paul, *California Crackup: How Reform Broke the Golden State and How We Can Fix It* (University of California Press, 2010).

5. Mark Baldassare and Cheryl Katz, *The Coming Age of Direct Democracy: California's Recall and Beyond* (Lanham, MD: Rowman and Littlefield, 2008).

6. Mathews and Paul, 166–170. Only one measure, to limit pay to legislatures when not passing a budget by the beginning of the year, passed.

7. For details on Boxer's background, gender stereotyping, and reelection campaigns see Jean Reith Schroedel, Marcia L. Godwin, and Ling Cao, "Boxer Defeats Fong in California's Senate Race," *The Roads to Congress 1998*, ed. Robert Dewhirst and Sunil Ahuja, (Belmont, CA: Wadsworth, 2000), 225–250 and Marcia L. Godwin, "Redefining Barbara Boxer: Boxer Defeats Jones in California's Senate Race," *The Road to Congress 2004*, ed. Sunil Ahuja and Robert Dewhirst, (New York: Nova Science Publishers, 2005), 65–80.

8. Barbara Boxer with Mary-Rose Hayes, *A Time to Run,* (San Francisco: Chronicle Books, 2005).

9. Barbara Boxer with Mary-Rose Hayes, *Blind Trust,* (San Francisco: Chronicle Books, 2009).

10. Michael Barone with Richard E. Cohen, *The Almanac of American Politics 2010,* (Washington, DC: National Journal, 2009), 143–146.

11. Rob Hotakainen, "Critics Pounce as Sen. Boxer Says No to 'Ma'Am,'" *Sacramento Bee*, June 23, 2009, A3.

12. Maeve Reston, "Fiorina Ad Focuses on Boxer's '09 Remark," *Los Angeles Times*, Sept. 24, 2010, AA4. While anecdotal, the author found that a co-ed group of students taking Gender and Politics in Spring 2010 thought that the issue was a non-starter.

13. Carly Fiorina, *Tough Choices: A Memoir*, (New York: Portfolio/Penguin Group, 2006), 4.

14. Fiorina, 80–85. For a critical view of Fiorina's career, see Peter Burrow, *Backfire: Carly Fiorina's High-Stakes Battle for the Soul of Hewlett-Packard*, (New York: John Wiley and Sons, 2003). For a more balanced evaluation see George Anders, *Perfect Enough: Carly Fiorina and the Reinvention of Hewlett-Packard*, (New York: Portfolio, 2003).

15. Fiorina, 37.

16. Anders, 49.

17. Charles H. House and Raymond L. Price, *The HP Phenomenon: Innovation and Business Transformation,* (Stanford: Stanford Business Books, 2009), 514.

18. Mary Anne Ostrom, "Is Politics Carly Fiorina's True Calling?" *San Jose Mercury News*, July 27, 2008.

19. Leslie Wayne, "The C.E.O. Challenge," *New York Times*, Sept. 17, 2008, A20, and Carla Marinucci, "McCain, Obama Not CEO Material?" *San Francisco Chronicle*, Sept. 17, 2008, A12.

20. Carla Marinucci and Joe Garofoli, "Fiorina Boldly Takes on Top Foe—Her Cancer," *San Francisco Chronicle*, Nov. 7, 2009, A1. Keven Yamamura, "Health Policy Very Personal for Fiorina," *Sacramento Bee*, Nov. 26, 2009, A1.

21. Joe Garofoli, "Fiorina's Sheep Video Gets Laughs, but Could Backfire," *San Francisco Chronicle*, Feb. 5, 2010, A1.

22. As of January 2011, the original demon sheep ad was widely available on YouTube and the Democratic response was available both on YouTube and www.demonsheepmovie.com. Both warrant viewing.

23. Mike Zapler, "Fiorina Ad Launches Opening Salvo in Possible Battle Against Boxer," *San Jose Mercury News*, June 2, 2010.

24. California Secretary of State, *Statement of Vote June 8, 2010 Statewide Direct Primary Election,* (Sacramento: California Secretary of State, 2010), www.sos.ca.gov.

25. John Fund, "She Wants to Reboot California," *Wall Street Journal*, November 28, 2009, A13.

26. Mike Zapler, "Boxer, Fiorina in Hard-Hitting Debate," *San Jose Mercury News*, Sept. 1, 2010. Maeve Reston and Seema Mehta, "Boxer and Fiorina Stage an Air War," *Los Angeles Times*, Sept. 30, 2010, AA1.

27. Maeve Reston, "Boxer Ad Casts Fiorina as Elitist," *Los Angeles Times*, Sept. 16, 2010, AA5.

28. Maeve Reston, "Fiorina Ad Focuses on Boxer's '09 Remark," *Los Angeles Times*, Sept. 24, 2010, AA4.

29. Joe Garofoli, "Poll: Voters Favoring Status Quo," *San Francisco Chronicle*, Oct. 21, 2010, C1, and author, personal observation.

30. Maeve Reston, "Boxer Overcame Significant Hurdles," *Los Angeles Times*, Nov. 4, 2010, AA9.

31. Maeve Reston, "Boxer Outraised, Outspent Fiorina," *Los Angeles Times*, Dec. 3, 2010, AA3.

32. Reston, "Boxer Outraised, Outspent Fiorina."

33. Cited by Daniel B. Wood, "In All-Blue California Election Results, Lessons for Democratic Party," *Christian Science Monitor*, Nov. 3, 2010.

34. The actual amount was reported as closer to $142 million in some reports and $175 million in others, but the $150 million figure was most commonly used. A popular water-cooler topic among Californians was to give suggestions on how $150 million could have been spent to help the economy.

35. Arnold Steinberg, "Why She Lost," *Los Angeles Times*, Nov. 4, 2010, A25.

36. The author repeatedly had difficulty convincing friends, colleagues, and students that Fiorina had spent only a fraction of the amount spent by Whitman.

37. Maeve Reston, "Fiorina is Hospitalized with Infection," *Los Angeles Times*, Oct. 27, 2010, AA4, and Daniel B. Wood, "Carly Fiorina Out of Hospital: How Does Illness Affect a Campaign?" *Christian Science Monitor*, Oct. 27, 2010.

38. California Secretary of State, *Statement of Vote November 2, 2010 General Election*. Sacramento: California Secretary of State, 2010, www.sos.ca.gov.

39. Counties won calculated by author, based on *Statement of Vote* reports.

40. California Secretary of State, *15-Day Report of Registration October 18, 2010 for the November 2, 2010, General Election*, (Sacramento: California Secretary of State, 2010), www.sos.ca.gov, 1.

41. USC/Los Angeles Times Poll, *California Statewide Survey Results November 3–14, 2010*, (Los Angeles: USC/Los Angeles Times, 2010, www.greenbergresearch .com_(Reports).

42. Mark Baldassare, Dean Bonner, Sonja Petek, and Nicole Willcoxon, *PPIC Statewide Survey: Californians and Their Government, December 2010*, (San Francisco: Public Policy Institute of California, 2010).

Chapter 11

Colorado Senate Race (Buck v. Bennet)

Incumbency Success in an Anti-Incumbency Year

Josh M. Ryan, E. Scott Adler, and Anand Edward Sokhey

Ken Buck
Party: Republican
Age: 51
Race: White
Education: B.A., Princeton University; J.D., University of Wyoming
Religion: Protestant
Occupation: Prosecutor
Political Experience: Weld County District Attorney, (2004–present)

Michael Bennet
Party: Democrat
Age: 45
Race: White
Education: B.A., Wesleyan; J.D., Yale University
Religion: Believes in God, but does not affiliate with any religion[1]
Occupation: Law; Business; Public service
Political Experience: Chief of Staff to Denver mayor John Hickenlooper, (2003–2005); Superintendent, Denver Public Schools, (2005–09); U.S. Senator (2009–present)

The 2010 Colorado Senate race pitted Ken Buck (R-CO) against Michael Bennet (D-CO). The Republican nominee rode anti-establishment and Tea Party waves to win the nomination over a more established Republican candidate, but lost the general election because he had trouble connecting with Colorado's unaffiliated voters and some important demographic groups (particularly women and Latinos). As the Democratic incumbent, Bennet struggled through a difficult primary race against a candidate who had obtained the backing of several prominent Democrats, including former President Bill Clinton. However, Bennet was aided by an ability to raise large amounts of money and avoid mistakes on the campaign trail. His general election win was particularly surprising, given that he was perceived as vulnerable due to his limited time in office and political inexperience.

Overall, the 2010 Colorado Senate election was unique, because in spite of Colorado's status as a swing state, the results resisted the national trend toward Republicans. In particular, the election demonstrated that despite the pervasive anti-incumbent mood in the state (and around the country), poor campaigning and ideological views perceived to be out of step with the electorate could still doom a challenger. Bennet ran a smart and nearly flawless, if unexciting campaign. He had no "gotcha" moments, and seemed to get stronger after defeating his primary challenger, Andrew Romanoff. On the other hand, Buck was more aggressive, but also more mistake-prone; his conservative, Tea Party-inspired message failed to resonate with Colorado's moderate voters. Colorado experienced a weak Republican wave, but the party was disappointed by its losses in the Senate and the other high profile state race for the governorship.

CHARACTERISTICS OF COLORADO

Party Balance

Republicans hold a 39 percent to 33.5 percent registration advantage over Democrats, with about 26 percent of voters unaffiliated.[2] These ideologically moderate, unaffiliated voters are the key to winning statewide office in Colorado.

While both parties have recently experienced internal divisions, the ideological conflict between party moderates and extremists has been more pronounced among Republicans. After the 2010 election, each side blamed the other for Republican failures, particularly in the disastrous governor's race. *The Colorado Statesmen* (a statewide political newspaper) reported that, "The anti-establishment activists not only want to replace [Dick] Wadhams (the state Republican chair), but also restructure the party's bylaws and propose legislation to cure perceived election pitfalls."[3]

Voting and Electoral History

Colorado gave Barack Obama an 8.5 percent margin of victory over John McCain in 2008, and elected Democratic senators in 2004 and 2008 (though Republicans have won the state in eight of the last 10 presidential elections). Democrats have been more successful in races for statewide office–in the ten years prior to the 2010 election, Democrats took control of the state Senate (in 2000), the state House (in 2004), and the governor's office (in 2006).[4]

Republicans did markedly better in 2010, capturing a one-seat majority in the Colorado state house, winning both the third and fourth congressional districts, and capturing two other statewide positions (Secretary of State and State Treasurer).

Demographic Character of the Electorate

Colorado is typical of many western states; it has been one of the fastest growing states in the country, and now has a population of more than five million. The major city, Denver, has a large Latino population, and tends to be the home of younger, more liberal voters. Denver also has the state's only sizable African-American population.

Other areas that are largely Latino, such as Pueblo and counties in southern Colorado, are also reliably Democratic. Wealthier areas, such as Boulder—home to the University of Colorado—and some mountain towns such as Breckenridge, Vail, and Aspen, are overwhelmingly white, but also liberal. Rural areas without large Latino populations (e.g., the far eastern and western parts of the state), including the city of Grand Junction; mountain areas, such as Glenwood Springs; and Grand, Park and Garfield counties, tend to be more Republican but are fairly sparsely populated.[5]

Colorado Springs, in El Paso County, is the second largest city in the state, and one of the most conservative communities in the United States; it is home to the Air Force Academy, a large military population, and is also the site of numerous, large evangelical churches and organizations. In statewide elections, Democrats tend to count on support in cities like Denver and Boulder, while Colorado Springs serves as a Republican stronghold.

Key Voting Blocks

In close races, Latino voters are among the state's most important voting blocs. According to exit polls, Latinos made up about 12 percent of the Colorado Senate electorate in 2010 (by comparison, African Americans made up only about three percent of Colorado Senate voters).[6] There are few other sizable racial minorities in the state.

Major Urban Areas and Employment/Occupational Characteristics

More than half of the state population lives in the Denver metropolitan area. This area—referred to as the "Front Range" and the center of the state's population boom for the last 20 years—includes Boulder, Greeley and Fort Collins to the north, as well as the suburbs that surround Denver. The only other significant population centers lie on the Front Range south of Denver along Interstate 25, and include Colorado Springs and Pueblo.

Given Colorado's demographic characteristics, the key to winning state-wide office is appealing to the white, moderate, swing voters who live in suburban communities along the Front Range urban corridor (this includes the counties of Jefferson, Adams, Broomfield, Arapahoe, Weld, and Douglas, as well as Larimer County to the north, home to Colorado State University in Ft. Collins). Republicans usually count on support from more rural Weld County, whose far southern border is near Denver (and encompasses some of its suburban communities), as well as Douglas County (south of Denver), which is wealthier and more conservative.

DEMOCRATIC PRIMARY

The Candidates

Michael Bennet, previously superintendent of Denver public schools, was appointed by Governor Bill Ritter in January 2009 to fill the Senate vacancy created after Ken Salazar accepted the position of U.S. Secretary of the Interior. Ritter's choice surprised many, as Bennet had never previously held elected office.[7]

Andrew Romanoff, Bennet's primary challenger, was an experienced and shrewd campaigner. He had previously been Speaker of the Colorado House, and was given credit by many in the state for the Democratic resurgence, most notably the takeover of the state House in 2004.[8] Many thought Romanoff would be Governor Ritter's pick for Salazar's vacated Senate seat, given Romanoff's credentials and his public campaign for the position.[9]

CAMPAIGN ISSUES

PAC and Soft Money

Bennet's voting record (for his two years) in the Senate was generally supportive of President Barak Obama; he received an enthusiastic endorsement from the president, but he was not the outspoken liberal that many Colorado Democrats would have liked. *The New York Times* described both Bennet and Romanoff as, "more policy wonks than firebrands." Romanoff did his best to energize liberal Democrats in the state,[10] emphasizing his "outsider" status, and attempting to make political contributions and the influence of corporate money an issue. Romanoff constantly reminded voters of Michael Bennet's willingness to take money from PACs–for example, saying "My opponent in this race is now No. 2 in Senate Democrats (in contributions) . . . from big oil. That's not a competition I want to win."[11]

Anti-Establishment Credentials

Though both candidates recognized the anti-incumbent mood in Washington and played up their anti-establishment credentials, the policy differences between them were minor.[12] That being said, Romanoff's challenge did seem to cause Bennet to become an outspoken advocate of the "public option" during debates on health care reform. Romanoff later accused Bennet of not trying hard enough to gather support for the policy in the Senate.[13]

White House attempt to Prevent Romanoff's Challenge

One of the only other campaign issues to make news during the Democratic primary was a controversy about whether the White House offered Romanoff political appointments to forgo his challenge to Bennet. President Obama had come to see Bennet as a valuable ally in the Senate, and wanted to ensure he stayed in power; Romanoff confirmed that a White House deputy said three jobs "would be available," though Romanoff and the White House claimed that specific offers were never made.[14] The effect of the scandal on the primary was probably negligible, though Republicans consistently tried to use it to attack Obama.[15]

CAMPAIGN STRATEGY

Media

The campaign was nasty, and the media coverage reflected the animosity between the two candidates. Many stories emphasized Romanoff's background in Colorado and his attempt to portray himself as more liberal than Michael Bennet. Stories also focused on the large amount of money being spent by Bennet, which seemed to support Romanoff's claim that unregulated campaign spending was hurting voters. Romanoff's message on this point was made even clearer by his heavily publicized decision to sell his house in order to finance his campaign.[16]

Image and Advertising

Bennet initially ran positive ads intended to serve as a way of introducing himself to Colorado voters, though his ads quickly turned negative. On the other hand, Romanoff's advertising campaign was negative from the start—his first buy in early July compared Washington to a rigged casino.[17] Another ad, called "Greed,"[18] accused Michael Bennet of "looting" money from his former employers. A *Denver Post* editorial called Romanoff's ads "below-the-belt," but this criticism did not change the tone of subsequent advertisements from his campaign.[19]

Finance

Romanoff's decision not to accept money from PACs or other outside groups pleased his Democratic supporters, but also seemed to handicap him in the race. Bennet outspent Romanoff by more than 3 to 1 as the race became the most expensive primary in state history.[20]

There was also some controversy as to whether Romanoff would accept PAC money in the general election, should he win the primary. Romanoff admitted that in order to keep up with his Republican opponent, he would accept money from the Democratic Senatorial Campaign Committee (DSCC) after the primary ended (though he stated he would ask the DSCC to exclude any PAC money in their donations to him). Predictably, the Bennet campaign called this a "stunning flip-flop."[21]

Grassroots

While Michael Bennet attempted to increase his name recognition and generate campaign excitement, Andrew Romanoff tried to tap into his grassroots support and core of enthusiastic supporters. At the start of the campaign, Romanoff had a strong, Democratic base already in place, and was "far more organized" according to news reports.[22]

Bennet lost the first two minor tests of the primary season, both of which were driven by Democratic party activists. In March 2010 at the state party caucus (precinct-level straw polls), Bennet's delegates won fewer seats than Romanoff's.[23] Because the delegates selected at the caucus go to the party convention, this meant that at the May convention Romanoff won a large victory, garnering votes from almost 60 percent of convention goers. Ultimately, these "losses" had little effect on the outcome of the election, though they did mean that Romanoff would be listed first on the primary ballot.

Bases of Support

Most of Bennet's support was drawn from the Democratic establishment based in Denver. Romanoff's supporters took to calling this group the

"17th Street elite," referring to the financial center of downtown Denver.[24] Romanoff's support came from Democratic party activists, voters younger than 50, Latino and liberals according to a poll conducted about a week before the election.[25] Romanoff was also endorsed by important organized labor groups in the state.[26] In his endorsement of Romanoff, former president Bill Clinton specifically cited Romanoff's role in helping craft the Democratic majority in the House, saying, "Andrew led the effort to win a majority in the Colorado House of Representatives for the first time in 30 years, and to keep that majority for the first time in more than 40 years."[27]

DEMOCRATIC PRIMARY ELECTION RESULTS

Polls taken about a week before the election showed Romanoff tied with or leading Bennet.[28] Most Colorado counties now use mail-in ballots only, and while Romanoff seemed to have the momentum, many voters had already voted by early August.[29] Bennet beat Romanoff with surprising ease, 54 percent to 46 percent, in the statewide primary election that ended on August 12, 2010. Though the candidates did their best to publicly reconcile after a bruising primary campaign, Romanoff was largely absent from Bennet's general election bid.

Analysis from a statewide poll of early-voters largely mirrored previous polling results:[30] wealthier, stronger Democratic party identifiers were more likely to vote for Bennet, but more liberal primary voters were more likely to go with Romanoff. Substantively, the ideological divide between the bases of support was clear: an extremely liberal, college educated, self-identified Democrat in a household making between $75,000–$100,000 was about 38 percent more likely to vote for Romanoff than a similarly profiled individual holding moderate ideological beliefs.[31]

REPUBLICAN PRIMARY

The Candidates

Prior to his Senate run, as the Weld County District Attorney Ken Buck became well-known in the state by pursuing illegal immigrants. This included the use of a controversial tactic of seizing tax records from a preparation company that catered to the Spanish speaking community. The Colorado Supreme Court later ruled this unconstitutional, but his actions endeared him to Tea Party supporters and other conservative groups.[32]

Buck's opponent, Jane Norton, was the former Lieutenant Governor and director of the Colorado Department of Public Health and Environment–a post to which she was appointed by Republican Governor Bill Owens. She was supported by most prominent Republicans in the state, including former Republican Senators William Armstrong and Hank Brown, as well as the popular former Governor Owens.[33]

CAMPAIGN ISSUES

The Right vs. The Extreme Right

Arguably, Buck took the more conservative view of the two Republicans on a number of social issues including gay marriage and illegal immigration. However, it should be emphasized that the actual policy differences between the candidates were quite small—rather, each candidate did their best to portray themselves as more conservative then their opponent.

Gender

Interestingly, gender became an issue in the campaign after Buck said that voters should choose him because he does not "wear high heels." This statement was made in response to a Norton television advertisement that challenged Buck to "be a man" and attack her directly instead of using what the ad called "shady interest groups." Buck followed up on his initial statement during a stump speech by making the high heels comment again, while going on to say, "I have cowboy boots. They have real bullsh-- on them." This exact line was then used in a Norton campaign advertisement, with the tag line, "Ken Buck wants to go to Washington? He'd fit right in."[34] Norton often commented that she would be the first female Senator from the state, just as she was the first female Republican Lieutenant Governor;[35] she also claimed that she would be more appealing to female voters during the general election—a constituency perceived as critical to a Republican's chances in Colorado (and a group that Buck would go on to do poorly with in the general election).

Anti-Establishment Credentials

The only other major issue of the Republican primary centered on which candidate was "more outside the Beltway." Cinamon Watson—a spokeswoman for Jane Norton—said:

Ken Buck may characterize himself as an outsider, but he's been a government lawyer for most of his career. He worked in the Clinton administration, he's been elected DA and, in fact, the current governor, Bill Ritter, was the best man in his wedding. To characterize himself as an outsider, like Sharron Angle or something, is absolutely false.[36]

Buck countered by repeatedly calling his opponent "the establishment candidate." The day before the primary, (after John McCain (R-AZ) campaigned with Jane Norton), he noted: "We have very different beliefs on who senators should represent. I'm focused on the grassroots, while my opponent is focused on the Washington establishment. That is more apparent today than ever before."[37]

CAMPAIGN STRATEGY

Media

While Buck seemed to receive a fair amount of positive press, Norton was routinely criticized. Much of this came from Republican party activists, especially after she made the decision to skip both the party caucus and the party convention. Aside from her high profile endorsements, there was little positive coverage of her in the summer of 2010. Overall, Norton never generated much positive momentum, and the media coverage of her reflected that.

Image and Advertising

As with Bennet and Romanoff, the Republican campaign was a negative one–the candidates focused their attacks on each other, but also took advantage of the national anti-incumbent mood to attack the Democratic party; specifically, both the Norton and Buck campaigns ran ads criticizing the health care reform legislation. The *Associated Press* noted that Buck's primary campaign "played up his no-compromise conservatism and ties to Tea Party groups."[38] Even though the policy differences between the two candidates were small, Norton was perceived as being less conservative. At one point Sarah Palin called her a "mama grizzly," though a widely expected endorsement from Palin never came.[39]

Finance

Buck received a large amount of money from outside groups associated with the Tea Party, such as Jim Demint's (R-SC) *Senate Conservatives Fund,* and another pro-business group called *Americans for Job Security.* Despite Norton's early advantages, Buck raised nearly as much money as Norton.

Norton criticized the role that the outside groups supporting Buck played throughout the campaign, likely because she received relatively little help from conservative PACs. Still, she spent nearly $4 million, while Buck spent only $1.6 million.

Grassroots

Norton had trouble connecting with grassroots Republicans. Specifically, her decision to skip the party conventions and petition her way onto the ballot earned her the ire of party activists.[40] Norton also replaced her campaign manager with Josh Penry, a popular former state Senate minority leader.

Buck's campaign, on the other hand, was almost entirely designed to be "grassroots-fed," and he used this term multiple times to characterize his strategy. It seemed to gain traction among party activists after the caucus victory. This was noted by Walt Klein, a Colorado Republican consultant and member of Buck's campaign team:

> I think when the history of this campaign cycle is written, there'll be a short, maybe somewhat painful chapter that ends on March 16—the date of the straw poll. Money froze up, and we were operating on a small budget—not spending much, but powered by the strength of Ken as a grassroots candidate.[41]

Bases of Support

Buck's support came from fiscal conservatives and individuals who identified with the Tea Party. Jane Norton may have been preferred by most well-known Republicans in the state, but she did not gain support from rank-and-file Republicans.

PRIMARY ELECTION RESULTS

About 68,000 more Republicans than Democrats voted in the primary.[42] Norton's inability to excite Republican primary voters and her listless campaign probably doomed her. A survey taken in June showed Buck leading 53 percent to 37 percent.[43] Norton fought hard and managed to close the gap—her campaign energized by the fight over the "high heels" comment–but Buck won by four percentage points.

Analysis from a statewide poll of early-voters largely confirmed conventional wisdom about the campaign:[44] more ideologically conservative, self-identified Tea Party supporters were likely to back Buck; women were more likely to support Norton. An extremely conservative, college educated, self-identified Republican in a household making between $75,000–$100,000 was about 32 percent more likely to vote for Buck than a similarly profiled individual holding moderate ideological beliefs; an extremely conservative, male Tea Party member with the same demographic characteristics was about 10 percent more likely to support Buck relative to a similarly profiled female.[45]

GENERAL ELECTION

Michael Bennet did a good job "managing" his limited campaign experience by raising huge sums of money, avoiding mistakes, and running a well-organized campaign. He made a quick transition from the primary to the general election, and because he had been the more moderate candidate during the primary, seemed to have an easier time than Ken Buck turning his appeal away from his party's base and toward remaining moderates and independents throughout the state.

CAMPAIGN ISSUES

Buck's Extremism

Buck had a more difficult time finding a message that resonated with moderate voters. The day after the primary, a coalition of liberal interest groups developed the "Too Crazy for Colorado" tagline, and planned to run television commercials which included Buck's quotes from the primary campaign.[46] Bennet repeated this theme throughout the general election, using the line, "Ken Buck: Too Extreme for Colorado." Bennet's campaign additionally targeted Buck for advocating the elimination of the Departments of Education and Energy, Amtrak, and the U.S. Postal Service.[47]

Social and Gender Issues

Just as they had in the Republican primary, social and gender issues came to the fore in the general election. First, advocacy groups brought up Buck's refusal to prosecute a rape case as Weld County District Attorney, and his apparent insensitivity to the victim. At one point, Buck told the Greeley Tribune that the victim had "buyer's remorse."[48] While Buck's decision not to prosecute the alleged attacker was supported by other attorneys, it became a campaign issue that would not go away. Bennet brought it up on the candidates' "Meet the

Press" debate on October 16, 2010,[49] and advocacy groups ran commercials specifically mentioning the "buyer's remorse" comment.

On another "Meet the Press" show, Buck compared homosexuality to alcoholism when discussing his support of the military's "Don't Ask, Don't Tell" policy. Again, Buck came under fire from liberal advocacy groups, and *The Denver Post* announced that Buck "elevated the culture wars from minor player to center stage."[50] Bennet continued to focus on social issues during the candidates' last debate—he tried to make abortion an issue after Buck said that he did not believe abortions should be legal in cases of rape or incest.[51]

President Obama and the Democratic Agenda

In an attempt to take advantage of anti-incumbency sentiment, Buck tried to make the race about Bennet and his support of President Obama's agenda. He repeatedly criticized the health care bill, and focused his message on creating jobs and reducing the deficit. Despite the anti-Washington mood throughout the country, one which was present in both primary campaigns, policy issues like health care and the economy received less attention in the Colorado Senate general election. For example, Bennet's stump speeches and television advertisements successfully kept the focus on "moral values," criticizing Buck's views on abortion, the separation between church and state, and birth control.[52]

CAMPAIGN STRATEGY

Media

The Denver Post gave Bennet a lukewarm endorsement, saying "Bennet has the potential to lead a bipartisan coalition of centrist U.S. senators."[53] However, the paper criticized him for being too beholden to the president and the Democratic leadership's agenda in his two years in office; it went on to say that he has "[s]o much potential yet not enough spine." This line was later used in an attack ad by Buck (though the ad failed to mention that the *Post* article also criticized Buck for his attempts to move back to a more centrist position after winning the primary on his conservative credentials).

Image and Advertising

Buck's conservative image served him well during the primary election, but proved to be a liability during the general election. Bennet's strategy seemed to avoid policy issues, while keeping the focus on Buck's social positions–his television advertisements were almost entirely negative.

Finance

The campaign became the most expensive in Colorado history. Bennet spent close to $13 million, while Buck spent about $5 million. Additionally, outside interest groups and political parties spent nearly $33.5 million on the race, with money supporting the Republican totaling nearly $18 million, and Democratic spending about $15.5 million.[54]

Grassroots

Both candidates had strong grassroots operations, though most observers agree that Buck was hurt by the divisiveness in the Republican party over the nomination of Dan Maes for Governor. Maes defeated a more established, moderate primary candidate by unifying conservatives, but he was unattractive to the general electorate and after a number of campaign gaffes his poll numbers sank quickly. Tom Tancredo—a former U.S. representative and anti-illegal immigration crusader—jumped into the race as a third party candidate, but Democrat John Hickenlooper easily defeated both candidates. The gubernatorial race may have discouraged grassroots Republicans as it created a perception that the state Republican Party was disorganized.

Bases of Support

Denver County voted for Bennet at a 71 percent rate, giving him about 15 percent of his overall total. Interestingly, Buck only did three points better in the Republican base of El Paso County than the Republican Senate candidate did in 2008 (who lost by nearly 10 points); he only performed about 1.3 points better in Denver County–Bennet's base—than the 2008 GOP candidate.

GENERAL ELECTION RESULTS

In a narrow but surprising victory, Bennet won 48 percent to 46 percent. The polls immediately prior to the election showed Buck with anywhere from a 1 to 4 point lead. Real Clear Politics Poll Tracker showed Buck with an average lead of 3 points, and *The New York Times'* FiveThirtyEight blog gave Bennet only a 35 percent chance of winning.

Unfortunately for Buck, Bennet won small majorities in all the crucial suburbs around Denver except Douglas and Weld counties.[55] Exit polls emphasize how badly Buck did among women, and how he was perceived as too extreme by many voters. Women favored Bennet 56 percent to 39 percent; Buck did nine points worse among women than the 2004 Republican Senate candidate. Critically, Bennet captured about 80 percent of the Latino vote in Colorado–indeed, Buck did little better with this group than did Tancredo in the gubernatorial race (perhaps not surprisingly, given the perceptions of extremity).[56] As the *Colorado Independent* pointed out, "had Buck done just a little better among either women or Hispanics he would have won."[57]

A glaring problem for Republicans was Buck's failure to connect with moderate voters. According to the exit polls, Bennet won self-identified moderates by 24 percent; he won among individuals who have "neutral" feelings toward the Tea Party by 9 percent. In 2010, 18 percent of Colorado voters said that their most important candidate quality was that the candidate was "not too extreme." Individuals who stated that moderation was most important favored Bennet 68 percent to 27 percent. Tellingly, voters who said that they either had a "strongly favorable opinion" or "had reservations" about the candidate they voted for preferred Ken Buck. However, among the 28 percent of voters who said that their opinion of the candidate was based on disliking his opponent, Bennet won 57 percent to 38 percent.

CONCLUSION

The last decade has seen a Democratic resurgence in Colorado, particularly as Democrats have done a better job nominating candidates who can appeal to middle-of-the-road, suburban voters. Republican candidates could not have asked for a better political climate in 2010, something made clear by the national results. Yet while Republicans made some significant gains at the local level, their statewide candidates disappointed because they were out of step with Colorado voters.

NOTES

1. Though Bennet's father was Christian and his mother was Jewish, he has said he believes in God, but does not regularly attend any church. Strasser, Max. "What is Michael Bennet's Religion?" *Politics Daily*. Accessed at www.politicsdaily.com/2010/10/26/what-is-michael-bennets-religion/ on January 23, 2011.

2. Colorado Secretary of State. Accessed at www.sos.state.co.us/pubs/elections/VoterRegNumbers/2010/November/VotersByParty_Status.pdf on December 27, 2010.

3. Jorgensen, Leslie. December 22, 2010. "GOP Chair Wadhams caught in crosshairs." *The Colorado Statesmen.* Accessed at www.coloradostatesman.com/content/992372-gop-chair-wadhams-caught-crosshairs on December 27, 2010.

4. In 2006, the Democrats won the 3rd Congressional District, and in 2008 they won the 4th CD, giving them five of the seven districts in the state. Both districts are heavily Republican, and the Democrats lost both in 2010.

5. City-data.com. Accessed at www.city-data.com/city/Colorado.html on January 23, 2011.

6. CNN Politics, Election Center Exit Polls. Accessed at www.cnn.com/ELECTION/2010/results/polls/#COS01p1 on January 5, 2011.

7. Zalubowski, David. January 6, 2009. "Colorado's new senator relatively unknown." Associated Press. Accessed at www.msnbc.msn.com/id/28519582/ns/politics-capitol_hill/ on January 5, 2011.

8. Riley, Michael and Lynn Bartels. September 13, 2009. "Rival Colorado Democrats play game of one-upmanship." *The Denver Post.* Accessed at www.denverpost.com/politics/ci_13325723 on February 8, 2011.

9. Elliott, Philip. June 2, 2010. "Senate Candidate Says White House Discussed 3 Jobs." Associated Press. Accessed at abcnews.go.com/Politics/wireStory?id=10809242&page=1 on January 23, 2011.

10. Frosch, Dan. September 29, 2009. "Colorado Democrats Brace for Senate Primary." *New York Times.* Accessed at www.nytimes.com/2009/09/30/us/politics/30colorado.html on January 23, 2011.

11. Lawrence, Mike. July 7, 2010. "Romanoff questions Bennet's campaign contributions in Steamboat visit." *Steamboat Today.* Accessed at www.steamboattoday.com/news/2010/jul/07/romanoff-questions-contributions-steamboat-visit/ on January 23, 2011.

12. Brown, Jennifer. August 12, 2010. "Bennet, Buck Win Senate Races." *Grand Junction Free Press.* Accessed at www.gjfreepress.com/article/20100810/COMMUNITY_NEWS/100819987/1006&parentprofile=1059 on December 27, 2010

13. Riley, Michael. March 23, 2010. "Bennet urged to add public option." *The Denver Post.* Accessed at www.denverpost.com/ci_14735946 on January 6, 2011.

14. Booth, Michael. June 3, 2010. "Romanoff confirms White House job discussion." *The Denver Post.* Accessed at www.denverpost.com/ci_15213784 on January 6, 2011.

15. Booth, "Romanoff confirms White House job discussions."

16. Booth, Michael. July 26, 2010. "Romanoff goes all in, sells house and loans campaign $325,000." *The Denver Post.* Accessed at blogs.denverpost.com/thespot/2010/07/26/romanoff-goes-all-in-sells-house-and-loans-campaign-325000/12440/ on January 23, 2011.

17. *Huffington Post.* July 7, 2010. "Andrew Romanoff's 'Casino' Ad to Air in Colorado." Huffington Post. Accessed at www.huffingtonpost.com/2010/07/07/andrew-romanoffs-casino-a_n_638357.html on January 23, 2011.

18. Murphy, Patricia. August 8, 2010. "Colorado Cliffhanger: Bennet and Romanoff Battle for Dem Senate Nod." *Politics Daily.* Accessed at www.politics-

daily.com/2010/08/09/michael-bennet-vs-andrew-romanoff-for-dem-senate-nod-in-colorad/ on January 23, 2011.

19. Denver Post Editorial. July 31, 2010. "Romanoff's ad is over the top." *The Denver Post*. Accessed at www.denverpost.com/opinion/ci_15642940 on January 23, 2011.

20. Sherry, Allison and Burt Hubbard. August 8, 2010. "Bennet: 'No choice but to respond' to Romanoff attack ads." *The Denver Post*. Accessed at www.denverpost.com/news/ci_15663719 on January 5, 2011.

21. Luning, Ernest. August 8, 2010. "Romanoff says he'll take DSCC funds after primary." *The Colorado Statesman*. Accessed at www.coloradostatesman.com/content/992025-romanoff-says-he percent3Fll-take-dscc-funds-after-primary on January 6, 2011.

22. Kleefeld, Eric. May 24, 2010. "Romanoff Beats Bennet At Colorado Dem Convention—But The Primary Has Just Begun." Talking Points Memo. Accessed at tpmdc.talkingpointsmemo.com/2010/05/romanoff-beats-bennet-at-colorado-dem-convention——but-the-primary-has-just-begun.php on January 5, 2011.

23. Ingold, John and Jessica Fender. March 17, 2010 "Underdogs Buck, Romanoff make strong inroads at caucuses." *The Denver Post*. Accessed at www.denverpost.com/election/ci_14689087 on January 23, 2011.

24. Bartels, Lynn. March 7, 2010. "Uphill Senate race doesn't keep Romanoff down." *The Denver Post*. Accessed at www.denverpost.com/ci_14527070 on January 23, 2011.

25. Catanese, David. August 2, 2010. "Poll: Andrew Romanoff catches Sen. Michael Bennet." Politico.com. Accessed at www.politico.com/news/stories/0810/40532.html on January 23, 2011.

26. Riley, Michael. February 10, 2010. "Labor groups endorse Romanoff." *The Denver Post*. Accessed at blogs.denverpost.com/thespot/2010/02/10/labor-groups-endorse-romanoff/5263/ on January 23, 2011.

27. Montanaro, Domenico. June 29, 2010. "Bill Clinton Backs Romanoff." Associated Press. Accessed at firstread.msnbc.msn.com/_news/2010/06/29/4582829-bill-clinton-backs-romanoff on January 11, 2011.

28. Sherry, Allison. August 1, 2010. "Romanoff pulls even with Bennet, poll finds." *The Denver Post*. Accessed at www.denverpost.com/election2010/ci_15650614 on January 23, 2011

29. Crummy, Karen. August 5, 2010. "Colorado primary turnout nears record amid hotly contested races." *The Denver Post*. Accessed at www.denverpost.com/election2010/ci_15679560 on January 23, 2011.

30. Sokhey, Anand Edward, Michael Barber, Chris Mann, Quin Monson, and Kelly Patterson. 2010. "The Colorado Primary Election Survey."

31. Results are predicted probabilities obtained from a logistic regression model estimating vote choice between Romanoff and Bennet.

32. Wyatt, Kristen. June 30, 2010. "Bucking GOP establishment in Colorado Senate race." Associated Press. Accessed at www.boston.com/news/nation/

articles/2010/06/30/bucking_gop_establishment_in_colorado_senate_race/?page=2 on December 30, 2010.

33. Roper, Peter. July 22, 2010. "Buck: Immigration a federal issue." Pueblo Chieftain. Accessed at www.chieftain.com/news/local/article_6d33473c-954c-11df-a2fe-001cc4c03286.html on January 5, 2011.

34. Montopoli, Brian. July 22, 2010. "GOP Rivals Jane Norton, Ken Buck Fight Over 'High Heels' and Manhood." Cbsnews.com. Accessed at www.cbsnews.com/8301-503544_162-20011333-503544.html on January 5, 2011.

35. Wyatt, Kristen. July 21, 2010. "Colo. GOP Candidates Spar Over Gender." Associated Press. Accessed at abcnews.go.com/Politics/wireStory?id=11222001 on January 5, 2011.

36. Miller, Sean J. June 10, 2010. "Colorado Republican looks to avoid becoming next Tea Party victim." *The Hill*. Accessed at thehill.com/blogs/ballot-box/senate-races/102569-colorado-republican-looks-to-avoid-becoming-the-next-tea-party-victim?page=1 on January 5, 2010.

37. Davis, Gene. August 9, 2010. "McCain stumps for Norton." *The Denver Daily News*. Accessed at www.thedenverdailynews.com/article.php?aID=9534 on January 5, 2011.

38. Wyatt, Kristen. August 11, 2010. "Colorado's Senate slate already moving to center." Associated Press. Accessed at www.greeleytribune.com/article/20100811/NEWS/100819942/1008&parentprofile=1001 on December 27, 2010.

39. Allen, Nicole. July 22, 2010. "In Colorado, A Mama Grizzly Fights the Tea Party." *The Atlantic*. Accessed at www.theatlantic.com/politics/archive/2010/07/in-colorado-a-mama-grizzly-fights-the-tea-party/60232/ on January 24, 2011.

40. Ashby, Charles. April 14, 2010. "Norton bypassing GOP delegates in Senate primary bid." *The Grand Junction Daily Sentinel*. Accessed at www.gjsentinel.com/articles/print/norton_bypassing_gop_delegates on January 23, 2011.

41. Roberts, Michael. April 15, 2010. "Ken Buck on a Tea Party binge—and consultant thinks Jane Norton is running scared." *Denver Westword*. Accessed at blogs.westword.com/latestword/2010/04/ken_buck_on_a_tea_party_binge.php on January 24, 2011.

42. Zeleny, Jeff. August 11, 2010. "Concern Over Centrists as G.O.P. Leans Right." *Washington Post*. Accessed at www.nytimes.com/2010/08/12/us/politics/12assess.html on January 5, 2011.

43. Allen, Nicole. July 22, 2010. "In Colorado, A Mama Grizzly Fights the Tea Party." *The Atlantic*. Accessed at www.theatlantic.com/politics/archive/2010/07/in-colorado-a-mama-grizzly-fights-the-tea-party/60232/ on January 24, 2011.

44. Sokhey, Anand Edward, Michael Barber, Chris Mann, Quin Monson, and Kelly Patterson. 2010. "The Colorado Primary Election Survey."

45. Results are predicted probabilities obtained from a logistic regression model estimating vote choice between Buck and Norton.

46. Wyatt, Kristen. August 11, 2010. "Colorado's Senate slate already moving to center." Associated Press. Accessed at www.greeleytribune.com/article/20100811/NEWS/100819942/1008&parentprofile=1001 on December 27, 2010.

47. Zeleny, Jeff. August 11, 2010. "Concern Over Centrists as G.O.P. Leans Right." *Washington Post.* Accessed at www.nytimes.com/2010/08/12/us/politics/12assess .html on January 5, 2011.

48. Kersgaard, Scot. October 10, 2010. "Buck's refusal to prosecute 2005 rape case reverberates in U.S. Senate race." *The Colorado Independent.* Accessed at coloradoindependent.com/63491/bucks-refusal-to-prosecute-2005-rape-case-reverberates-in-u-s-senate-race on January 5, 2011.

49. Plungis, Jeff and Nicole Gaouette. "Colorado's Senate Candidates Bennet, Buck Spar Over Rape Case." *Bloomberg's Business Week.* Accessed at www. businessweek.com/news/2010–10–17/colorado-s-senate-candidates-bennet-buck-spar-over-rape-case.html on December 27, 2010.

50. Riley, Michael. October 17, 2010. "Buck's remarks on homosexuality loom after Meet the Press debate." *The Denver Post.* Accessed at www.denverpost.com/news/ci_16362834 on January 6, 2011.

51. Booth, Michael. October 23, 2010. "Buck, Bennet take on social issues in final debate." *The Denver Post.* Accessed at www.denverpost.com/news/ci_16418583?source=pkg on January 24, 2011.

52. Sherry, Allison. September 19, 2010. "Buck softens stance on abortion and 'personhood.'" *The Denver Post.* Accessed at www.denverpost.com/election2010/ci_16114433 on January 24, 2011.

53. Denver Post Editorial. October 15, 2010. "Michael Bennet for U.S. Senate." *The Denver Post.* Accessed at www.denverpost.com/opinion/ci_16342042 on December 27, 2010.

54. OpenSecrets.org, Center for Responsive Politics. "2010 Colorado Senate Race." Accessed at www.opensecrets.org/races/summary.php?cycle=2010&id=COS1 on February 2, 2011.

55. Specifically, Bennet won Jefferson County 48 percent to 46 percent, Broomfield 49 percent to 46 percent, Adams, 50 percent to 43 percent, Larimer 48 percent to 46 percent, and Arapahoe 49 percent to 46 percent.

56. Kersgaard, Scot. November 5, 2010. "Numbers show Hispanic voters carried the day for Colorado Democrats." *The Colorado Independent.* Accessed at coloradoindependent.com/66544/numbers-show-hispanic-voters-carried-the-day-for-colorado-democrats.

57. Kersgaard, Scot. December 28, 2010. "Top campaign stories of 2010-You had to see it to believe it." *The Colorado Independent.* Accessed at colorado independent.com/70645/top-campaign-stories-of-2010-you-had-to-see-it-to-believe-it on January 5, 2011.

Chapter 12

Connecticut Senate Race (McMahon v. Blumenthal)

Blumenthal Beats McMahon in a Race that Set State Records for Spending

Kevin Buterbaugh

Linda McMahon
Party: Republican
Age: 52
Sex: Female
Race: Caucasian
Religion: Catholic
Education: B.S. in French from East Carolina University with teacher certification
Occupation: CEO, World Wrestling Entertainment, (1993–2009). Involved in managing the WWE since 1980.
Political Experience: None

Richard Blumenthal
Party: Democrat
Age: 63
Sex: Male
Race: Caucasian
Religion: Jewish
Education: B.A., Harvard, 1967; J.D., Yale Law, 1973
Occupation: Public Service
Political Experience: Clerk for U.S. Supreme Court Justice Harry Blackmun, (1974–1975); U.S. Attorney for Connecticut, (1977–1981); CT State Representative, (1984–1987); CT State Senator, (1987–1990); CT State Attorney General, (1990–2010)

In a year where Republicans dominated the electoral landscape, Connecticut stood as an exception. Democrats swept all major offices in the state. This included the U.S. Senate race where the long-time Democratic Attorney General Richard Blumenthal rather easily defeated the Republican candidate Linda McMahon 55 percent to 43 percent. It may appear that Blumenthal had an easy path to victory; however, this was not the case. In late September 2010, Blumenthal's lead in the polls had fallen to a mere three percent. This was within the margin of error of the tracking polls. At that time, state Democratic leaders feared that Blumenthal's campaign had lost its way, and was on the verge of losing a seat that everyone thought he should win easily. McMahon, a novice in politics, turned out to be a more formidable candidate than expected largely because of the resources she brought to her campaign. She spent more than $50 million of her own money during the campaign, and this money allowed her to quickly build name recognition in the state and also to undermine Blumenthal's image as a trustworthy and reliable public official.

However, money was not enough to give McMahon the victory, and in fact, McMahon's efforts add to the growing evidence that self-funded candidates usually lose. Historically, only about 20 to 30 percent of candidates who self fund win elections. And the more these self-funding candidates spend, it seems, the more likely they are to lose. The campaign also shows us that outspending your opponent does not equal victory. The political science literature on elections sees candidates as needing a sufficient amount of money to run their campaigns, not to spend more than their opponents, and this clearly describes the case in this year's Connecticut senate race. Blumenthal, while outspent six to one by McMahon, had more than enough money to campaign and get out his message.

One thing that makes this race particularly unique is that the campaign dealt little with actual issues of the day. Both candidates focused on character—their own and their opponent's—as the core item in the campaigns. Both candidates were criticized in the media for refusing to answer questions about specific policies or to take stands on the issues of the day. Finally, in a year when the Tea Party, a conservative splinter movement, had a significant effect at the polls across the nation, McMahon largely painted herself as a moderate centrist Republican and distanced herself from the anger and issues that motivated Tea Party supporters. This distancing may have been one reason she failed to win the election.

This race would not have happened if not for the retirement of long-time Senator Christopher Dodd. Just three years prior, Dodd was popular enough in the state, and he thought nationally, to make a run for the presidency. By January 2010, Dodd, a Democrat, was forced to retire after a series of ethical blunders undermined his support both within his party and among the voters of Connecticut. Dodd's weaknesses led to McMahon becoming a candidate in September 2009, and without the ethical blunders it is unlikely that a candidate with the resources or abilities of McMahon would have entered the race. Dodd won more than 66 percent of the vote in 2004 and 65 percent of the vote in 1998. These high vote totals are usually enough to deter quality candidates from attempting to unseat an incumbent.

Before examining the problems that led to Dodd's retirement, the candidates, their paths to nomination, and their actions during the general election, we first need to examine Connecticut and the various factors that affect its politics.

CHARACTERISTICS OF CONNECTICUT

Connecticut is geographically the third smallest state in the country. Only Delaware and Rhode Island are smaller. The state is about 110 miles across east to west and 70 miles from north to south. These small distances make campaigning different in Connecticut than elsewhere. Candidates have little trouble traveling the state to meet voters. So retail or personal politicking is much more possible than in a large state like Texas or Florida. The small size also means that candidates must buy advertising only in the major markets of the state—Hartford and New Haven—since these outlets are able to broadcast across the entire state.[1] This makes it easier for candidates to disseminate their messages and should, in theory at least, reduce the costs of campaigning.

While Connecticut is one of the smallest states geographically, it is in the middle of the pack in regard to population.[2] Connecticut has about 3.5 million people ranking it 29th among states. This also means that Connecticut is one of the most densely populated states in the country. The U.S. Census estimates that Connecticut has about 738 people per square mile. This places the state sixth in population density and well above the national average of 87 people per square mile. High density also means that most people in the state live in an urban area with more than 87 percent doing so in 2000; this is about eight percent above the rate for the country as a whole. The higher level of urbanization makes it easier for candidates to access voters since they are more concentrated.

Connecticut is one of the wealthiest states in the country. Depending on how one measures wealth it is either the wealthiest or in the top five in regard to wealth. Per capita income ($56,300) places Connecticut first, median income ($68,600) places it fourth, and mean income ($103,000) places it first among states. However, Connecticut also has one of the highest levels of income inequality among the 50 states. 2009 Census estimates place Connecticut 49th in income inequality—only New York State has a higher level of inequality than Connecticut. Its Gini Index[3] in 2009 was .48 while the index for the country as a whole was .47. What accounts for this high level of inequality? The state is home to several of the wealthiest cities in the country. Greenwich, Connecticut, for example, has a per capita income of more than $74,000. The city is home to many of the professionals who work in the financial industry in New York City. At the same time the state contains some of the poorest cities in the country. The Brookings Institution ranked Hartford, the state capital, as one of the poorest large cities in the country. Its per capita income of $13,400 in 2000 is less than 1/5th the income of Greenwich.

Much of the inequality is the result of economic changes over the last 50 years. Connecticut's major cities were hubs of industry through the 1970s producing a wide array of goods from hats, to weapons to brass to jet engines and military aircraft. Many of these industries disappeared during the 1970s, leaving cities hollow at their cores. Today the largest cities of Connecticut are all poorer—far poorer than the rest of Connecticut and poorer than most other cities across the nation. The wide disparity in wealth between the large cities and smaller cities of the state has a clear effect on state politics. The large cities vote overwhelmingly Democrat while the smaller cities either split their votes between the parties or in the wealthiest ones vote overwhelmingly Republican.

Racially the state is a bit less diverse than the nation as a whole. Blacks make up about 10.5 percent of the population while Hispanics make up about 12.5 percent. These compare to 13 percent and 16 percent for blacks and Hispanics respectively across the nation. Blacks and Hispanics are also concentrated in the largest cities of the state and contribute, especially the black population, to the high level of support the Democratic Party receives in those cities.

Connecticut also ranks second in the percent of residents with at least a bachelors degree with more than 35 percent of residents having one. This is one reason for the state's high level of wealth. It also may play a role in the state's support of Democratic politicians at the national level. National election surveys show that as a person's educational attainment increases so does support for the Democratic Party and liberal ideology generally.

Chart 12.1 shows the general trends in party affiliation in the state since 1960. As one can see, most voters in the state are registered as unaffiliated or independent. This has generally been the case since data was first collected by the Secretary of State in the 1950s. Between 1975 and 1995 Democrats made up the largest percent of the electorate, but independents became the largest group of voters again in 1995 and they increased their vote share until the Obama campaign in 2008.

Chart 12.1 Party Affiliation of Registered Voters in Connecticut 1960–2010

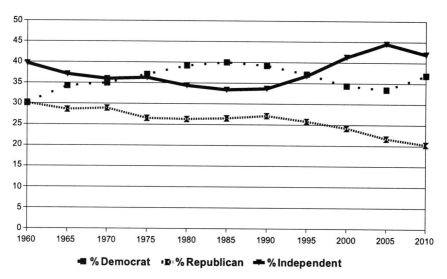

— ■ —% Democrat ·◻·% Republican —▲—% Independent

Source: Connecticut Secretary of the State

There has been an important shift, however, from Republican to Democrat over the last 50 years. In 1960, Republicans and Democrats rather evenly split the electorate with each party having 30 percent of registered voters. Republicans have since lost about 10 percent of their support while Democrats have gained about 6 percent. Thus, Republicans now have only 20 percent of the registered voters while Democrats have 36 percent. The changes in party affiliation have made it more difficult for Republicans to win state wide elections. They must now garner a sizeable majority of the independent vote to offset the much larger base of support that the Democrats possess. This change in party affiliation is related to the general changes we have seen in the American electorate with the south becoming more Republican, much more Republican since the mid 1960s, and the Northeast becoming more Democrat.

THE CANDIDATES

The Creation of an Open Seat: The Retirement of Senator Dodd

Senator Chris Dodd was first elected to the Senate in 1980. He became known for his legislative skills during the Clinton administration and steadily rose among Democrats in the Senate. In the 2004 election, Dodd won more than

65 percent of the vote. His margin of victory may have led him to believe that he was safe and to make choices and take actions that in the end forced him to retire by the time his next election arose. Four actions are key to the explanation of Dodd's fall.

The first was running for the presidency in 2008. Connecticut voters were displeased that he moved his entire family to Iowa during 2007 and spent more time campaigning in that state than in Connecticut or performing his duties in the Senate. The second was revelations in 2008, just as the financial crisis was beginning, that Dodd had received low interest mortgages and other perks from Countrywide Financial as part of a VIP list created by the head of company. This raised serious questions about whether Dodd had misused his position as Chair of the Senate Banking, Housing and Urban Affairs Committee to enrich himself. The third was the discovery in February 2009 that Dodd as chair of that committee removed from legislation approving bailouts for large financial institutions a clause that would have limited bonuses to executives in companies receiving the bailouts. Dodd's action allowed AIG executives to pocket more than $180 million in bonuses despite being bailed out by the U.S. government. In essence, the government transferred money directly from tax payers into the pockets of AIG executives.

The fourth was in February 2009 it also became known that Dodd had participated in the purchase of a property in Ireland in 1994 with a partner. The partner sold his share in the property to Dodd in 2002 for a price that was significantly below the value of what other properties in the area were selling. This raised serious questions about whether Dodd was being paid off by the partner for some type of services rendered. One commentator felt Dodd may have been paid off for supporting a pardon request by an individual convicted of securities fraud in the 1990s.[4]

This string of allegations led to Dodd's approval ratings plummeting. As a result, Robert Simmons, a longtime Republican Congressman, who had lost his seat in 2008, entered the race against Dodd in spring 2009. In September 2009, Linda McMahon also decided to enter the race. Both Simmons and McMahon had large war chests and polls showed them well ahead of Dodd in approval among voters. Democratic leaders in the state began to publicly suggest that Dodd should leave the race and retire. Failure to do so, they warned, might lead to the loss of the seat by the Democrats. The loss of support from state Democrats led Dodd to announce his retirement on January 6, 2010. On the same day, Attorney General Richard Blumenthal announced that he was entering the Senate Race and would seek the Democratic Party nomination for the seat.

Linda McMahon

Linda McMahon was born on October 4, 1948, in North Carolina. She graduated from East Carolina University with a degree in French and a teaching certificate. In an interview with the *Hartford Courant* she was quoted as saying that she expected to be a French teacher when she left the university.[5] However, instead of becoming a teacher, she entered the wrestling business with her husband, Vince McMahon, in the early 1980s. Together Linda and her husband built a small wrestling company, purchased from Vince's father, into World Wrestling Entertainment, Inc. It is the largest wrestling company in the world with more than 500 employees and offices around the world. The company is also the source of Linda McMahon's wealth. Prior to 2002 the McMahons were ranked by Forbes magazine as one of the 400 richest families in the U.S. with a net worth over $ 1 billion dollars.[6] However, disclosure reports filed by Linda McMahon during the race placed her net worth around $335 million.[7] McMahon's wealth allowed her to almost entirely self fund her campaign. Out of the $50 million used by her campaign less than $200,000 came from outside donations.[8]

Not only was the WWE the source of Linda's wealth helping to make her a viable candidate, it was also the source of most of the attacks used by her opponents during the race. The WWE has had a rather controversial history. It has been attacked for its negative depictions of women, and for the poor treatment of the "talent" it uses in the ring.[9] In 2007 the WWE was the focus of a Congressional hearing which concluded that drug and steroid use were pervasive among the wrestlers. This was after a high profile drug death of one wrestler in 2006 and the hearing was followed by a murder suicide perpetrated by a second wrestler in 2007. Seven wrestlers died between March 2009 and October 2010. Four of these wrestlers were found to have either narcotics in their blood at the time of their deaths or had waged public battles with addiction. Simmons, McMahon's Republican opponent, used these issues to raise questions about McMahon's fitness for office, and Blumenthal used them again during the general election to raise similar questions. Blumenthal stressed, in particular, the depictions of women within the WWE, and these may have led to women failing to support McMahon in the general election.

McMahon had no real political experience prior to her run as a candidate. In 2009 she was appointed by the governor to serve on the Connecticut Board of Education. She resigned from the board in April 2010. She also has served as a trustee of Sacred Heart University. She had never run for office prior to this election.

Richard Blumenthal

Richard Blumenthal was born February 13, 1946, in Brooklyn, New York. He graduated from Harvard in 1967 and Yale Law School in 1973. Between graduating from Harvard and attending Yale, Blumenthal served as an aide to Senator Daniel Moynihan. This was the first of what would be an entire career working in public positions. After law school Blumenthal served as a clerk for Supreme Court Justice Harry Blackmun. He was then appointed to the U.S. Attorney position in Connecticut by President Jimmy Carter. Blumenthal was only 31 years old when made U.S. Attorney, at the time, he was the youngest U.S. Attorney in American history. During the 1980s Blumenthal won a seat first in the Connecticut House and then the Connecticut Senate. He moved to the Attorney General's office in 1990 and easily won reelection every four years until 2010 when he decided to leave the Attorney General's position and campaign for the U.S. Senate.

Polls have consistently shown Blumenthal as one of the most respected public figures in the state. He had a long reputation for propriety and for using the Attorney General's office to protect the citizens of Connecticut. However, Blumenthal's image was damaged during the general election campaign and this damage may be why Blumenthal had difficulty in the early part of the race creating distance between himself and McMahon.

Blumenthal is also known for his use of the media. Within the state there is a joke that "if there is a garage door opening within the state, Dick Blumenthal will be there." Opponents of Blumenthal have commented "that the most dangerous place to be in the state was between a camera and Dick Blumenthal."[10] Both of these describe his ubiquitous presence in the media. It is clear that Blumenthal saw a constant presence in the local media as a way to ensure reelection to office by developing name recognition and actively cultivating support among Connecticut citizens.

NOMINATION AND PRIMARY CAMPAIGN

Connecticut parties control the nomination process of candidates far more than parties in most other states. Candidates for the major parties are required to obtain 15 percent of the votes from delegates to state party conventions in order to force a primary for the U.S. Senate. Convention votes are largely controlled by party town committees and in order for a candidate to succeed, she must lobby town committee members and bargain for their support. Town committee chairs are powerful enough that they can close out candidates not supported by the party leadership in the state. A town committee cannot be forced by a candidate to give her access to town committee meetings or even to consider her for nomination. This makes it difficult for outsiders to win the nomination of either party. However, candidates failing to obtain 15 percent of the convention votes may still force a primary if they collect 2 percent of the state's total party registrants in the district or state on a petition.[11] Since the Senate is a statewide office a candidate failing to win 15 percent of the convention delegates would be forced to collect 2 percent of all major party registrants in order to force a primary.

Blumenthal benefited significantly from these rules. Merrick Alpert, a businessman from Mystic, Connecticut, entered the race for Senate in 2009 several months before Dodd announced his retirement. Alpert hoped that Dodd's difficulties would allow him to obtain the needed support to force a primary election. However, with Dodd's retirement and Blumenthal's entrance into the race, Alpert found access to town committees to be difficult if not impossible.

Alpert did succeed in getting Blumenthal to agree to a debate in March 2010. However, after exit polls and media comment showed that Alpert was considered the winner of the debate, Blumenthal refused to participate in further debates with Alpert. Alpert's victory did not turn into convention votes, nor did it open access to town committees in the state. On May 21, 2010, Blumenthal was nominated by acclaim at the state Democratic convention. This was after Alpert officially removed his name as a candidate for the U.S. Senate. The press reported after the convention that Alpert was denied access to the podium by convention leaders until he had withdrawn himself as a candidate. Alpert later released a copy of the speech he wanted to make at the convention appealing for the need of a primary.[12]

Linda McMahon entered the Senate race on September 16, 2009, after resigning as CEO of World Wrestling Entertainment, Inc. At the time Simmons, a long time Congressman, had been in the race since the previous spring. Moreover, Simmons had been urged to seek the nomination by top national Republican Party officials. Simmons was well funded and had a large amount of name recognition within the state. He was also a candidate with a rather high level of approval; 46 percent of voters in a Q poll performed on September 17, 2009, stated that they had a favorable opinion of Simmons compared to only 11 percent having an unfavorable opinion.[13] However, 46 percent of those polled said they did not know enough about Simmons to make a judgment. Two other candidates were also in the race for the nomination. Tom Foley—who would later withdraw in order to run for the open governor's office—and Peter Schiff. Schiff stayed in the race until the end but was never a significant factor.

McMahon's campaign hit the ground running. She began airing her first campaign advertisements on September 23, 2009, just seven days after entering the race. Her early ads both introduced who she was to the citizens of Connecticut and targeted Dodd and his ethical lapses and errors. McMahon's campaign war chest was so large that she was able to place ads during high profile events like Notre Dame football broadcasts on Saturdays and during prime-time programming. An examination of her ads shows that she had a clear strategy of ignoring the other Republicans in the race for the nomination.[14] It appears that she decided to present herself as the clear frontrunner in the race and for people to consider her standing against the likely Democrat in the race, first Dodd, then Blumenthal, instead of how she stood against the various Republicans. McMahon also argued that she was an outsider. She was not a career politician and thus would be able to make changes or accomplish things in Washington that career politicians could not. No names were given in these ads about who was the career politician. So, her ads could be used against both Dodd and Simmons.

By December 2009, three months after entering the race, McMahon had already spent more than $5 million on her campaign. Most of this spending went to advertising in the major media outlets of Connecticut or to direct mail. McMahon blanketed the state with direct mailings throughout the entire campaign leading to complaints about voter fatigue and overexposure of the candidate.

McMahon's activities bore fruit rather quickly. Chart 12.2 shows the trends in voter support measured by the Q Poll from November 2009 until July 2010. One can see that by the middle of January 2010, McMahon had caught Simmons in the polls and from that point onward her lead increased steadily.

The Simmons campaign began to actively target McMahon in December 2009. First, Simmons staffers released information to the press showing that McMahon had donated more than $35,000 to Democratic candidates over the last decade. They also presented evidence raising doubts about whether she had voted in previous elections. This was a clear attempt to show that McMahon was not a true Republican and that her interest in politics was not sincere. Simmons also began publicly arguing that McMahon was attempting to buy the race. Finally, the Simmons campaign began attacking McMahon's record as head of the WWE. In particular, they raised questions about the business practices of the WWE under her watch, arguing that she had ignored drug abuse within the ranks of the WWE and that this had led to the deaths of wrestlers. The implication was that the WWE used wrestlers to make money, but did little to ensure their health. This could be seen in the WWE employing wrestlers as private contractors and not employees so that the WWE would not be responsible for providing them with health care. Simmons stated that as head of the WWE McMahon showed a lack of support for the traditional family values held by the Republican Party.

Chart 12.2   Percent Support for McMahon and Simmons: September 2009–August 2010

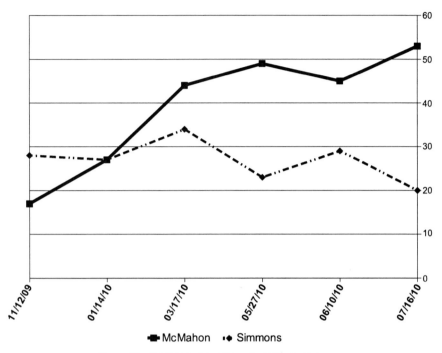

◼ McMahon   ◆ Simmons

Source: The QPoll: Quinnipiac University Polling Institute

McMahon responded to these attacks by arguing that the WWE had made major changes to its practices once the abuse of drugs had been discovered. She pointed to the use of testing of all wrestlers and the development of a well-ness program to ensure that the health of wrestlers was not adversely affected by their activities in the ring. On the issue of family values, McMahon argued that her business was a type of show business, a soap opera, and should not be taken seriously. Moreover, she claimed that many of the excesses Simmons criticized were things the WWE had done during the 1990s. She argued that today's WWE was more family friendly and less extreme. She pointed to herself as a mother and long time wife of Vince McMahon to establish her strong family values.

Despite the attacks by Simmons, McMahon's lead in the polls continued to widen. Simmons' support among Republican leaders also began to fade. Party leaders went from encouraging Simmons to run for the Senate to openly stating that a primary would be the best method for choosing the party's candidate. These events made McMahon confident enough in winning the nomination of the Republican Party that she began running advertisements against Blumenthal, the likely Democratic nominee, four days before the Republican state nominating convention.

On May 21, 2010, McMahon won the Republican Party endorsement by a vote of 737 to 632 at the state party convention. However, the Simmons campaign did not withdraw from the race and stated that it would call for a primary election to decide the party's candidate. On May 25th, Simmons changed his mind and announced that he was suspending his campaign for Senate. Through the summer, Peter Schiff continued to campaign against McMahon for the Republican nomination. But it was assumed that McMahon would easily win the primary election. McMahon's campaign focused entirely on Blumenthal and not the primary.

In mid July, Simmons reentered the race. He claimed that he had never left the field of candidates, merely that he had stopped campaigning. Thus, his name remained on the ballot. He once again began to actively campaign for the nomination including the release of two new advertisements. Simmons may have decided to rejoin the race when polls showed that among all voters he performed as well against Blumenthal as McMahon did. Simmons' renewed efforts won him the endorsement of several media outlets including the *Hartford Courant,* the most important newspaper in the state. However, these efforts were not enough to displace McMahon.

On August 10, 2010, the primary election was held. McMahon easily won the primary winning 49 percent of the vote to Robert Simmons' 28 percent and Peter Schiff's 23 percent. McMahon's campaign in winning the nomination of the Republican Party had already spent $22 million on the race.

GENERAL ELECTION

Blumenthal's campaign largely disappeared from view during the summer months after he received the nomination of his party, while the McMahon campaign actively attacked Blumenthal and worked to develop more name recognition for its candidate. As stated previously, the McMahon campaign began running ads against Blumenthal even before it had received the endorsement of the Republican nominating convention. Moreover, McMahon staffers fed information to *The New York Times* that Blumenthal had regularly inflated his military experience over the years. On May 17, four days before the Democratic Party state convention, *The New York Times* had a front page story that Blumenthal had made statements to veterans groups in the state that he had served in Vietnam. The facts, however, showed that Blumenthal had received five deferments allowing him to avoid the war, and he was then admitted into the Marine Corps Reserve which ensured that he would not be deployed to Vietnam. The story went on to show that the statements about serving in Vietnam had been made repeatedly over the years. Furthermore, the story stated

> that what is striking about Mr. Blumenthal's record is the contrast between the many steps he took that allowed him to avoid Vietnam, and the misleading way he often speaks about that period of his life now, especially when he is speaking at veterans' ceremonies or other patriotic events. Sometimes his remarks have been plainly untrue, as in his speech to the group in Norwalk. At other times, he has used more ambiguous language, but the impression left on audiences can be similar.[15]

Blumenthal initially stated that he had misspoken at various events, but that he had not meant to deceive anyone about his military record. At a press conference the day after the story ran in *The New York Times,* Blumenthal stated, "on a few occasions I have misspoken about my service, and I regret that and I take full responsibility . . . but I will not allow anyone to take a few misplaced words and impugn my record of service to our country." Several veterans surrounded Blumenthal during the press conference as a show of support for him and his record.

This issue did not go away. McMahon returned to Blumenthal's misstatements repeatedly through the rest of the campaign in order to undermine Blumenthal's credibility and approval among voters. It is hard to say how much impact the issue had in the end. Blumenthal's overall approval ratings declined, but a Q Poll taken September 14 showed that 55 percent of Connecticut voters had a favorable opinion of Blumenthal while 57 percent of voters thought that he was trustworthy. These compared to 45 percent of voters having a favorable impression of McMahon with 58 percent saying she was trustworthy.

Blumenthal's campaign was so quiet during the summer that some Democratic leaders in the state worried that he was becoming complacent and that he might end up losing the Senate race much like the Democratic Attorney General had lost in her bid to replace Democrat Ted Kennedy as senator in Massachusetts. Worries were magnified by the fact that not only was Blumenthal's campaign quiet, but that Blumenthal had become far less ubiquitous in the media.[16]

Chart 12.3 shows that McMahon's efforts paid dividends as she slowly closed the gap in tracking polls between herself and Blumenthal. At the start of the summer, McMahon was 20 percentage points behind Blumenthal, by the middle of August she had closed to within 10 points, and by the middle of September she was only 6 points behind Blumenthal in the polls.

Chart 12.3   Percent Support for Blumenthal and McMahon: March to October 2010

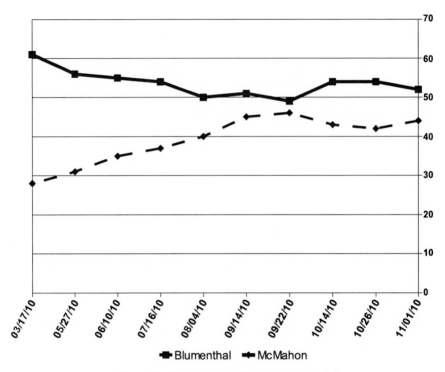

Source: The QPoll: Quinnipiac University Polling Institute

Her strategy throughout was to paint Blumenthal as a political insider and to show that he was far less reliable than people were led to believe during his 20 years as Attorney General. In a July advertisement, the McMahon campaign showed Blumenthal stating that he never accepted PAC money and never would. The ad then showed Blumenthal at a fund raising event in Vancouver, Canada, accepting money from the American Trial Lawyers Association. Other ads were released in September and October with similar types of attacks. Each ad showed a statement by Blumenthal and then attempted to show that the statement was false or that events he had promised would not occur from his actions had occurred. The *Hartford Courant* found two of these ads to be at best misleading, and at worse false.[17]

She also blanketed the state with direct mail and broadcast media advertisements. Between September 1 and October 7 the McMahon campaign spent $5.4 million on television ads alone.[18] On one station, the NBC affiliate based in West Hartford, McMahon purchased more than 700 ad spots between September 27 and November 2.[19] There were so many McMahon ads that voters may have begun to feel candidate fatigue. In any case, McMahon's campaign hit its high-water mark in late September when she pulled to within 3 points of Blumenthal in the race. From that point on, she steadily lost ground, as shown in Chart 12.3.

The Blumenthal campaign became more active after Labor Day, but it did not begin to really catch fire until McMahon had closed the gap in the polls in late September. It was then that both Bill Clinton and President Barack Obama came to the state to campaign for Blumenthal. Clinton's visit in particular, seemed to have energized the campaign as well as Democrats. Clinton at a rally in New Haven exhorted Democrats to mobilize and work to ensure the election of Blumenthal.

Like McMahon, Blumenthal attacked the character of his opponent as a primary strategy. Blumenthal's Twitter site linked to video showing the treatment of women in WWE wrestling matches. One video titled by Blumenthal's campaign was, "Sex, Violence and the Abusive Treatment of Women." It showed Vince McMahon demanding that a female wrestler get on her knees and bark like a dog. Blumenthal also ran advertisements showing that as CEO of WWE McMahon had laid off employees of the company while receiving more than $45 million in compensation. Blumenthal continued the attacks launched by Simmons that the WWE mistreated its wrestlers and had done little to prevent drug abuse within its ranks. As part of this, the Blumenthal campaign paid for the father of a wrestler to come to Connecticut to discuss how his son had died from drug abuse and mistreatment while a wrestler for the WWE.

Finally, the Blumenthal campaign spent heavily on television ads as well. His campaign spent more than $600,000 on ads in the last five weeks of the campaign, and almost $2 million on ads between September 1 and October 7.[20]

The candidates participated in three debates during the early part of October. The debates took place on October 4, October 7, and October 12. Neither candidate made any serious mistakes during the debates. Both candidates continued their attempts to attack the character of the other, while attempting to buttress their own image. McMahon emphasized her outsider status and leadership role of a company, while repeating that Blumenthal had lied about his service record. Blumenthal argued that he had always been a defender of Connecticut citizens as Attorney General and that McMahon's leadership of the WWE had harmed wrestlers and demeaned women. From the tracking poll data in Chart 12.3 it seems that Blumenthal was the winner of these debates. His numbers jumped dramatically after the debates and McMahon would never close the gap again.

A final issue arose as Election Day neared. The Secretary of State's Office in late October announced that wearing WWE paraphernalia to the polls would constitute electioneering for McMahon. Poll workers were initially instructed to tell any voter wearing or carrying WWE paraphernalia to cover it up or to go home and change before they would be allowed to vote. Vince McMahon, Linda's husband and current CEO of the WWE, threatened to sue the state if this order was allowed to stand. This threat led the Secretary of State to retract her ruling. However, Vince McMahon used the issue to say that the WWE was being harassed and unfairly treated by Democratic leaders of the state, and he organized a fan appreciation day for October 31 just two days before the election. The rally for the WWE in Hartford drew over 17,000 people and Vince McMahon exhorted fans to vote on Election Day while also giving out free WWE paraphernalia.

McMahon spent more than $50 million on her campaign. Blumenthal spent more than $8 million during the campaign, raising about seventy percent from both PACs and individuals. Opensecrets.org reports that about two thirds of Blumenthal's PAC money was contributed by labor and liberal ideological and single issue organizations. Their donations equaled about $500,000. Most individual contributions came from four sectors: retired individuals, lawyers, securities and investment professionals, and real estate. The four sectors accounted for more than one-fifth of the almost $5 million raised from individuals by the Blumenthal campaign.

Combined the two candidates spent almost $60 million. This is twice the level of the old record of spending on a Connecticut election set in the 2006 race between Joe Lieberman and Ned Lamont.

ELECTION RESULTS

On November 2, 2010, Blumenthal defeated McMahon 55 percent to 43 percent. This was slightly higher than what the final tracking polls predicted. The question became, why did a candidate as well funded as McMahon do so poorly? Part of the answer came from the nature of self funding. Candidates who self fund do not build the type of campaign organization that candidates who rely on donations must. To obtain money through donations a campaign must embed itself among voters. On Election Day this gives the campaign an advantage in getting people to the polls. Second, donations are a form of signaling. Good candidates are able to gain donations, bad candidates are not. In essence, money flows to the person that is seen as the most viable and popular. Finally, a donation to a candidate often leads to the donor working for the candidate in some way. In particular, the person is likely to work to convince others to also support the candidate in order to help ensure that one's donation is not wasted. Word of mouth can be a powerful tool to recruit supporters to a candidate. The fact that Blumenthal raised 70 percent of his $8 million from individuals and groups shows that he had much wider support than McMahon within the state.

Exit polls from the race show that Blumenthal won almost every category of voter.[21] The only category he failed to win were those with conservative ideologies. He won the majority of votes from all income categories, and he either tied McMahon or won the majority of votes from all education categories as well. Blumenthal also won the majority of votes from both men and women, dominating among women with 60 percent of their vote. From this it appears that Blumenthal's tactic of painting McMahon's WWE as anti woman paid dividends. While Blumenthal lost decisively among conservative voters winning only 20 percent, he did better than McMahon's 8 percent support from liberal voters. He also decisively won the moderate voter of Connecticut 57 percent to 41 percent. For a Republican to win in Connecticut, she must capture the lion's share of the independent vote—most of whom lie in the moderate category ideologically.

CONCLUSION

Money may allow a candidate to compete, but it does not mean that the candidate will win. McMahon outspent Blumenthal by a 6 to 1 margin. However, Blumenthal's $8 million was more than sufficient to ensure that his message could be heard. In the end, Blumenthal did what was expected when he entered the race. He won handily. However, McMahon made him work for victory and at one point made it appear that Blumenthal may lose.

NOTES

1. Candidates often buy some media spots in the New York City market as well since it overlaps with the southwestern corner of the state.
2. All economic and demographic data comes from the U.S. Census Bureau.
3. The Gini Index is a measure of inequality that varies from 0 to 1. A score of 1 means that one person makes all income in the state while a score of 0 indicates that all people have the same incomes.
4. Kevin Rennie, "Dodd's 'Cottage': A Cozy Purchase," *Hartford Courant,* February 22, 2009, p.C3.
5. Daniela Altimari, "Wrestling in a New Ring: Politics; Linda McMahon," *Hartford Courant,* December 20, 2009, p.A1.

6. Altimari, "Wrestling."

7. Ken Dixon, "The Running of the Rich: Is Wealth Changing Connecticut Politics?" *The Connecticut Post,* March 14, 2010. Found at www.ctpost.com/news/article/The-running-of-the-rich-Is-wealth-changing-406355.php.

8. All campaign finance data for this chapter comes from www.opensecrets.org.

9. WWE employees use the term "talent" for wrestlers. The wrestlers are not employees of the company but private contractors. Material for this paragraph comes from: Daniela Altimari, "An Act Cleaned Up? Substance Abuse in WWE Dogs McMahon Run." *Hartford Courant,* October 14, 2010, p. A1.

10. David Plotz, "Richard Blumenthal: He was Supposed to be President. So Why is he only Connecticut's Attorney General?" *Slate,* September 15, 2000. Found at www.slate.com/id/89649/. During the campaign Richard Blumenthal commented proudly about the garage door opening joke using it to highlight his service to Connecticut citizens.

11. State Republican Party Rules make it unclear whether a candidate receiving less than 15 percent of the convention vote can force a primary through a petition containing 2 percent of the total party voters within the state for the U.S. Senate. This paragraph come from the Connecticut Democratic State Party Rules approved in 2006 and the Connecticut Republican State Central Committee Rules and Bylaws approved in 2006. Both can be found at www.ct.gov/sots/cwp/view.asp?a=3179&q=392236&SOTSNav_GID=1846.

12. Chris Keating, "Democrats: Blumenthal Admits 'Mistakes' but Pledges not to Back Down," *Hartford Courant,* May 22, 2010, p. A1.

13. All tracking polls and preelection poll results in this chapter come from the Q Poll. This is a poll conducted by the Quinnipiac University Polling Institute. The Institute conducted polls almost monthly during the primary and general election season and provides a reliable base of information on Connecticut attitudes towards the candidates and issues in the election. The Q Poll also allows the following of trends in support for candidates and issues since the same questions are asked over time. The Q Polls for the senate race can be found at www.quinnipiac.edu/x1291.xml.

14. The author was not able to find a single advertisement through various web searches, perusing McMahon's website or on Youtube.com that made mention of Simmons, Foley, or Peter Schiff.

15. Raymond Hernandez, "Candidate's Words on Vietnam Service Differ From History," *New York Times,* May 17, 2010, p.A1.

16. Tedd Man, "Blumenthal Maintaining a Low Profile—but Why? Attorney General's Campaign Strangely Quiet." *The New London Day,* July 6, 2010. Found at www.theday.com/article/20100706/NWS01/307069953/1018.

17. Matthew Kauffman, "Claim Check: 'Blumenthal Energy Tax'; Television Ad from Republican Linda McMahon's Campaign for Senate," *Hartford Courant,* October 1, 2010, p. B2 and Matthew Kauffman, "Claim Check: 'Biggest Lie'; Television Ad from Republican Linda McMahon's Senate Campaign," *Hartford Courant,* October 22, 2010, p. B2.

18. Advertisement spending numbers for both McMahon and Blumenthal come from, Susan Haigh and Everton Bailey Jr., "McMahon Dominates Conn. TV Ad Spending in Election," *The Associated Press,* Friday October, 22, 2010. Found at finance.yahoo.com/news/McMahon-dominates-Conn-TV-ad-apf-4176763389 .html?x=0&.v=1.

19. McMahon's 730 ad spots on WVIT—the NBC affiliate—cost $275,222. This means that each ad cost on average $377. Using this figure we can calculate that she purchased about 13,700 ads in the period from September 1 to October 7. This figure comes from dividing the $5.2 million her campaign spent by $377.

20. Using the same formula used to estimate the number of ads for McMahon, Blumenthal bought about 1600 ads during the final five weeks of the campaign.

21. Exit Polls come from *The New York Times* website and can be found at elections.nytimes.com/2010/results/senate/exit-polls#connecticut.

Chapter 13

Florida Senate Race
(Crist v. Meek v. Rubio)

The Rise of Rubio and Fall of Crist

Sean D. Foreman

Charlie Crist
Party: No Party Affiliation
Age: 54
Sex: Male
Race: Caucasian
Religion: Methodist
Education: B.A. Florida State University, J.D. Cumberland School of Law
Occupation: Public Service; Law
Political Experience: Florida Senate, (1992–1998); Nominee for U.S. Senate, (1998); Florida Secretary of Education, (2001–2003); Florida Attorney General, (2003–2007); Governor, (2007–2011)

Kendrick Meek
Party: Democrat
Age: 44
Sex: Male
Race: African American
Religion: Baptist
Education: B.S. Florida A&M University, 1989
Occupation: Public Service; Former State Trooper
Political Experience: Florida House of Representatives, (1994–1998); Florida Senate, (1998–2002); U.S. House of Representatives, (2003–2011)

Marco Rubio
Party: Republican
Age: 39
Sex: Male

Race/Ethnicity: White/Hispanic
Religion: Roman Catholic
Education: B.A., University of Florida, 1993; J.D. University of Miami, 1996
Occupation: Public Service; Law
Political Experience: West Miami City Council, (1998–2000); Florida House
of Representatives, (2000–2008), House Speaker, (2006–2008).

It started as a *David v Goliath* battle between Marco Rubio and Charlie Crist
within the Republican Party and turned into a spirited race between three
Florida political insiders. Rubio, Crist, and Kendrick Meek, three of the most
experienced and connected politicians in the sunshine state, competed for the
Senate seat that opened when first term Republican Mel Martinez opted for
early retirement.

Marco Rubio entered the race for U.S. Senate as a 30-point underdog
to Governor Charlie Crist. Over the next year the tides turned and Rubio
emerged as a national political star for both the Republican Party and the
conservative Tea Party movement. On Election Day, Republicans swept the
sunshine state, winning all statewide executive offices, defeating four incumbent House Democrats and putting the 39-year-old Cuban-American son of
working class immigrants in the U.S. Senate.

In a year of political outsiders, Florida's race for a Senate seat involved
three career politicians. Crist's decision to vacate the governor's seat and run
for the open Senate seat led to a domino effect. There are no "do-overs" in
campaigns but if Charlie Crist had this decision to do over again, he might
very well have stayed put in the Florida governor's mansion. Crist was a
popular first term governor and a rising national public figure, respected
by members of both political parties, who was on the short list for John
McCain's selection of a running mate in 2008. If Crist had run for reelection
as governor he probably would have only faced token opposition in both the
Republican primary and from a Democratic opponent. Florida would have
had a boring political season, a word not usually used to describe Florida
politics. But when Mel Martinez announced he was vacating his U.S. Senate
seat, Crist saw an opportunity to jump into the prestigious upper chamber of
Congress, a position with a platform on national and international issues and
without term limits.

Martinez narrowly defeated Betty Castor in 2006 by 49.4 percent to 48.3
percent (by 82,663 votes out more than of 7.2 million).[1] But in 2009 he
decided not to seek reelection and then to give up his seat early. That allowed
Governor Crist, then a Republican, to appoint a successor, and it tempted the
tanned and popular first term governor to run for the seat. Crist appointed
his former campaign chief and political advisor George LeMieux, who had

left the governor's staff to return to practice law. Crist passed over many experienced politicians with Washington experience to pick LeMieux, who was known as "the Maestro" for his role in orchestrating Crist's campaigns for Attorney General in 2002 and Governor in 2006. The common wisdom was that LeMieux would be a "seat warmer" as Crist would run for the seat and pass up a clear path to reelection as the chief executive of the 4th largest state in the union.

CHARACTERISTICS OF FLORIDA

Party Balance

Democrats had 600,000 more registered voters than Republicans but got swept statewide in 2010. The voter registration for Florida as of the general election showed 4,631,068 Democrats and 4,039,259 Republicans. There were 2,186,246 no party affiliations (NPA) and another 360,811 registered with minor parties out of the 11,217,384 registered voters in Florida.[2] Marco Rubio won the Senate seat and Republicans carried the statewide executive offices of Governor, Attorney General, Chief Financial Officer, and Secretary of Agriculture and Consumer Services.

Even as registered Democrats have outnumbered Republicans for decades, Republicans have been the dominant party electorally since capturing the state Senate in 1994 and the state House in 1996. In 1994, incumbent governor Democrat Lawton Chiles narrowly defeated Republican Jeb Bush by 50.8 percent to 49.2 percent, a 63,940 vote margin. Bush went on to win the governor's race in 1998 by 11 percent and in 2002 by 13 percent. Bush, term limited, was succeeded by Crist in 2006.

Voting and Electoral History

Florida was traditionally a southern Democrat state from World War II until the 1990s.[3] During the 1990s the state flipped to being majority Republican in the state legislature and in the Congressional delegation. The last elected Democratic governor was Lawton Chiles who died days before leaving office in 1999. Chiles defeated Republican Jeb Bush in 1994 but then Bush won the gubernatorial elections of 1998 and 2002. Crist, a moderate Republican, won in 2006. In 2010, Rick Scott won the gubernatorial election by a one percent margin over Democrat Alex Sink.

For the past 30 years Florida has usually had one Democrat and one Republican representing them in the Senate. The Class 1 seat is held by

Democrat Bill Nelson who won in 2000 and was reelected in 2006. Nelson took over that seat after Republican Connie Mack III, a two-term Senator retired. Before that Chiles, a Democrat, held the seat for three terms from 1971–1989.

The Class 3 seat that Mel Martinez won in 2004 was previously held for three terms by Democrat Bob Graham. In 1986, Graham defeated Republican Paula Hawkins, Florida's first and only female Senator. Graham retired from the Senate in 2004. Martinez defeated Democrat Betty Castor in 2004 after serving as Secretary of Housing and Urban Development in the George W. Bush administration. Martinez was recruited by Bush supporters and got strong national party support. Martinez, who left Cuba at age 15 and became the first Cuban-American U.S. Senator, served as the Republican National Committee chair. The time spent campaigning and raising money for other candidates was seen as taking time away from Martinez getting a good start on fundraising to support his own reelection. Martinez quit the Senate in August 2009, saying he wanted to spend time with his family and to return to the private sector.[4] This allowed Governor Crist to appoint LeMieux to fill the term until the 2010 election. When it became clear that Rubio would defeat Crist in the primary and the governor left the Republican Party, LeMieux publicly abandoned his political mentor and said that he would support the party nominee, Rubio.

Voter turnout was 49.7 percent statewide for the 2010 elections. That was higher than the 46.8 percent in 2006 but down from the 55.3 percent turnout in 2002. Beyond the usual reasons for a midterm election to elicit lower turnout than a presidential election, other factors for the lower turnout may have included a lack of interest in the gubernatorial candidates, the lack of suspense at the end of the campaign for the Senate race, and the general negativity of the statewide campaigns.

Demographic Character of the Electorate

Florida, the nation's fourth largest state with a population estimate of 18,537,969 in 2009, has a diverse and growing population. It had 79 percent white population and 16 percent black with 60 percent white, non Hispanic and 22 percent Hispanic or Latino according to 2009 Census data.[5] While the Hispanic population was historically concentrated in Miami and Tampa is has slowly and steadily permeated the central and northern portions of the state. The Black populations are concentrated in the large urban areas and in the rural northern part of the state.

According to the Florida Division of Elections, White non-Hispanic voters totaled 7,693,268, Black non-Hispanic numbered 1,459,831, and Hispanic voters added to 1,425,804 in October 2010. There were 3,388,491 Whites, 445,353 Hispanics and 58,875 Black non-Hispanics registered as Republicans. Democrats included 2,632,694 White non-Hispanics, 1,218,787 Black non-Hispanics, and 550,799 Hispanics.

Within Hispanics it is important to note that Cuban-Americans typically vote Republican and are concentrated in the Greater Miami area while Puerto Ricans and Dominicans tend to vote more for Democrats and have large concentrations in Central Florida. It is inaccurate to think of Hispanic voters as a monolithic block or to treat them that way in terms of campaigning.

White voters are split between the urban and rural areas in terms of ideology. In cities like Miami, Ft. Lauderdale, Palm Beach there are many White liberals. But in the central and northern part of the state the White voters are more traditionally conservative.

Key Voting Blocs

Key constituencies in Florida include retirees and seniors, Hispanics, and newly arriving immigrants, and military interests. There are more than 20 military bases in Florida. Members of the military tend to be more conservative than their civilian counterparts.

Florida has an aging population with 17.2 percent of residents 65 or older compared with 12.9 percent nationally. This makes health care and Social Security pertinent issues and visits to retirement communities vitally important in campaigns.

The percent of foreign born persons in Florida was 16.7 percent in 2000 compared to 11.1 percent nationally. 23.1 percent of Floridians speak a language other than English at home compared to 17.9 percent across the country. The higher level of immigrants suggests that there will be people who are newer residents of the state and less familiar with state politics. They may also get their news and information from sources that use languages other than English. In South Florida Spanish language radio and television are a big part of the political dialogue.

Major Urban Areas and Employment/Occupational Characteristics

Florida has 10 media markets, though there is great disparity in size.[6] Miami/ Ft. Lauderdale and Palm Beach in the south and Tampa and Orlando in the center are the largest urban areas. Tallahassee, the state capital, and Gainesville are large college towns in the north central. Jacksonville in the northeast and Pensacola in the northwest have major military installations. Five counties, Miami-Dade, Broward, Palm Beach, Hillsborough and Orange, have more than 1 million people while 26 out of 67 counties have fewer than 50,000 residents.

Tourism, Agriculture, and Growth and Development are the major employment categories. A main attraction in Florida is the Disney parks and resorts around Orlando and other parks in Tampa. The "I-4 corridor" is the fastest growing part of the state in terms of population and economic development. The beaches from Pensacola in the north to Miami Beach in the south draw millions of visitors each year.

THE CANDIDATES

Marco Rubio

Marco Rubio was born in West Miami to parents who emigrated from Cuba in 1959.[7] Rubio attended South Miami High School where, as an undersized defensive back, he was a leader on the football team. He earned a scholarship to Tarkio College in Missouri, transferred to a junior college in Florida, and then graduated in 1993 from University of Florida. In 1996, Rubio earned a J.D. from the University of Miami.[8]

Rubio worked for the campaign of Republican presidential candidate Bob Dole in 1996 and made critical political connections. Al Cardenas, a prominent lawyer who later became chair of the Republican Party of Florida, took an interest in Rubio. While Dole's chances were not good Florida or nationally, Cardenas saw a winner in Rubio. "I said to myself, 'This is what we need, someone so young that failure is not an option, who hasn't gone through everything to have a more practical outlook,'" Cardenas later said.[9] Cardenas hired Rubio as his law firm, Tew Cardenas.

In 1998, at age 27, he ran for the West Miami city commission. Rubio won the race and, according to a fellow commissioner who also won that night, received a phone call from future Governor Jeb Bush congratulating him for his win.[10] "He was the anointed golden child, even then," said Enrique Gonzalez.[11]

The following year Rubio ran for an open state House seat winning a run-off primary election by 64 votes and cruising to a general election victory in the heavily Republican-leaning district. Because he won a special election he was able to serve in the spring legislative session in 2000 and get a head start on other freshman members elected in November. Term limits started in the legislature that year and Rubio was first in a class of new legislators to gain experience and network with colleagues. This gave him an advantage in winning a race for Speaker in a highly competitive process of fundraising and vote gathering.[12]

Rubio spent the next eight years in the House, the final two (2006–2008) as Speaker. He was the first Cuban-American speaker in Florida. When he became speaker, Governor Bush presented Rubio with a sword from a "great conservative warrior."[13] It was an unusual gesture but a sure sign that the popular governor had taken the young speaker under his wing.

Rubio sat out the 2008 election cycle and turned to practicing law. He also served as a political analyst for *Univision* while teaching courses on state politics at Florida International University.[14] During that time Rubio quietly began building a base for a statewide run for office.

Observers thought that Rubio was angling for Attorney General or for Governor. The conventional wisdom was that if Governor Charlie Crist ran for the U.S. Senate, Rubio would run for governor. Rubio even said in January 2009 that "Crist would be the best candidate" if he ran for Senate.[15] Crist wavered about his intentions saying that he would not announce until after the 2009 legislative session that ran through May 1. Crist also made some moves that fueled conservative opposition including accepting the Democratic passed federal stimulus dollars and opposing oil drilling off of Florida's shores. Rubio made the decision to jump into the race for Senate, announcing by YouTube video on May 9, 2009, before Crist despite low poll numbers and weak initial fundraising.

Despite Crist's broad popularity and broad public appeal, former Speaker of the Florida House Rubio decided to challenge Crist for the GOP nomination. As Rubio often said on the campaign trail, there were only a handful people who thought he could win and most were in his home and four were under age 10.[16] Rubio persisted and slowly gained attention and momentum by attending tea parties, speaking on conservative radio and television programs, raising money, and pounding the pavement around the state.

Charlie Crist

Charlie Crist, a descendent of Greek Cypriot immigrants, was born in Altoona, Pennsylvania and moved to St. Petersburg, Florida as a child. Crist climbed the state political ladder. After law school he worked as general counsel for Minor League baseball and then as a staff member for former Senator Connie Mack III. Crist was elected to the state Senate in 1992 and earned a reputation as a law and order politician, even gaining the nickname "chain gang Charlie" for sponsoring legislation to reintroduce physical labor for inmates. Later he was elected Education Commissioner, Attorney General and, in 2006, was elected Governor.

Crist won the Republican nomination for U.S. Senate in 1998 but lost the race to Bob Graham. Crist was punching above his weight against Graham in 1998 but a dozen years later the sitting governor was the state's political heavyweight and was viewed as a major favorite to win the Senate seat when he declared his intent to run in May 2009.

Crist had endorsed Arizona Senator John McCain for the 2008 Republican nomination even after he had given his word to Rudy Giuliani that he would support the former New York City mayor. Crist's endorsement of McCain was craftily timed and seen as giving McCain the edge he needed to win the Florida primary. That win propelled McCain on the path to the nomination and put Crist on the shortlist of vice presidential candidates. [17]

Initially Crist was 20 points ahead; a year later Rubio was 20 points ahead and Crist left the Republican Party and quit the primary to run as an independent with no party affiliation. The kiss—or hug—of death came in February 2009 when Crist and President Barack Obama embraced on a stage in Ft. Meyers. Crist reluctantly embraced the president as he more readily accepted federal stimulus dollars for the state budget. The photos of the hug proved to be a perception that Crist could not escape—that he embraced the president's agenda. When Crist told Mike Wallace in a Fox debate with Rubio that he would have voted for the stimulus as a Senator it marked the end of support from Florida Republicans for his candidacy. Crist ultimately found his nomination to the Republican nomination blocked by Rubio. He decided to run as an independent candidate, formally called No Party Affiliation (NPA) in Florida, and hoped to secure moderate voters from the center of both the Republican and Democratic Parties.[18] He enjoyed fundraising success, name recognition, a platform as governor, and a reputation as a friendly and likable politician.

Eventually Rubio had the support of the state party establishment including the most popular Florida Republican, former Governor Jeb Bush. Bush campaigned for Rubio and cut commercials for him. This open support was a driving force in putting Rubio on the path to pushing Crist out of the Republican Party. While Rubio was able to avoid a primary battle with Crist and cruise to the nomination, he created a tough situation where he would then have to face both Crist and the Democratic nominee in November.

Kendrick Meek

Kendrick Meek was born and raised in Miami. He played high school and college football and became a State Trooper. Meek had a long but largely undistinguished career in public service following in the path blazed by his pioneering mother, Carrie Meek. She was the first African-American woman elected to the Florida Senate and then the first Black woman elected to Congress from Florida. When she ran for Congress in 1992, Meek took her seat in the state Senate. When she decided not to run for reelection to the U.S. House in 2002 days before the filing deadline it cleared the field for Kendrick to win the nomination uncontested. The 17th Congressional District in North Miami is a majority-minority district, the smallest geographic district in the state and the poorest. Meek has a large physical stature but was not very intimidating politically. His most notable accomplishments in the legislature were a sit-in he conducted in then-Governor Jeb Bush's office over education policy and his support for a class size limit amendment to the state constitution. In Congress, he was criticized for not getting a significant piece of legislation passed and having a weak record on bills he proposed.

After Barack Obama won Florida in 2008, Meek was convinced by a colleague in the House, Alcee Hastings, to run for the Senate. Ironically, Meek was a big backer of Hillary Rodham Clinton in the 2008 primary campaign and remained loyal to the Clintons and friendly with Bill Clinton. The former president was an early supporter and fundraiser for Meek and this helped clear the Democratic field from challengers.

Meek, a four term Congressman, was the party establishment candidate.[19] While recognized politicians sat out the campaign, billionaire businessman Jeff Greene got into the race days before the filing deadline and spent $23 million of his own money on advertising. It was an aggressive and nasty race between Meek and Greene. The contested primary pushed Meek to hone his message and debate skills and better prepared him to take on Rubio and Crist. Still, Meek's campaign emerged from the primary bruised while Rubio's was clicking on all cylinders.

As the general campaign progressed Meek got more aggressive and his political fight awakened. "I'm the only candidate who's fighting for the middle class and I'm not going anywhere except the United States Senate. . . . Because if they want to go back to the Bush years, they're going to have to go through this six foot three inch former state trooper," he said in a campaign statement after rumors surfaced that he would drop out of the race and endorse Crist.[20] Still, he seemed like a political lightweight against the more polished public speakers Crist and Rubio.[21]

CAMPAIGN ISSUES

The main issues of this campaign were the personal integrity of the candidates, the national health care law passed in March 2009, and discussions over Social Security reform and economic debates related to unemployment and housing. Questions about each candidate's integrity, their political associates and the past decisions in which they were involved dominated commercials and debates and overshadowed the focus on substantive and policy-related issues.

Personal Integrity

The character and integrity of each candidate was the main issue in advertisements and in debates. Crist and Rubio were both tied to ethical issues involving the Republican Party of Florida. Crist hand selected Jim Greer, a city councilman from Ovideo and local party chair, to be chair of the state party. Greer's tenure was fraught with incompetence and illegal activity. Greer was eventually removed from the position and faced six felony charges for creating a fake company and funneling party funds to it.[22] While Greer was closely tied to Crist the downfall of the party chair did not have a major impact on Crist's campaign as he was largely able to brush off the guilt by association charges. Rubio's camp did not push this issue since Rubio was the GOP nominee and did not want to highlight the problems in the state party, which also included a credit card scandal.

Rubio was dogged throughout the primary and general campaigns by allegations that he mismanaged his own finances and abused use of a Republican Party issued credit card. It was documented that Rubio used the state GOP card for personal expenses including car repairs and plane tickets that were double expensed along with reimbursements from the legislature. Rubio claimed to repay all personal expenses, after the issue became public, and that other expenses were party related. Crist's campaign accused Rubio of using public office for personal gain while Rubio claimed that Crist's campaign leaked the credit card records to the media.[23] Crist and Meek used this issue to question Rubio's fiscal conservatism. Crist tried to carefully push this story while also avoiding backlash to his campaign. While Crist did not have a party credit card many of his staff members did, and his ally, GOP Chairman Greer, misused party money.

Meek had his own issues to address during the campaign. A highly public case involved an earmark Meek helped to secure in Congress for a low-income housing project in his home district. The developer of the project, Dennis Stackhouse, stole nearly $1 million of the $4 million secured from Congress and the project was never developed. Stackhouse allegedly hired Meek's mother and bought her a luxury car for her services. Also one of Meek's former staff members had received a sweetheart deal on a home mortgage soon after the earmark was approved. The developer went to jail but the failed project tainted the Meek name in their home neighborhood.[24] Questions also arose about a security firm for which Meek once worked that overbilled Miami Dade County and for whom both his mother and wife had lobbied.[25]

Crist's integrity was questioned because he had denied that he would leave the Republican Party up to the deadline for candidate filing. He had said repeatedly he would not run as an independent during a Fox News debate with Rubio hosted by Mike Wallace. Because he switched to no party affiliation, embraced the Democratic president and stimulus package as a Republican governor, and late in the 2010 legislative session vetoed a series of bills pushed by the Republican leadership including one to eliminate teacher tenure that he originally supported, his opponents raised questions about his character and political principles.

All three candidates had the unenviable honor of being named to the Crooked Candidates 2010 list of "the most egregious violators of the public trust" by the Citizens for Responsibility and Ethics in Washington.[26]

Health Care Reform

The national health care debate became one of the main issues in this race. Meek held several town hall events in 2009–2010 in his district and voted for the final bill in March as a House member. He was basically in lockstep with the Democratic position, and would have supported a public option favored by more liberal representatives.

Rubio essentially took the Republican position and talked about the need to repeal the health care law. When pushed he admitted that repeal was not realistic and that he would like to keep some parts of the bill, including the provision that prevents insurance companies from denying coverage to people with preexisting conditions

Crist was in an awkward position over his stances on health care. As a Republican candidate on March 21 he called for repeal of the bill. By July 20, when he was running without party affiliation, Crist's position was that he would not have voted for the law and he was not for repealing it but instead wanted to see the bill be modified. Then on August 27, Crist told a local television reporter that he would have voted for it though he thought that there could have been a better bill. Then two hours later Crist's campaign released a statement where he backtracked from his comments in the television interview.

> If I misspoke, I want to be abundantly clear: the health care bill was too big, too expensive, and expanded the role of government far too much. Had I been in the United States Senate at the time, I would have voted against the bill because of unacceptable provisions like the cuts to the Medicare Advantage program. But being an independent, I have the freedom to be an honest broker for the people of Florida without regard for political party, and the reality is this: despite its serious flaws, the health care bill does have some positive aspects.[27]

From these twists and turns Rubio claimed that Crist had "6 different positions" on health care. PolitiFact Florida, a project of the *St. Petersburg Times* and *The Miami Herald* to investigate campaign claims, found the claim to be "half true" as Crist did not have that many distinct positions though he flipped back and forth on whether or not he would have voted for the bill.[28] These and other position changes led voters to question Crist's honesty and integrity and whether he would say whatever it took to get elected.

Economy

Economic issues were at the forefront nationally, and it was no different in Florida. The unemployment rate in October 2010 was 11.9 percent in Florida compared to 9.7 percent nationally. The housing crisis hit Florida particularly hard. Values drastically dropped, and nearly one in five houses in Florida was in foreclosure in 2010. Despite all of the concerns about the economy, none of the candidates had specific plans for improving the situation. Rubio followed the Republican line of lower taxes and less government spending while Meek defended the economic stimulus package.

Social Security reform was a major component of economic discussions. Most people agree that entitlement reform is needed, but talking about touching Social Security is truly the "third rail" in Florida with the high level of seniors in the state. Rubio discussed increasing the eligibility age for younger citizens and introducing means testing. Crist tried to capitalize on these statements to scare seniors aware from voting for Rubio in television advertisements.[29]

CAMPAIGN STRATEGY

Media

Crist entered the race with the greatest name recognition as the sitting governor. Both Meek and Rubio were well known in their home territories in Miami-Dade County and also were recognized in Tallahassee where both were high profile legislators. But in other parts of the state they needed to get known. The two approaches to doing that were by traveling the state and meeting with grassroots groups and by running high profile media campaigns.

Florida has 10 major media markets, making it very expensive and time consuming to travel the state and cover it with advertisements. Nearly two-thirds of voters live in the three largest markets. The Tampa Bay market is home to the largest share of registered voters (24.4 percent) followed by Miami/Fort Lauderdale (20.5 percent) and Orlando at (19 percent).[30] The most ads were focused in these regions.

Image and Advertising

The popular press tried to portray Rubio as a Tea Party–backed candidate. Rubio tried to present himself as a Ronald Reagan Republican. He used his American Dream-style story as the son of working class Cuban immigrants and his young and photogenic wife and four children to depict a family man image. Rubio often spoke of American Exceptionalism on the campaign trail and appealed to the nation's founding principles.

Crist had high popularity numbers as governor and was personally liked even if his policies were not. After he left the Republican Party he was criticized for "flip-flopping" on several positions including abortion, education reform, the health care law, and offshore oil drilling. Crist ran commercials criticizing partisanship and trying to position himself as a centrist that could appeal to both sides of the spectrum.

As the campaign progressed Crist got more liberal. At the end of the legislative session in April he vetoed three bills championed by conservative Republican leaders, one reestablishing leadership PACS, one that virtually eliminated tenure for public school teachers, and another that mandated an ultrasound before an abortion. During the summer as oil gushed from the Deepwater Horizon oil rig explosion that sent nearly 5 million gallons of oil into the gulf, Crist called for a special session to ban offshore oil drilling. The Republican legislative leaders generally supported expanding drilling and blocked the session and neutralized Crist's ability to politicize the issue. Then during the campaign Crist embraced the economic stimulus package.

Meek had an image of a "political lightweight" who had gotten his political positions with the help of his mother. After a tough primary fight, Meek became a stronger campaigner. His first campaign ad introduced him to Floridians as an everyman who was involved in some way in all of the state's important issues. As the campaign progressed he attacked both Rubio and Crist saying that he was the only true champion of middle class Floridians. Yet Meek was ultimately overshadowed by Rubio and Crist nationally, and Florida Democrats appeared to pay more attention to trying to win the governor's race than to supporting his Senate bid.

CAMPAIGN FINANCE

Crist beefed up his front runner status early by raising a Florida record $4.3 million over 50 days in the second quarter of 2009. Crist gained quick endorsements by many state Republicans and by the National Republican Senatorial Committee and its chairman John Cornyn citing their desire to avoid a costly and divisive primary.

Conservative Senator Jim DeMint of South Carolina embraced Rubio and helped to raise his national profile. DeMint helped Rubio tap into the momentum of the growing Tea Party movement nationally.[31] Rubio gained traction by becoming a frequent guest on conservative radio and television shows and then got a big boost from his headlining speech at the 2010 Conservative Political Action Conference. Mike Huckabee, 2008 presidential candidate, endorsed Rubio, who had supported the former Arkansas governor in the presidential race. Rubio also got the endorsement of former House Majority Leader Dick Armey, which helped him to tap into national conservative fundraising circles. Armey's group FreedomWorks identified the Florida race as a main target for the conservative movement in 2010.[32]

The attention sparked more attention. An MSNBC interviewer introduced Rubio the "GOP's Barack Obama."[33] The *National Review*, a conservative magazine, placed Rubio on the cover in September with the headline, "Yes, HE CAN: Florida conservative Marco Rubio's play for the GOP future." Conservative columnist George Will predicted Rubio would be the next Senator from Florida and on ABC's *This Week*, Will said, "Absolutely, he will win."[34] The conservative Club for Growth helped Rubio raise money. Sean Hannity booked Rubio as a frequent guest and political strategist Karl Rove took an interest in his campaign. Later, moderate presidential candidates Mitt Romney, former Massachusetts governor, and former New York City mayor Rudy Giuliani, jumped on board.[35]

In October 2009, Rubio announced raising $1 million in the quarter. While Crist raised $2.4 million during the same period and still had a 5-to-1 advantage in money, it showed that Rubio was competitive. By 2010, Rubio was raising more money than Crist. Rubio raised $4.5 million in the summer 2010 quarter and broke Crist's record of $4.3 million from the prior year.

Crist's fundraising ability decreased when he left the Republican Party but as the sitting governor Crist could travel the state on official business and schedule campaign activities in off hours. He enjoyed free media appearances from April through September due to the oil spill in the Gulf of Mexico from the explosion of the Deepwater Horizon rig. He also got lots of free publicity due to his unusual independent bid.

There were many calls for Crist to return donations to Republican donors after he left the party but Crist resisted. He ended up returning $220,133 to various sources but only about $20,000 was returned after he left the Republican Party. Despite reports that Crist would return contributions to convicted former state party chair Jim Greer, according to FEC records the money was not returned.[36]

Although Meek was the first announced major candidate in the race and the congressman enjoyed a cozy relationship with former president Clinton, he was unable to keep up with the fundraising prowess of Rubio and Crist. Clinton appeared at least nine fundraisers in Florida and New York and send out emails soliciting funds for Meek. The money support ended when the former president intervened in mid-October to try to convince Meek to drop out and endorse Crist. The hope among Democrats was to rally around one candidate to defeat Rubio, and Crist appeared to have the broader statewide appeal.[37] Several attempts by Clinton to get Meek to quick the race were unsuccessful.

In total, Rubio raised $21,748,330 and spent $21,638,315. $19.4 million (89 percent) was from individuals and $1.2 million (6 percent) from PACs. Crist gathered $13,655,044; individual contributions totaled $12.6 million and $622,291 from PACs. Meek raised $8.8 million and spent $9.2 million with $7 million from individuals and $1.4 million from PACs.[38] Rubio benefited from outside spending by the U.S. Chamber of Commerce, Club for Growth and Karl Rove's "super PAC" American Crossroads.[39] In mid-October the Republican Party pulled $4 million of advertisements in support of Rubio to use the money in other states where it was more needed. The decision indicated that Rubio was sure to defeat Crist and Meek.

Grassroots and Bases of Support

Rubio enjoyed support from the grassroots-based Tea Party movement in Florida. His ability to knock Crist out of the Republican Party stemmed from his successful tour of local conservative clubs and small county party organizations. The movement to help Rubio rise to the top of the ticket came from grassroots support as much as it came from establishment party backers.

Barack Obama's campaign set up a formidable grassroots organization with Organizing for America in 2008 on the way to winning Florida. But the Meek campaign could not tap in to that same network or energize the base in similar ways. The biggest criticism of Democrats during the campaign is that they did not excite the base nor did they mobilize them very well for either Meek's Senate run or for gubernatorial candidate Alex Sink.

Crist lacked grassroots support from the time he left the Republican Party. He tried to tap into his base as a popular governor but was unable to get much organizational traction. He selected his sister to be his campaign manager and ran a populist campaign presenting himself as the "people's governor" and the "people's candidate." Because he had been at the top of state politics for several years, the image was inauthentic and ultimately did not take hold.

ELECTION RESULTS

Rubio won the Senate seat with 49 percent (2,615,262) of the vote to 30 percent (1,588,821) for Crist and 20 percent (1,076,028) for Meek. Rubio won all of

Florida's 67 counties except four.[40] Crist won heavily Democratic Broward and Palm Beach Counties as well as Leon County, home of state capital Tallahassee, where Crist was serving as governor. Meek won Gadsden County, with a heavily African American population east of Leon and on the Georgia border.[41]

Exit polls showed Rubio with an advantage in most categories. Rubio won a majority of Whites (74 percent of total voters with 55 percent support for Rubio) and Latinos (12 percent of voters with 55 percent support for Rubio). Meek, who is African American, won 74 percent of the Black vote (11 percent of voters). Rubio won a plurality or majority of all age and income groups. Rubio won a majority of all education groups except those at the postgraduate level which Crist won by 42 percent to 40 percent over Rubio. Of those people who said that the economy was the number one issue facing the country Rubio got 50 percent of the vote.[42]

Rubio won a majority of males and a plurality of females. He got 55 percent of the male vote compared to 28 percent for Crist and 17 percent for Meek. Among females Rubio gained 44 percent of the vote compared to 33 percent for Crist and 22 percent for Meek. Breaking it down for both race and gender Rubio got 61 percent of White men and 50 percent of White women which were 33 percent and 41 percent of the total, respectively. He won 54 percent of Latino men and 55 percent of Latino women which each accounted for 6 percent of the total voters. Meek got 72 percent of Black men (6 percent of total) and 75 percent of Black women (7 percent of total) while Crist scored 21 percent of each group and Rubio got 6 percent and 3 percent respectively.

Rubio got a plurality of voters with income (39 percent) under $30,000 and of those earning $30-$50,000 (45 percent) while getting a majority of those making $50–75,000 (52 percent), $75–100,000 (58 percent), $100–200,000 (56 percent) and $200,000 or more (52 percent). Meek came in second place amongst the lowest earners but Crist came in second among all other categories mainly around the 30 percent of the vote that he received for the entire election.

By education, Rubio got a majority of high school graduates (53 percent to 24 percent for Crist and 22 percent for Meek) while getting 50 percent of the people with some college (31 percent of voters) and 50 percent of the college graduates (32 percent of voters). These vote totals mirrored the overall results.

The party identification question shows that Rubio got 87 percent of Republicans (36 percent of total) while Crist got 12 percent. Rubio got 51 percent of Independent voters (29 percent of total) while Crist got 38 percent and Meek got 10 percent support. Meek won the Democrat vote (36 percent of total) with 47 percent to 44 percent for Crist and 8 percent for Rubio.

Not surprisingly, Rubio got 86 percent support from those who said they supported the Tea Party (40 percent of voters) and 44 percent from voters who were neutral to the Tea Party (24 percent). Crist gained 55 percent of the voters who opposed the Tea Party while Meek got support from 39 percent of those voters (32 percent of the total). While those who supported the Tea Party overwhelmingly voted for Rubio, 61 percent of exit poll respondents said that the Tea Party was not a factor in their overall vote decision.[43]

CONCLUSION

There are several reasons why Marco Rubio won this race. First, he got more votes among most demographics across the state. It helped that Crist and Meek split independent and moderate votes, but Rubio had solid support across education and income categories, reliable support from Hispanic voters, and a majority of white voters.

Second, it was a Republican year nationally and in Florida. Republicans, already strong in Florida, swept the state elections and their solid turnout buoyed by Tea Party support helped to elect Rubio and to keep the seat in Republican hands.

Next, Rubio ran a largely flawless campaign. He was the youngest candidate in the race but he was also the most disciplined campaigner. He mainly avoided personal attacks on his opponents. While he was largely critical of the Obama administration's policies, he resisted temptations to personally criticize the president. He stayed on message, used social media, and benefited from a national conservative movement that made him a media star. After an early flap over the use of Twitter to communicate private information about himself and his wife, Rubio used social media responsibly and reliably throughout the campaign to inform his supporters without making any gaffes or providing fodder for his opponents.[44]

While each of the candidates could be attacked about financial issues and relations with people attached to their campaigns, Rubio did a good job deflecting media and popular criticism while keeping focus on his opponents' flaws.

Finally, and maybe most importantly, Rubio raised more money than Crist and Meek. Rubio's $22 million was nearly more than Crist's $13.5 million and Meek's $8.8 million combined. Rubio also benefited from expenditures by outside groups.

Rubio exploded onto the national political stage as a poster boy for the Tea Party movement and the face of the next generation of Republican leaders.[45] But he was not a Tea Party candidate. He is tied to the Republican establishment and also has support from the Tea Party movement. Rubio has one foot in each camp but his head and heart are with the GOP establishment. Many people already mentioned Rubio as a vice presidential candidate for

2012 before he was inaugurated to the U.S. Senate. Some even suggested that he should run for president. In this political environment, one never knows. What is clear is that Rubio will be a force for the GOP's next generation and his party is already looking to him for leadership.

NOTES

1. Florida Division of Elections. election.dos.state.fl.us/elections/resultsarchive/Index.asp?ElectionDate=11/2/2004&DATAMODE=.

2. Florida Division of Elections. election.dos.state.fl.us/voter-registration/statistics/elections.shtml#2010.

3. David Colburn and Lance DeHaven-Smith. 2010. *Florida's Megatrends: Critical Issues in Florida*, Second Edition. University Press of Florida.

4. Alex Leary and Adam C. Smith. "Sen. Mel Martinez resigns; Crist will appoint replacement," *St. Petersburg Times*. August 8, 2009. www.tampabay.com/news/politics/national/article1025671.ece.

5. Florida QuickFacts, U.S. Census Bureau. quickfacts.census.gov/qfd/states/12000.html.

6. Kevin Hill, Susan A. MacManus, and Dario Moreno, eds. and contributors, *Florida Politics: Ten Media Markets, One Powerful State*. Tallahassee, FL: Florida Institute of Government, 2004.

7. Rubio's father passed away two months before Election Day prompting Rubio to take some time off from the campaign. His father' illness caused Rubio to cancel a *Meet the Press* appearance scheduled with Meek.

8. Tim Elfrink, "Marco Rubio, Tea Party pretty boy," *Miami New Times*. July 22, 2010.; Project Vote Smart. Senator Marco Rubio (FL). www.votesmart.org/bio.php?can_id=1601 (accessed February 25, 2011).

9. Alex Leary, "Marco Rubio's meteoric rise in Florida politics," *St. Petersburg Times*. October 9, 2010.

10. Elfrink 2010.; Bush won the gubernatorial office that November.

11. Elfrink 2010; Leary 2010.

12. Michael Worley, "The Rise of Marco Rubio," (paper presented at American University, November 2010).

13. Leary 2010.

14. Controversy surrounded his appointment at Florida International University as he earned an unadvertised teaching position as the public university was undergoing budget cuts. Rubio was responsible for fund raising half of his salary and exceeded that expectation.

15. Adam C. Smith, "In Shift, Marco Rubio is willing to battle Charlie Crist for Senate," *St. Petersburg Times*. April 14, 2009.

16. Rubio and his wife have 4 children.

17. In December 2008, Crist married Carole Rome, a wealthy New York socialite who also had a home on Fisher Island in Miami Beach. There was skepticism about

the marriage as rumors circulated that Crist was gay, a story that was perpetuated in the movie *Outrage*.

18. Peter Wallsten. "Crist Uses His Old Party as a New Foil: Senate Push Gains as Florida Governor Sets Himself Off against State's GOP, with Some Firepower from Obama Camp," *Wall Street Journal* Online. July 20, 2010. online.wsj.com/article/SB10001424052748704229004575371810495691530. html?KEYWORDS=crist.

19. Susan MacManus with the assistance of David J. Bonanza. "Voter Demographics: Florida Registration and Voting Patterns by Media Market," 2010. SayfieReview.com www.sayfiereview.com/documents/Media_Market_Makeup.pdfelection. dos.state.fl.us/elections/resultsarchive/Index.asp?ElectionDate=8/24/2010&DATAM ODE= (accessed February 28, 2011).

20. "Rumors of Meek's Drop Out Greatly Exaggerated." NBCMiami.com. October 13, 2010. www.nbcmiami.com/news/local/Rumors-of-Meeks-Drop-Out-Greatly-Exaggerated—104588344.html.

21. Jane Musgrave. "Fear of Rubio helps Crist get Democrats; The governor is siphoning," *Palm Beach Post*. September 23, 2010. findarticles.com/p/news-articles/ palm-beach-post/mi_8163/is_20100923/fear-rubio-helps-crist-democrats/ai_n55358517

22. Aaron Deslatte and Rene Stutzman. "Florida GOP ex-Chairman Jim Greer leaves jail after being indicted," *Orlando Sentinel*. June 2, 2010. articles.orlandosentinel. com/2010–06–02/news/os-republican-jim-greer-arrested-20100602_1_victory-strategies-llc-jim-greer-mr-greer (accessed March 10, 2011); Marc Caputo. "Ex-Florida GOP chairman Jim Greer arrested on 6 felony charges," *The Miami Herald*. June 2, 2010. www.miamiherald.com/2010/06/02/1659715/ex-florida-gop-chairman-jim-greer.html#ixzz1KBnvZWQo.

23. William March. "Credit use has Rubio on spot," *The Tampa Tribune*. www2 .tbo.com/content/2010/feb/26/na-credit-use-has-rubio-on-spot/news-politics/?utm_ source=feedburner&utm_medium=feed&utm_campaign=Feed%3A+tbo%2Fpolitics +%28TBO+%3E+Politics%29 (accessed January 25, 2010). The car repairs occurred after Rubio's vehicle was allegedly damaged by a valet parker at a party event. Other charges included local grocery stores and a computer store near Rubio's home and an undetermined charge of $130 at a barber shop. When Rubio was vague in explaining the charge, Crist claimed on Fox News that "maybe it was a back wax." Andy Barr. "Charlie Crist suggests Marco Rubio got 'back wax'" *Politico*. www.politico.com/ news/stories/0310/34117.html (accessed February 24, 2011).

24. PolitiFact Florida. "Is Kendrick Meek the second most corrupt Democrat in Congress," August 3, 2010. www.politifact.com/florida/statements/2010/ aug/03/jeff-greene/kendrick-meek-second-most-corrupt-democrat-congres/; Jason Grotto. "Developer reaped millions for biotech park never built," *The Miami Herald*. June 24, 2007. www.miamiherald.com/multimedia/news/povped/part1/index .html#ixzz1KBqMpDOW.

25. Beth Reinhard. "Kendrick Meek downplays his ties to controversial Wackenhut," *The Miami Herald*. August 10, 2010. www.miamiherald.com/2010/08/10/1768738/ kendrick-meek-downplays-his-ties.html#ixzz1KBu5dnGQ.

26. Crooked Candidates 2010. www.citizensforethics.org/crookedcandidates2010 (accessed February 26, 2011).

27. PolitiFact Florida. "Marco Rubio says Charlie Crist has taken 'six different positions' on health care law," PolitiFact.com. politifact.com/florida/statements/2010/sep/02/marco-rubio/rubio-says-crist-has-taken-six-different-positions/ September 2, 2010.

28. PolitiFact Florida. "Marco Rubio says Charlie Crist has taken 'six different positions.'"

29. Beth Reinhard. "Heading into Wednesday's debate, Crist hammers Rubio over Social Security," *The Miami Herald.* October 6, 2010.

30. MacManus with Bonanza.

31. Steven F. Hayes. "It was Rubio's Tuesday: The most important freshman senator," WeeklyStandard.com. November 15, 2010. www.weeklystandard.com/articles/it-was-rubio-s-tuesday_515082.html (accessed January 27, 2011.

32. Peter Wallsten. "Crist Faces Test From Right in Bid for Senate," *The Wall Street Journal.* November 4, 2009.

33. www.nbcmiami.com/news/local/Rubio-Coined-the-Next-Obama.html (accessed February 26, 2011).

34. George Will. "A Ripe time for Florida's Marco Rubio," *Washington Post* September 27, 2009, www.washingtonpost.com/wp-dyn/content/article/2009/09/25/AR2009092502470.html; www.youtube.com/watch?v=xodQI8sAms8 (accessed February 26, 2011).

35. Guiliani's move was popularly viewed as payback to Crist who had promised to endorse him in the 2008 presidential campaign only to switch to McCain right before the Florida primary, a move that is seen as helping McCain to win Florida and ultimately the Republican nomination.

36. FEC.gov www.fec.gov/DisclosureSearch/HSProcessContributorList.do.

37. Ben Smith. "Bill Clinton pushed Meek to quit Florida race," *Politico.* October 28, 2010. www.politico.com/news/stories/1010/44337.html.

38. Open Secrets. 2010 race: Florida Senate. www.opensecrets.org/races/summary.php?id=FLS2&cycle=2010# (accessed March 7, 2011).

39. Beth Reinhard. "Outsider 'super PAC' a boost for Marco Rubio," The Miami Herald. September 30, 2010. www.miamiherald.com/2010/09/30/1849537/outsider-super-pac-a-boost-for.html (accessed March 10, 2011).

40. *elections.nytimes.com/2010/results/florida* (date accessed January 20, 2011).

41. Damien Cave. "Rubio Continues Quick Rise in G.O.P. With Win in Florida Senate Race," *The New York Times.* November 2, 2010. www.nytimes.com/2010/11/03/us/politics/03florida.html (accessed January 20, 2011).

42. CNN Election Center. www.cnn.com/ELECTION/2010/results/polls/#val=FLS01p1 (accessed March 7, 2011).

43. CNN Election Center.

44. miamiherald.typepad.com/nakedpolitics/2009/05/rubios-wife-takes-forever-to-blowdry-her-hair.html#ixzz1HYcmrNAd (accessed March 22, 2011).

45. Mark Leibovich. "The First Senator From the Tea Party?" *The New York Times.* January 6, 2010. www.nytimes.com/2010/01/10/magazine/10florida-t.html.

Chapter 14

Missouri Senate Race (Blunt v. Carnahan)

Still a National Bellwether State

Daniel E. Smith

Roy D. Blunt
Party: Republican
Age: 60
Sex: Male
Race: Caucasian
Religion: Baptist
Education: B.A., Southwest Baptist University; M.A., Missouri State University
Occupation: History teacher; President of Southwest Baptist University (1993–96)
Political Experience: Green Co. Clerk (1973–1984); MO Secretary of State (1984–1993); U.S. House (1997–2010)

Robin Carnahan
Party: Democrat
Age: 49
Sex: Female
Race: Caucasian
Religion: Baptist
Education: B.A., William Jewel College; J.D., University of Virginia
Occupation: Practicing attorney; National Democratic Institute; U.S. Import-Export Bank
Political Experience: MO Secretary of State, (2005–present)

In 2006, nationally all eyes were on the Missouri Senate race, and Missouri lived up to its billing as a bellwether state. When Rep. Roy Blunt (R-MO) and

Missouri Secretary of State Robin Carnahan announced their candidacies in 2009, attention turned once again to Missouri, and not simply because it was an open seat and the contenders represented two Missouri political dynasties. Unlike 2006, however, the 2010 Senate race never lived up to its potential as a close, competitive battleground race, and attention of the politicos turned elsewhere. Rather, a combination of predictable state, local and national trends, including a significant partisan wave, plus significant gaps both in funding and campaign effectiveness, resulted in a comfortable win for the more entrenched, establishment candidate.

CHARACTERISTICS OF MISSOURI

Missouri has long been perceived as a bellwether state for national elections—presidential and Senate races. First, Missourians had voted for the winner in all but two presidential elections in the past 100 years. Until 2010, the state's seats in the House of Representatives were nearly evenly divided, with incumbents of both parties winning reelection handily through 2008, while it was common for the state's two Senators to be from different parties. In terms of political demographics, the state's two large urban centers, St. Louis and Kansas City, vote heavily Democratic—the inner cities overwhelmingly so, while the suburbs are more competitive—whereas with a handful of exceptions, the entire rest of the state votes decisively Republican in national and statewide elections. In addition, the state's geopolitical status tracks its physical location—near the center of the nation, straddling the Midwestern and southern Bible belts, yet still connected to the urban upper Midwest.

Second, in the elections cycles leading up to 2010, Missouri was for a time viewed as "leaning red," poised to become a solid Republican state. In addition to supporting President George W. Bush in 2000 and 2004 by solid margins, Missouri voters elected a Republican governor, Matt Blunt in 2004, following two Democratic governors; replaced Democratic Senator Jean Carnahan with Sen. Jim Talent in a 2002 special election; and have steadily expanded Republican majorities in both houses of the state legislature since early this century. This Republican majority enacted a number of core conservative agenda items, including term limits for state legislators, a sweeping ban on same-sex unions, an allowance for concealed weapons, and in 2010, a symbolic rejection of the federal healthcare reform act. The Senate election in 2006 bucked this trend, yet in 2008 Republican candidate John McCain (R-AZ) carried the state, albeit by the thinnest of margins. One question tested by the 2010 Senate race, then, was whether Claire McCaskill's (D-MO) victory in 2006 and the razor-thin McCain win were part of a larger statewide shift away from the "leaning red" tendency, widespread dissatisfaction with President Bush and his allies, candidate-driven success, or simply a temporary "throttling back" from trending Republican.[1] In this regard, the Missouri Senate race was a measuring stick for the national mood toward President Barak Obama, his policies, and his party; and the ability of the opposition party—this time the Republicans—to capitalize on a hostile political environment for the party in power reminiscent not merely of 2006, but 1994.

Third, both the primary and general elections included ballot measures further testing the state's bellwether status. Although these issues were not nearly as high-profile as stem cell research or the minimum wage increase in 2006, three of these issues—the anti-health insurance mandate on the ballot during the August primary election, and several anti-tax measures on the general election ballot—embodied important state and national election narratives: anger toward President Obama and the Democratic party; anti-establishment and anti-government; and the power of conservative groups to dominate the political discourse. These ballot measures tracked Republican legislators' efforts to further cement Missouri as a low tax, low public services state; in 2009 the state spent $3,852 per capita, ranking forty-fifth among the states and well below the national average of $5,038.[2] As will be discussed, unlike 2006 or 2008, these issues did have an impact on the Senate race.

DEMOGRAPHIC CHARACTER OF THE ELECTORATE

Population

Based on the 2010 Census, Missouri was home to approximately six million people at the time of the 2010 election; over half the total population and close to 60 percent of the state's eligible voters resided in the St. Louis or Kansas City suburban areas.[3] The state's population density of 86.9 is closer to the national average than any other state, however, aside from the two large urban areas, and a handful of smaller cities which hold up to 5,100 people per square mile, the population density tracks that of most rural states in the United States; the vast majority of the state is classified as rural and small town.

Income

Median household annual income was $46,847, based on 2008 estimates, over $5,000 less than the national average. 13.5 percent have incomes below the poverty line, which is above the national average. Nevertheless, the vast majority of the state's residents, over 70 percent (2000 Census data), own their own homes, which is common in a predominantly rural state.

Education

81.3 percent of the state's residents above age 25 have completed high school, which is slightly above the national average; however, the percentage holding bachelor's degrees, 21.6 percent is nearly three points below the national average (2000 Census data).

Race, Ethnicity, Gender, and Age

Even accounting for its large urban centers, Missouri is not known for its racial or ethnic diversity. According to 2009 data, the state is 89.1 percent white, non-Hispanic, 11.6 percent African American, 3.4 percent Hispanic, 1.5 percent Asian, and 0.5 percent Native American. 96.4 percent of the total state population is foreign-born, and just 4 percent speak a primary language other than English. Just over half the population, 51.1 percent, is female; 13.7 percent are over 65, and 23.9 percent are under 18.

Religion

The state is overwhelmingly Christian, with representation of other religious groups below the national average. Approximately 77 percent of state residents describe themselves as Christians—45 percent Baptist, Methodist or another Protestant denomination, and 19 percent Catholic. 15 percent of state residents describe themselves as non-religious; only 2 percent self-identify as religious but non-Christian. Muslims, Jews and Hindus are present in the urban areas, particularly Kansas City, but their combined numbers are less than 2 percent.[4] According to a January 2009 Gallup poll, 68 percent of Missourians consider religion to be an important part of their daily lives.[5] Based on 2006 data, 46 percent attend religious services regularly;[6] however, this number is closer to 50 percent in many of the state's rural areas.

PARTY BALANCE AND ELECTORAL HISTORY

As noted earlier, the Missouri electoral map is unusual. It is, of course, common for urban areas to be bastions of Democratic strength, and for rural areas to be heavily Republican. Missouri, however, takes these characteristics to extremes. In recent statewide elections Democrats have won St. Louis and Kansas City, typically by wide margins; while Republicans have won everywhere else by even wider margins. Statewide races over the past decade have been decided by turnout in St. Louis and Kansas City, and the overall margin of victory for Republicans in the entire rest of the state. These electoral characteristics are the result of Missouri being essentially two states politically, economically, culturally, and demographically.[7]

This dramatic partisan divide was not always the case. Along with its track record of choosing winners in presidential elections, Missouri has a long history of electing moderates of both parties to national and statewide office, of splitting its two Senators between the parties, and of electing governors and Senators of different parties; these trends have continued during the past decade. But from the mid-1990s until 2006, Democrats essentially conceded rural Missouri to Republicans in statewide races, all the while losing significant ground in the statehouse; and those areas moved steadily towards more conservative positions. Of course partisanship is often quite different at the local level. Many of the thousands of small towns throughout rural Missouri elect Democrats to local office. However, there is often little difference between voters and local candidates in these areas, and on social issues in particular, conservative Democrats will vote Republican in statewide elections.

The 2006 Senate race and the 2008 presidential race slowed this trend. After narrowly losing the gubernatorial race in 2004, Senator McCaskill made a conscious, sustained effort to compete statewide, by crafting a message that would resonate with small-town and rural voters, and by actively traveling to the most remote areas during the campaign. She did not win rural Missouri, but she successfully closed the partisan gap and was able to win the election. In 2008 then-candidate Obama followed the McCaskill game plan, even employing the Senator extensively in the state, and fought to a virtual tie in the statewide vote.

Key Voting Blocs

The geographic and demographic duality of the state also largely determines its key voting blocs. The rural, less populated expanses of the state are socially conservative, generally suspicious of government regulation, yet focused on aid and support for the agricultural industries. By contrast, the urban areas of St. Louis and Kansas City are more ethnically diverse, and face the plethora of economic and social issues associated with urban decay, struggling schools and high poverty rates; for these voters, government is viewed far more favorably, particularly regarding provision of services. The suburban areas are distinct as well—more white collar and service industry jobs, higher per capita incomes, more economic and social stability, yet less homogeneous and social conservative value-driven voting patterns. As a result, the suburbs are more evenly divided politically than the urban or rural portions of the states.

Missouri also has a significant senior citizen population, representing nearly 14 percent of the public (and a higher percentage of voters).[8] Again, however, age tends to manifest itself consistent with the geographic and other demographic patterns, that is, older urban voters vote differently than older rural voters. In addition, due to the lack of racial, ethnic, religious and cultural diversity in most of the state, and the concentration of such diversity the two urban areas, candidates can routinely treat the socially conservative white majority, and the more liberal, diverse minority, as distinct voting blocs which can be targeted, or shielded, in campaign strategy. This results in candidates, especially Republican candidates, touting socially conservative credentials and assailing even the slightest deviation from those values, in canvassing efforts, while backing off such efforts in large media buys.

THE CANDIDATES

Roy D. Blunt

At the time of the election, Roy Blunt was completing his seventh term as U.S. Representative of the 7th District of Missouri. The 7th District, located in the Ozark Mountains of southwestern Missouri, encompasses the cities of Springfield and Joplin, and is arguably the most conservative district in the state. Blunt was first elected in 1996 when the incumbent, Republican Mel Hancock, honored a term limit pledge and did not seek reelection. Blunt was then reelected six times without serious opposition. Prior to serving in Congress, Blunt served as Missouri's Secretary of State from 1985 to 1993; ran unsuccessfully for governor in 1992; then served as President of Southwest Baptist University from 1993 to 1996. He also served a number of years as Clerk of Greene County, beginning in 1972.

While in the House of Representatives, Blunt initially served on the House Committees on Agriculture, Transportation and International Relations; he eventually moved up to the more powerful committees on Energy and Commerce, and Intelligence. More significantly, he also rose rapidly in the Republican Party organization under Speaker Newt Gingrich and Majority Leader Tom Delay. He served as Chief Deputy Whip from 1999–2003, then another four years as Majority Whip from 2003–2007.[9] He became Acting Majority Leader when Rep. Delay resigned his office in 2005, but in 2006 was defeated by John Boehner in his effort to become Majority Leader. His defeat was due in part to the party's concerns about his close ties with Mr. Delay and scandals surrounding the same.[10] In addition to being Delay's close associate and hand-picked successor, Blunt served as the Republican House's key liaison for the "K Street Project," an organization that coordinated contributions from political action committees to Republican members of Congress. He was accused of benefiting clients of convicted lobbyist Jack Abramoff while accepting campaign contributions from Abramoff; he was also alleged to have introduced, and attempted to introduce, legislative proposals which directly benefited clients of his then-girlfriend (now wife) and one of his sons, who were lobbyists for Philip Morris and UPS, respectively.[11] While he was never indicted, the political fall of Delay and Abramoff's conviction diminished Blunt's political stock in the House, and created a potential Achilles heel for his Senate campaign.

The Blunt family is heavily involved in politics, which led many to describe the 2010 Senate race as a battle of dynasties. This is partly accurate. Blunt's father served a number of years in the state legislature; his son Matt is a former Governor of Missouri; his wife and youngest son from his first marriage are Washington lobbyists; and his son Andy has run his and Matt's campaigns.[12] However, Blunt himself has established a family legacy, rather than being born into one. He married his current wife in 2003; the couple adopted a young Russian orphan, Alexander Charles, in 2006. Blunt has three adult children from his first marriage, and six grandchildren.

Blunt is solidly conservative both on social and economic issues. His opposition to abortion, same-sex marriage and gay adoption, and his support for school prayer and Second Amendment rights have earned him over 90 percent ratings from the American Conservative Union and the Christian Coalition, and an A rating from the NRA.[13] On health care, he not only has been a vocal opponent of the recent legislation, but he is on record questioning the creation and continued existence of Medicare.[14] His opposition to financial regulations has earned him a 97 percent rating from the U.S. Chamber of Commerce,[15] and his opposition to environmental measures have earned him disdain from the League of Conservation Voters.[16] He does, however, have a record of bipartisanship on a handful of issues; three examples include his opposition to an expanded school voucher program; his work across the aisle to legislate restrictions on precursors to methamphetamines, and on revisions to the Foreign Intelligence Surveillance Act.[17]

During the primary season, there was a flurry of activity from the conservative wing of the Republican Party. Ultra-conservative candidate Chuck Pergason mounted an insurgent campaign, criticizing Blunt's support for the TARP program, his Washington insider status, and his unwillingness to cut government spending. Ultimately, however, Pergason was unable to raise sufficient funds to run a competitive primary challenge, winning just over 13 percent of the primary vote. Kristi Nichols, a self-styled Tea Party candidate, also sought the Republican nomination, winning 7 percent of the vote. Blunt won nearly 72 percent of the primary vote,[18] meaning that his challengers did not provide a sufficient threat to his *bona fides* as Republican standard-bearer.

Robin Carnahan

Like her opponent, Robin Carnahan comes from a political family, but her "legacy" is more extensive. Her grandfather served multiple terms in the U.S. House of Representatives, and her father Mel Carnahan served two terms as governor of the state before being elected to U.S. Senate posthumously in 2000, after losing his life in a tragic plane accident during the Senate campaign. Her mother Jean Carnahan served as U.S. Senator following the 2000 election until she was defeated in a special election by James Talent in 2002. And her brother Russ Carnahan is the current U.S. Representative for Missouri's 3rd District, a position he has held since 2005.

Carnahan was elected Missouri Secretary of State, her first political office, in 2004; and was easily reelected in 2008. Prior to her election, she practiced law in St. Louis, then spent several years in central Europe working for the National Democratic Institute, an organization which assists emerging democracies through leadership training, drafting laws and monitoring elections. She has also served as assistant to the Chairman of the United States Export-Import Bank. While Secretary of State, Carnahan co-chaired the Elections Committee of the bipartisan National Association of Secretaries of State, and chaired the Democratic Association of Secretaries of State.[19] In her professional career prior to holding elected office, and as Secretary of State, she has developed a reputation for working across party lines; nonetheless, she has also been extremely active in the Democratic Party, both as an official and in support of candidates nationally and statewide.

In addition to her duties as Secretary of State, Carnahan continued to manage her family's farm and cattle operation outside of Rolla, Missouri. She is also an avid pilot, and frequently flew herself to and from campaign stops. Her husband—who unlike other members of her family and the Blunt family maintained a remarkably low profile, if not total invisibility, during the campaign—works in the computer field. Finally, Carnahan has a compelling personal story, which leading up to the Senate race had helped endear her to the public: not only did she lose her father—a popular public servant—to a tragic accident, but she is a breast cancer survivor, having been diagnosed during her first term as Secretary of State.[20]

Carnahan has staked out moderate to center-left positions on a variety of issues. On social issues, she is pro-choice, opposes gay marriage but is open to extending legal rights to same-sex couples. She has actively supported government investment in green jobs, most notably the 2009 American Recovery and Reinvestment Act (aka the "stimulus plan"), but stated that she would have opposed the 2008 TARP bailout legislation. She supported the healthcare reform legislation, and would have supported a "public option" in that legislation.[21] These positions, particularly her support for the healthcare and stimulus initiatives of President Obama, left her vulnerable to attack in the campaign.

CAMPAIGN ISSUES

A number of policy issues were addressed by the candidates in the campaign. Sadly, as has become the norm in hyper-partisan political campaigns, serious discussion of the issues deteriorated quite rapidly in a series of generalizations, talking points and personal attacks by both campaigns. Given the weak national economy, bleak job picture, and public frustration with the national government's efforts to address conditions, economic issues were front and center, often framed as referenda on President Obama and the Democratic Party.

The Economy: Stimulus, Bailouts, and Taxes

A weak economy is typically a boon for minority party candidates, particularly when the White House is held by the opposing party. But perhaps the most interesting question of the 2010 Senate race was whether Blunt, a long-term Washington insider and part of the Republican leadership that took the fall for the economic collapse in 2008, would be able to capitalize on continued bleak economic news just two years later. Blunt was a leading player in the Republican-controlled national government that was widely blamed for widespread corruption, exploding deficits, two costly wars and, in particular, the financial meltdown, recession and job losses which began in 2007. The crown jewel of public anger, and an event which launched the Tea Party movement, was the TARP program, passed under President Bush shortly before the 2008 presidential election. Blunt played a vital role in securing passage of TARP, which came to be viewed by the public, correctly or not, as a taxpayer-funded bailout resulting in a windfall to the very large financial institutions that had caused the financial crisis, while ordinary Americans lost their homes, their savings and their pensions.

By 2010, however, public frustration had been redirected at the new Democratic president and his party, due in part to an aggressive public relations campaign by the Republican minority in Congress, but also due to two high-profile policy initiatives by President Obama and the Democratic-controlled Congress in 2009: the stimulus package and the auto industry bailout. The stimulus, which combined grants to the states—to preserve state jobs, rebuild/repair infrastructure and promote alternative energy—and tax cuts, had a price tag of nearly $800 billion, which exceeded the cost of the financial industry bailout the previous year. And while the non-partisan Congressional Budget Office has asserted, and economists have widely agreed, that the stimulus added or saved in the neighborhood of two million jobs, the widely held perception is that the program did not create jobs[22] and, in any case, was far too expensive. The auto industry bailout was also judged a success by non-partisan sources, in that Chrysler and American Motors were able to reorganize and continue operations; yet it was also perceived by large numbers of Missouri voters as another example of wasteful spending and government encroachment on the private sector. In particular, this smaller bailout presented the Republican party with an opportunity to hang the "bailout" label on President Obama, notwithstanding the fact that the TARP "bailout" was proposed by, and adopted under, President Bush. The candidates differed a bit less on other government spending questions. Carnahan advocated balancing the federal budget and an outright ban on congressional earmarks; nonetheless she also supported spending as a way to preserve Missouri public sector jobs and stimulate new business. Blunt defended the earmark process as a way to ensure that Missouri "gets our fair share," while also advocating reductions in federal spending. He opposed virtually all of President Obama's economic efforts, but supported, at least in the abstract, efforts to stimulate job creation, particularly in U.S.-based energy.[23]

A related set of campaign issues dealt with the status of the Bush tax cuts, which had been adopted in 2001 and were due to expire at the end of 2010. If Americans like tax cuts, Missourians are deeply, passionately in love with them, irrespective of the budgetary ramifications. Consequently, both candidates supported extending the tax cuts; the only debate between them was whether or not to make all of the tax cuts permanent down the road.

Health Care Policy: (Obamacare) and Health Care Reform

Another key component in the Blunt campaign's "big government" narrative was, of course, the landmark healthcare reform legislation, strategically labeled "Obamacare" by Republicans. Due to the law's length and complexity, the drawn-out legislative battles prior to passage, the gradual phasing in of many of the most important benefits, and conflicting reports about the projected fiscal ramifications; the law proved far easier to attack, and far more difficult to promote, than had been expected when President Obama and his party campaigned heavily on the issue in 2008. As of the 2010 election, the law proved to be remarkably unpopular in the state, as demonstrated in the August ballot initiative discussed below. The Carnahan campaign was forced to play defense regarding healthcare, stressing particular benefits for Missouri families.

Statewide Ballot Issues

There were several high-profile ballot issues in Missouri in 2010. It is difficult to calculate the impact of these issues on the Senate campaign, as they were not the subject of regular polling throughout the campaign season the way the stem cell and minimum wage issues were in 2006. We can, however, take note of these issues as indicative of the voters' attitudes towards economic policy, most notably taxes and government regulation.

The highest profile ballot issue was Proposition C, the largely symbolic opposition to the national health insurance mandate, which was presented on the August 2010 primary election ballot. The measure passed overwhelmingly, 71 percent to 29 percent, with over 920,000 votes cast.[24] Because the vote took place in the primary election, it is unlikely that Proposition C had any direct effect on the outcome of the general election, however, it did energize conservative Republican voters and reinforce the Republican narrative, used effectively by the Blunt campaign moving forward, that President Obama, and Robin Carnahan as a supporter of his agenda, stood for government expansion at the expense of individual freedom.[25]

Three other ballot measures, each of which was approved in the general election, also reinforced the dominant campaign themes. Constitutional Amendment 3 imposed a preemptive ban on creation of real estate transfer taxes. Proposition A repealed the authority of municipalities to impose local earnings taxes, and required municipalities with existing earnings taxes (Kansas City and St. Louis) to put continuance of those taxes to a popular vote every five years. These two proposals were presented and debated as anti-tax measures, and each passed by overwhelming margins; the fact that no transfer taxes had been proposed or were contemplated was irrelevant to Amendment 3; and the fiscal implications of Proposition A were not seriously discussed. The final ballot measure, Proposition B, was designed to curtail animal cruelty in so-called "puppy mills." Irrespective of the merits, debate over this proposal was cast as animal treatment versus government encroachment on business; the measure barely passed, 51.6 percent to 48.4 percent.[26] Missourians have a long and rich history of voting on ballot measures without regard, or impact, upon candidate selection.[27] Taken as a whole, however, these items reinforced a powerful anti-government theme, which was at the heart of the Senate race.

CAMPAIGN STRATEGY

As noted above, the principal theme of the campaign was voter anxiety regarding the poor state of the economy. This anxiety was coupled with a palpable anger towards the national government in general, and incumbents in particular, fueled by a sense of frustration with excessive, yet perceived ineffective government spending. In short, the public in Missouri was angry at government's inability to fix the economy, and angry at government for its efforts to do so; this anger magnified Missourians' pre-existing inclinations to oppose government on principle, and the perceived government expansion by the Obama administration in particular. Not surprisingly, the Blunt campaign sought to accomplish two primary objectives: (1) tie his opponent as closely as possible to President Obama and the national Democratic agenda; and (2) insulate the Congressman, to the extent possible, from attacks based on his Washington insider status. For its part, the Carnahan campaign attempted to claim "outsider" status, casting Blunt as part of the problem with Washington, and Robin Carnahan as a crusader for fiscal responsibility and ethics in government; and to tread a fine line between claiming the mantle of "change" and being associated with an unpopular President. Moreover, due to the complexity of the economic problems, neither candidate was particularly willing to engage the public, or the political opposition, in substantive debate on the economy. Each candidate therefore staked out a number of vague policy positions; took specific positions on symbolic, yet substantively minor issues; and relied upon largely negative messages about the opponent.

Carnahan focused much of her campaign efforts on government reform-fiscal responsibility and ethics. She also sought to turn the stagnant economy back onto her opponent, and his party's failures over the past decade: "We have been living with Congressman Roy Blunt's jobs plan [for the past several years;] that's what got us into this mess in the first place."[28] She proposed bans on earmarks; stricter government ethics laws, including restrictions on post-service lobbying; and pay cuts for Congress until the federal budget is balanced.[29] Each of those positions was designed not merely to cast herself as a Washington outsider and reformer, but also to highlight her opponent's insider status and ties to the causes of the poor economy. Blunt, for his part, maintained laser focus on his party's anti-big government message, calling for tax cuts, fewer restrictions on business, and opposition to healthcare reform and the stimulus plan.

Media

Not surprisingly, given the tens of millions of dollars raised by the campaigns and their independent supporters, both campaigns relied heavily on television and radio advertisements to make their cases to the voters. On occasion, the ads addressed real policy differences. More often than not, however, they relied on character attacks, which grew more personal, shriller, and gradually expanded into attacks on the opponents' families. Politico aptly described the two campaigns' media strategies as competing labels: 'Rubberstamp' Robin versus 'Bailout' Blunt.[30] "Rubberstamp" was designed to tie Carnahan to President Obama, whose approval in the state throughout 2010 was consistently polling in the low 40s, with unfavorables reaching the mid-50s by mid-summer. The term was used repeatedly in ads highlighting healthcare reform, the "failed" stimulus plan and energy policy in particular. As the campaign moved into the fall, the Blunt ads began targeting a particular grant in the stimulus: a $107 million grant to a wind farm project founded by Carnahan's brother. The ad claimed that no jobs were created by the project—a claim debunked by Factcheck.org[31]—and that the candidate's support for the legislation was designed to benefit her brother. Not to be outdone, the Carnahan campaign ran repeated ads criticizing Blunt's support for the TARP "bailout" program and his extensive use of earmarks. But the campaign also hit Blunt personally, highlighting allegations of corruption by Blunt—his alleged ties to wrongdoing by Tom Delay, "Duke" Cunningham and Jack Abramoff (several of which Factcheck also debunked)—and his family members working as lobbyists, essentially calling her opponent 'the most corrupt politician ever.' [32] Such personal attacks ultimately do not change many voters' minds, but the candidates sought to increase their opponent's negatives in an effort to dissuade voters.

Finance

Following the *Citizens United v. FEC* decision in early 2010, political observers predicted a dramatic influx of corporate electioneering spending, particularly in high-profile Senate races such as Missouri. Further, based on announcements by prominent political organizations, most notably the U.S. Chamber of Commerce,[33] it was anticipated that such influx would dramatically favor Republican candidates. The money did flow, and the imbalance did come to pass in Missouri, albeit the disparity was not by the staggering amounts seen in other, more competitive races nationwide. As shown in Table 14.1, the campaigns combined to spend over $22 million, with the

Table 14.1.   Total Raised and Spent 2010 Race: Missouri Senate

Candidate	Roy Blunt	Robin Carnahan
Amount Spent - Total	12,095,571	10,338,037
Individual Contributions	7,342,776	8,634,967
PACs	3,252,143	1,095,118
Total Independent Spending	8,151,614	5,532,513
For the Candidate	2,208,970	690,061
Against Opponent	3,979,670	4,055,276
Undesignated	1,962,974	608,780

Source: Open Secrets, http://www.opensecrets.org/races/summary.php?cycle=2010&id=MOS1.

Blunt campaign spending nearly $2 million more than did the Carnahan campaign. Interestingly, however, more money was actually raised and spent by the McCaskill and Talent campaigns in 2006—$11.3 million and $14.5 million, respectively;[34] this is due in part to the start-to-finish closeness of that race, as well as the likelihood that that race would determine the balance of power in the Senate. By contrast, it was unlikely in 2010 that the Republicans would be able to capture a majority in the Senate; and as it became increasingly clear that the race was not close, national interest and contributions slowed, and neither side felt the need to pour exorbitant sums of money into advertising in the final weeks of the campaign.

Total independent expenditures supporting or opposing the two candidates totaled another $13.5 million, a majority of which was spent in negative attacks on the opposition. As shown in Table 14.1, Blunt supporters had a more decisive advantage here. Again, however, the dramatic increase in independent group expenditures—at least reported expenditures—relative to 2006 did not pan out; in fact, total independent expenditures in the 2006 campaign exceeded 2010 expenditures by $10 million.[35]

Grassroots and Bases of Support

Both candidates entered the Senate race having run successful statewide campaigns in the past, and with an existing network of support in the state. In fact, Carnahan might have entered the race with a slight edge, having more recently run statewide campaigns and starting with a more favorable statewide profile, while Blunt's recent campaigns had been for his more homogeneous congressional district. Once the race began in earnest, though, the strength of the Blunt grassroots organization, and the effectiveness of his campaign team became clear. In addition, Blunt's ties to rural Missouri, culled over decades of public service, presented a more formidable challenge than had former Senator Talent in 2006. Both candidates made only half-hearted efforts to galvanize young voters, particularly college students, but the lack of young people engaged in the campaign clearly hurt the Democrat more than the Republican.[36]

The party apparatus—statewide and local party activists—formed the core of each candidate's campaign network. Consistent with the national trend, however, the Democratic organization was far less active, even compared to Carnahan's 2008 campaign for reelection as Secretary of State. Outside of Kansas City and St. Louis, Democratic campaign visibility was low. In-state endorsements were also remarkably predictable and contributed very little to the campaign. Essentially, Carnahan was endorsed by the newspapers in Kansas City and St. Louis; Blunt by all the other major papers in the state.[37]

ELECTION RESULTS

The Numbers

Ultimately, despite early indicators to the contrary, a close, competitive race never materialized. Senator Blunt was elected to the U.S. Senate by a comfortable margin, receiving just fewer than 55 percent of the popular vote.[38]

As was expected, Senator Blunt won by wide margins throughout most of the state, losing only in the Democratic strongholds of St. Louis and Kansas City.

Table 14.2. Vote Results Missouri Senate Race

Candidate	Total Votes	Percentage of Votes
Blunt, Roy (REP)	1,054,160	54.2%
Carnahan, Robin (DEM)	789,736	40.6%
Dine, Jonathan (LIB)	58,663	3.0%
Beck, Jerry (CST)	41,309	2.1%
Six Additional Candidates	31	0.1%
Total Votes	1,943,899	100%

Source: November 2, 2010 General Election Results, Missouri Secretary of State Office. http://www.sos. mo.gov/enrweb/allresults.asp?eid=300.

Table 14.3. Voter Turnout Missouri Senate Race

Year	Registered Voters	Total Votes Cast	% Turnout
2002	3,681,844	1,877,620	51%
2004	4,194,416	2,731,364	65.1%
2006	4,007,174	2,128,459	53.1%
2008	4,205,774	2,917,621	69.4%
2010	4,137,545	1,943,898	47%

Source: November 2, 2010 General Election Results, Missouri Secretary of State Office. http://www.sos. mo.gov/enrweb/allresults.asp?eid=300.

What closer review of the numbers illustrates is that 2010 was a remarkably low-turnout election in the state, not only compared to 2008 and 2004, but even compared to the two previous midterm elections.

This decline in voter turnout was magnified in the urban areas, as Democratic voters stayed home in far greater numbers than their Republican counterparts. In Kansas City proper, 2010 turnout was 38 percent; in St. Louis City, 37.9 percent. Collectively, the most heavily Democratic areas voted 9 percent below the statewide average.

In addition, 2010 marked an end to Democratic gains in the Republican rural strongholds that had propelled McCaskill to victory in 2006 and nearly won the state for President Obama in 2008. Blunt was able to recapture the rural vote lost in 2006 and 2008, and then some. As demonstrated in Table 4,

Table 14.4. Voter Turnout by Missouri County

County	Population	McCaskill 2004	McCaskill 2006	Carnahan 2010
Atchison	less than 10,000	34.9%	38.4%	25.2%
Carter	less than 10,000	39%	41%	33.7%
DeKalb	10,000–30,000	40.4%	43.7%	30.9%
Maries	less than 10,000	37.8%	40.5%	29.8%
McDonald	10,000–30,000	24.7%	32.4%	19.9%
Monroe	less than 10,000	38.9%	44.7%	33.8%
Newton	30,000–70,000	23.7%	30%	20.7%
Ozark	less than 10,000	34.8%	40%	27.2%
Pulaski	30,000–70,000	33.8%	38.6%	26%
Worth	less than 10,000	40.6%	40.7%	32.3%

Source: County-by-county ballot percentages are from the General Election Results, Missouri Secretary of State Office Election, for the respective election years; population data are from the Missouri Economic Research and Information Center (MERIC) 2010 population estimates.
http://www.missourieconomy.org/newsletter/2005countypop.htm.

Carnahan received far less percentage of the rural vote than did McCaskill in 2006, and also in 2004, when then-gubernatorial candidate McCaskill rarely ventured out of Kansas City or St. Louis. The pattern was fairly consistent in out-state counties, both small and moderate sized, across the state.[39]

Analysis

In a sense, the 2010 Missouri Senate election *was* a bellwether of sorts. The race, more than recent statewide elections, was about public unrest and anger, much of it national in scope and in focus. Blunt rode to victory on a wave of anti-incumbent, anti-Democrat, anti-Obama sentiment; driven in large measure by the poor economy, and magnified by powerful rhetoric which, true or not, directed much of the public's angst and fear at the President and party in power. Additional factors—the negative tone of the campaign, the lack of a successful rural strategy by the Democrat, the Republican fundraising edge—reinforced and built upon these advantages. Carnahan attempted to run an outsider candidacy, casting her longtime Washington insider as part of the incumbency problem, but her strategy did not gain traction, due in part to her perceived close ties to the President, and in part to her focus on issues—earmarks, runaway spending, and abuse of corporate power at the expense of "main street"—that were widely seen as Republican, not Democratic strengths. Similarly, Blunt was shielded from his most telling vulnerabilities, his close ties to President Bush's policies and, particularly, to Tom Delay and the scandal-ridden Republican establishment of the past decade, due to Missouri voters' impatience with the economy and, as a result, the Democratic Party.

There was, to be sure, a long list of failures, scandals, and political blunders by the Bush Administration, and its Republican allies in Congress, during President Bush's eight years in office—culminating with investigations and convictions of multiple House members and lobbyists, and the financial crisis. Yet 2010 demonstrated, once again, that voters have short memories and tend to vote retrospectively, defined in the very short term: "what have you done for me lately?"

After two election cycles of Democratic advantage, or at least parity, with Republican fundraising, the Republican monetary advantage returned with a vengeance in 2010. As noted above, the Blunt campaign raised and spent nearly $2 million more than did Carnahan. In addition, in the aftermath of the *Citizens United* decision, there was a large influx of money in support of the Blunt candidacy that Democratic independent sources were unable to match. The financial advantage was certainly a factor, yet it was not enough to explain Senator Blunt's comfortable win. The Democratic candidate was not overwhelmed by the fundraising disparity, and was able to compete for the most part. And despite the impact of *Citizens United,* both campaigns, and their independent supporters, actually spent less than was spent by their counterparts in the 2006 Missouri Senate campaign.

Ultimately, this election was about turnout, or more accurately, poor turnout, even relative to recent midterm elections. And the low turnout was not uniform, but was particularly acute in Democratic strongholds, and amongst demographics which typically vote Democratic.

Why was this the case? First, whether or not President Obama is rightfully to blame for the continued economic malaise, the initial excitement of his campaign and early months of his presidency gradually gave way to the stark reality that the economy is not coming back quickly—certainly not for the middle class. As a result, not merely the new voters of 2006 and 2008 stayed home, but also large numbers of moderate, conservative, even liberal Democrats disengaged from politics and passed on the 2010 election. Perhaps the most significant accomplishment of the Obama campaign was its ability to mitigate turnout bias—the vicious cycle whereby lower income, younger, urban, less educated voters disengage because the government does not respond to their interests. The Obama campaign engaged those voters, but for many of them 2010 was a return to past disappointments. As the exit polls demonstrate, Carnahan won well over 70 percent of the urban vote; she won among the working poor, split the middle class, won the under 30 vote, and won overwhelmingly among Democrats.[40] Democrats voted for Carnahan, and Republicans voted for Blunt, in substantially the same numbers that they voted for Obama and McCain in 2008, but this time more Democrats stayed home. Similarly, Republican-leaning independents broke for Blunt, whereas Democratic-leaning independents stayed home, a pattern that became increasingly likely as the campaign wore on.[41] Indeed, while Carnahan polled ahead of Blunt throughout 2009 and into early 2010, the polls of likely voters began a steady shift towards the Republican candidate, a shift that closely tracked dissatisfaction with the state of the economy, President Obama and the Democratic Party. By August 2010, Blunt was maintaining a sizable lead in substantially all of the polls, which in turn reinforced Democratic pessimism.

In addition, Carnahan was unable to maintain her party's gains in rural Missouri which had been achieved in 2006 and 2008. Republicans have dominated rural Missouri for decades, particularly in the smallest towns and counties. The McCaskill strategy in 2006 had not been to win those areas, but to compete successfully enough to reduce the loss margins. That campaign did so by focusing on the candidate's small town *bona fides,* by speaking directly to the voters on "kitchen table" issues, particularly economic issues, and by actively campaigning statewide, rather than relying exclusively on surrogates and advertising in rural areas. The Carnahan campaign, however, did not fully implement the McCaskill rural strategy, and to the extent it tried, the effort was nowhere near as successful. This failure is understandable: rural voters were far less susceptible to overtones by the party of Barack Obama in 2010; Roy Blunt's appeal to rural voters was far greater, and his organization far stronger, than that of the previous Republican candidate for Senate. In addition, the candidate and campaign employed a negative-driven strategy not geared towards maximizing turnout, which played to the advantage of the Blunt campaign. Finally, Robin Carnahan, despite her considerable political skills, simply did not appeal to rural voters as effectively.

With the bleak economic outlook, and being an off-year election, the historic tendency was already lower turnout, and turnout bias favoring Republican voters. Negative campaigns tend to further depress turnout, particularly among voters in urban areas where the television and radio ads are most heavily concentrated. As a result, the tenor of the campaign accentuated the challenger's difficulties. The Carnahan campaign's attacks on Blunt's scandal-ridden Washington, D.C. past-ties to corrupt lobbyists, pay-for-play deals and legislative favors for family members-failed to connect with voters already inclined to associate government failure with the current administration and party in power. And laying claim to outsider status, labeling your opponent the "business as usual" candidate when *your* party holds power and you are on record as an avid supporter of that party's objectives, is extraordinarily difficult to pull off, especially when embroiled in a predominantly negative campaign. It was perhaps the best strategy in a particularly difficult year for a Democratic candidate in Missouri; but it needed to be executed to perfection.

CONCLUSION

In sum, the 2010 Missouri Senate race played out as a true bellwether in a predictably low-turnout midterm election. The poor state of the economy soured Democrats on their party and their leadership. Blunt was not successful in winning independents or even more conservative Democrats in significant numbers. But his campaign did get out his base, and it did reinforce the tendencies of many Democrats to sit this one out. Robin Carnahan entered the race with high approval ratings, a clean record regarding ethics, and viewed as a rising star in her party. Yet from early in 2010 her negatives steadily climbed, shooting up a full ten percent from July to October.[42] By the end of the race her negatives were well over 50 percent, and Roy Blunt, a consummate Washington insider for the past fifteen years, was elected to the United States Senate by a margin that reflected the national political environment.

NOTES

1. David A. Lieb, "Neither blue nor red, Mo. is a battleground," *Columbia Missourian*, November 13, 2006.

2. "Total State Expenditures Per Capita, SFY2009," Kaiser Foundation. www
.statehealthfacts.org/comparemaptable.jsp?ind=32&cat=1&sub=10&yr=91&typ=4&
sort=a&rgnhl=27.

3. Demographic data in this section is taken from "Missouri QuickFacts from the
U.S. Census Bureau." quickfacts.census.gov/qfd/states/29000.html.

4. Mayer, Kosmin and Keysar, American Religious Identification Survey, The
City University of New York, 2001. www.gc.cuny.edu/faculty/research_briefs/aris/
key_findings.htm.

5. Frank Newport, State of the States: Importance of Religion. Gallup,
January 28, 2009. www.gallup.com/poll/114022/state-states-importance-religion.
aspx#2.

6. "Church or Synagogue Attendance by State." *The San Diego Tribune*, May
2, 2006.

7. Chad Garrison, "Voting Maps Show Political Divide in Missouri; St. Louis
and Kansas City vs. Everyone Else." *Riverfront Times*, November 4, 2010.

8. "Missouri QuickFacts from the U.S. Census Bureau," Garrison, 2010.

9. "About the Senator." Official Website for Senator Roy Blunt. blunt.senate.
gov/public/index.cfm/biography?p=about-the-senator.

10. Carl Hulse and David Stout, "Ohio Congressman Wins Majority Leader Race,
Replacing DeLay," *New York Times*, February 2, 2006.

11. Center for Responsibility and Ethics in Washington, "Congressman Roy
Blunt," CREW's Most Corrupt, Report Issued 2006. www.crewsmostcorrupt.org/
roy_blunt.

12. Tony Messenger, "For Roy Blunt, Politics is a Family Affair," *St. Louis
Post-Dispatch*, October 13, 2010.

13. Data obtained from "Roy Blunt," On the Issues, November 2010. www.
ontheissues.org/default.htm.

14. Bill Lambrecht, "Blunt: Medicare, Medicaid 'distorts the marketplace.'" *St.
Louis Post-Dispatch*, July 10, 2009.

15. "Roy Blunt," On the Issues, November 2010. www.ontheissues.org/default.
htm.

16. League of Conservation Voters, "LCV Names Roy Blunt to 2010 Dirty Dozen
List, Launches BigOilBlunt.com," March 10, 2010.

17. "Editorial Endorsement of Roy Blunt," *Springfield News Leader*, October 24,
2010.

18. August 3, 2010 Primary Election Results, Missouri Secretary of State Office.
www.sos.mo.gov/Enrweb/allresults.asp?arc=1&eid=283.

19. Biographical information obtained from "About Robin," Robin Carnahan,
Missouri Secretary of State (the official campaign site for the Robin Carnahan Senate
Campaign). www.robincarnahan.com/about.

20. At the time of the 2010 campaign, her cancer was in remission. Jake Wagman, "Carnahan, a breast cancer survivor, assembles team for Komen race," *St. Louis Post-Dispatch*, May 17, 2010.

21. Policy Positions summarized from "Robin Carnahan," On the Issues. www. issues2000.org/senate/Robin_Carnahan.htm.

22. Melissa Siegel, Kelsey Ferguson and Eugene Kiely, "Toss-ups: Missouri Mud-slinging," Factcheck.org., October 12, 2010.

23. Steve Kraske, "A Look at Where Senate Candidates Robin Carnahan and Roy Blunt Stand on the Issues," *Kansas City Star*, October 11, 2010.

24. Ballot Issues, August 3, 2010 Primary Election Results, Missouri Secretary of State Office. www.sos.mo.gov/enrweb/ballotissueresults.asp?eid=283&arc=1.

25. David Catanese, "Proposition C Spells Trouble for Robin Carnahan," Politico, August 6, 2010. www.politico.com/news/stories/0810/40716.html.

26. Descriptions of the ballot measures can be found at Ballot Issues, November 2, 2010 General Election, Missouri Secretary of State Office. www.sos .mo.gov/elections/2010ballot/.

Results can be found at Ballot Issues, November 2, 2010 General Election Results. www.sos.mo.gov/enrweb/ballotissueresults.asp?eid=283&arc=1.

27. David Lieb, "Stars join stem cell fight," *Dallas-Fort Worth Star-Telegram*, October 28, 2006.

28. Eli Yokley, "Carnahan Says Blunt's Jobs Plan 'Got Us Into this Mess,'" Polit-icMo, September 7, 2010.

29. Jo Mannies, "Carnahan Calls for Congressional Pay Cut So They Can Feel The Pain," *St. Louis Beacon*, September 8, 2010.

30. David Cantonese, "Complete Election Coverage: 'Rubberstamp' Robin Carna-han Fires Back at 'Bailout' Roy Blunt," Politico, May 13, 2010. www.politico.com/news/stories/0510/37232.html.

31. Factcheck.org, "Toss-ups, ibid.

32. Factcheck.org.

33. Jeanne Cummings and Chris Frates, "New Business Plan: Crushing Dems," *Politico*, August 3, 2010.

34. "James M. Talent, 2001–2006 Profile," OpenSecrets.org, Center for Respon-sive Politics, released January 25, 2007. www.opensecrets.org/politicians/summary. asp?CID=N00005004&cycle=2006.

35. Open Secrets, "Total Raised and Spent: 2006 Race: Missouri Senate. www. opensecrets.org/outsidespending/summ.php?cycle=2006&disp=R&pty=A&type=G

36. Tony Messenger, "Missouri State Rep: Young Democrats Hold Key to 2010 Election," St. Louis Post-Dispatch, August 20, 2010.

37. "Editorial Excerpts on Missouri's U.S. Senate Race," Daily Journal Online, October 25, 2010.

38. November 2, 2010 General Election Results, Missouri Secretary of State Office. www.sos.mo.gov/enrweb/allresults.asp?eid=300.

39. County-by-county ballot percentages are from the General Election Results, Mis-souri Secretary of State Office Election, for the respective election years; population

data are from the Missouri Economic Research and Information Center (MERIC) 2010 population estimates. www.missourieconomy.org/newsletter/2005countypop.htm.

40. 2010 Missouri Exit Polls, CNN Politics Election Center. www.cnn.com/ELECTION/2010/results/polls.

41. Public Policy Polling, "MO-Senate: Dems Suffering from Intensity Gap." Reposted on Daily Kos, August 17, 2010. www.dailykos.com/story/2010/08/17/893720/-MO-Sen:-Dems-suffering-from-intensity-gap.

42. Tony Messenger, "Blunt Maintains a Healthy Lead Over Carnahan," *St. Louis Post-Dispatch*, October 23, 2010.

Part IV

Conclusion

Chapter 15

The Legacy of the 2010 Congressional Elections

Robert Dewhirst

The Democrats, swept into power on the tide of voter discontent surrounding the "Great Recession" in 2008, were washed out of power in the House of Representatives in 2010 by the continuing economic downturn. The high reported unemployment rate, hovering around the 10 percent mark through much of the year of 2010, trumped all other issues. Moreover, the powerful unemployment rate was the major, but not sole, issue contributing to Democrats losing several Senate seats. It was a great year for the Republicans and their best "off-year" (non presidential) national election performance since 1994.

CHARACTERISTICS OF THE 2010 CONGRESSIONAL ELECTIONS

Economic Woes

Nationwide the Democrats' campaign efforts to retain their House and Senate majorities largely collapsed under the weight of several factors working against them. The state of the economy in general, and the continuing high unemployment rate in particular, clearly was the proverbial "800 pound gorilla in the room" for the American electorate. The outcomes of elections throughout the nation's political history have been hinged on the state of the economy, with the party in power traditionally being severely punished. In the twentieth century alone one-term presidents such as Herbert Hoover, Jimmy Carter, or George H. W. Bush had their White House stays cut short due to the electoral burden of a lagging economy. Likewise, in such times voter wrath in off-year elections traditionally was directed toward the party of the president in power, particularly in House of Representatives contests.

Traditional "Off Year" Election Voting Patterns

Unfortunately for the Democrats they were confronting a second traditional obstacle in 2010. Another pronounced electoral pattern was that the party of the president tended to lose seats in Congress in the first "off year" election two years into their first term. With only two exceptions during the past eight decades (1934 and 2002) voters opted to strengthen the hand of the party opposing the president.

The United States Supreme Court Influences the Campaign

A third factor playing a role in the 2010 congressional elections was a United States Supreme Court ruling early in the campaign season, *Citizens United v. Federal Election Commission.* Although this played a somewhat limited role overall (except in a few carefully targeted key races) in contributing to the outcome of 2010 elections, pundits and political professionals alike agreed that the ruling promised to become a major factor in future elections. In essence, the *Citizens United* decision allowed wealthy interest groups and individuals to donate unlimited amounts of money anonymously to influence election outcomes. Existing floodgates that previously had attempted to restrain the continuing massive expansion of campaign funding were suddenly burst open. Although some of the added donations made available by this ruling in 2010 went to the Democrats, the overwhelming majority of the money reportedly went to the Republicans from their traditional allies among wealthy Americans and corporations. The identity of these new funding sources could only be estimated by journalists, academics, and political watch dog groups because of the anonymity provisions of the highly controversial 5–4 court ruling,

To be sure, critics and supporters of the landmark ruling agreed that it likely would change the future of American politics. The balance of power, already tilting heavily in favor of wealthy interests, suddenly became an even more lopsided struggle. Nonetheless, observers speculated that these donations benefited Republican candidates over their Democratic rivals by at least a 7–1 ratio. For example, in Missouri Democrats reportedly received about $1 million in such donations while Republicans collected about $7.5 million. Major Republican benefactors included Harold Simmons, the Koch brothers (Charles and David), Trevor Rees-Jones, Robert Rowling, Paul Singer, Rupert Murdoch, and the U.S. Chamber of Commerce (which reportedly donated at least $75 million). Also contributing significant amounts of money were two fund gathering groups formed by Karl Rove. His American Crossroads group pledged to collect and spend at least $100 million to donate to Republican candidates.

On the other hand, the Republican National Committee, headed by Michael Steele, ironically was embroiled in one largely embarrassing controversy after another and was mired in an increasing debt throughout the 2010 campaign and provided no help to party congressional candidates. However, money continued to pour into congressional Republican candidate campaign war chests. Donations flowed through affiliated intermediary groups directly to the candidates.

On the other side of the financial equation, campaign spending in 2010 continued its twenty-first century trend of setting new outlay records in each campaign season. For example, spending on television advertising alone grew from $2.4 billion in 2006 (the last off year election) to $2.7 billion in 2008 to $3 billion in 2010.

Turnout

Voter turnout was a fourth factor which benefited Republican candidates in 2010. In some ways this followed a traditional pattern; Republican voters tend to be wealthier than their Democratic counterparts and therefore are more likely to go to the polls on Election Day. But in 2010 Republican turnout was aided by other factors. The Tea Party, a movement largely consisting of white, middle class, conservative Republicans, built momentum throughout the year. Their ire reportedly was directed mainly at what they saw as excessive government power in Washington, D.C., a reckless growth in government spending, a federal takeover of the nation's health care system, and a wasteful government bailout of the nation's banking and automotive industries.

Significantly, Rupert Murdoch's Fox television and radio networks endlessly promoted the Tea Party concerns, publicized, and even helped plan their rallies. Glenn Beck, Bill O'Reilly, and the rest of the Fox network lineup, plus Rush Limbaugh, continuously provided talking points and inspiration for the ever-expanding ranks of the Republican Tea Party faithful. In addition, a group led by Dick Armey, a former Republican Majority leader from Texas, provided critical direct financial support, reportedly as much as 95 percent, to fund advertisement and travel expenses to and from Tea Party demonstrations.

On the other hand, complaints about efforts to suppress the turnout of the poor and minorities were fewer in 2010 than in previous elections. This was a particular problem during the 2008 election when complaints were filed in numerous states of attempts to deceive or harass minority and poor voters.

ELECTION RESULTS

Republicans won control of the House of Representatives but fell short of their goal of capturing the Senate too. In the Senate, the Republicans picked up six seats to swell their ranks to 47 while the Democrats retained the majority with 53 members, including two independents that caucused with them. Democrats lost Senate seats in Arkansas, Illinois, Indiana, North Dakota, Pennsylvania, and Wisconsin. Meanwhile, across Capitol Hill Republicans won control of the House of Representatives with the final count at 242 Republicans and 193 Democrats.

As anticipated by political professionals in both parties, turnout among traditional Democrat constituencies such as African Americans, Hispanics, and women voters fell well below totals for the 2008 election. This trend, coupled with an energized base of traditional Republican voters, particularly social conservatives and wealthy whites, clearly were keys to the party's big victory.

Finally, the role the Internet played in the campaign continued to grow at an accelerated pace as it played an important role in disseminating news and information about the campaign and as a vehicle for making fund-raising appeals. Websites, Twitter, and YouTube appearances became commonplace as candidates and interest groups scrambled to take advantage of the new technology.

LOOKING TO THE FUTURE: CONFRONTATION AND CONFLICT

The 2010 congressional elections were held within the context of one of the most partisan and combative periods in American political history. The incivility and intensity of the rhetoric, begun years beforehand and continued throughout the year, promised to escalate even further as the politicians and media personalities ramped up their efforts in anticipation of the 2012 campaign. The partisan and ideological firestorm raged on.

Soon after the election the Republican leader in the Senate, Mitch McConnell of Kentucky, said the party's primary task in the upcoming congress would be to make certain that Barack Obama would be a one term president. Meanwhile, across Capitol Hill, the incoming Speaker of the House of Representatives, John Boehner (R-OH) vowed to repeal the Democrats' agenda passed during the 111th Congress. Other national Republicans vowed to use the mechanism of reducing federal expenditures to kill or weaken policies and programs such as Medicare, Medicaid, and Social Security that they had long opposed.

The 2012 campaign had begun.

Index

About the Contributors

EDITORS

Robert Dewhirst is Professor of Political Science at Northwest Missouri State University and serves on the Executive Board of the National Social Science Association. Before his academic career, Dewhirst served as a public affairs officer for the U.S. Army in Vietnam, a public affairs director for the Illinois state government, and a reporter for the *Kansas City Star* and several other newspapers in the Midwest. Dewhirst's teaching and research cover American government/politics, state politics, Congress, the American presidency, campaigns and elections, media and politics, political parties, and public policy. He has published several books and numerous book chapters, articles, and essays. His books include *Rites of Passage: Congress Makes Laws, Government at Work*, and *Congress Responds to the Twentieth Century*. He also directed such reference projects as *The Almanac of Missouri Politics* and *The Encyclopedia of the United States Congress* and co-edited several earlier editions of *The Roads to Congress* series.

Sean D. Foreman is Assistant Professor of Political Science at Barry University. He is author of a chapter on the Florida Districts 21 and 25 U.S. Congressional elections for the book *The Roads to Congress 2008* (Lexington Press, 2010) and of "Marco Rubio in Florida: The First Tea Party Senator—Or Not?" in *Stuck in the Middle to Lose: Tea Party Effects on 2010 U.S. Senate Elections* (Lexington Press, 2011). He hosts a weekly radio show called World of Politics on Barry's WBRY radio station that streams on the Internet at www.barry.edu/radiostation. Foreman is quoted in many publications on Florida and national elections and is a frequent guest on talk radio and television programs in Florida and around the United States and has been quoted in newspapers around the world.

CONTRIBUTORS

E. Scott Adler is Associate Professor of Political Science at the University of Colorado, Boulder. His areas of expertise are the U.S. Congress, elections, political institutions, and public policy making. Among his publications are his books *Why Congressional Reforms Fail: Reelection and the House Committee System* (University of Chicago Press, 2002) and *The Macropolitics of Congress* (Princeton University Press, 2006). His forthcoming book is *Congress and the Politics of Problem Solution* (Cambridge University Press).

Sunil Ahuja is Dean of Social Sciences and Human Services at Lorain County Community College. He received his Ph.D. in Political Science from the University of Nebraska-Lincoln. He was formerly a Professor of Political Science at Youngstown State University and has served on the faculty at Seton Hall University and at the University of Louisiana at Lafayette, specializing in American Politics.

Jeffrey Ashley is Professor of Political Science at Eastern Illinois University. He has written or coauthored three books and a number of articles on topics ranging from first ladies and environmental protection to congressional races and indigenous rights.

Margaret E. Banyan is an Assistant Professor at Florida Gulf Coast University and a Senior Faculty Associate for the SW Florida Center for Public and Social Policy. Dr. Banyan teaches in the Division of Public Affairs in the areas of land use planning, public administration, and political science. In addition, she is the Chair of the Lee County Community Sustainability Advisory Committee (formerly the Smart Growth Advisory Committee); member of the Florida Department of Transportation's 2060 Plan Community Sustainability, Environment, and Livability Advisory Committee; member of BikeWalkLee; and board member for the Lee County Homeless Coalition. Dr. Banyan's interests center on sustainability, public transit, special districts, and citizen involvement. Previously, she worked at Portland State University as the director of the Center for Public Participation and Hatfield Scholar for the National Policy Consensus Center.

Peter J. Bergerson is a Professor of Public Policy at Florida Gulf Coast University and teaches political science and public policy in the Division of

Public Affairs. His research and teaching interest include Political Institutions, Campaigns and Elections, Public Personnel Administration and Leadership in Public organizations. He earned his Ph.D. at Saint Louis University and has been a professor for over forty years, publishing several books and numerous articles as well as lecturing in Europe, the Middle East and Asia. He is actively engaged as a political analyst in local media outlets.

William Binning is Professor Emeritus of Political Science at Youngstown State University.

Kevin Buterbaugh is a Professor of Political Science at Southern Connecticut State University. He has published works on American Elections, U.S. Security Institutions and the World Trade Organization.

Marcia L. Godwin is Associate Professor of Public Administration at the University of La Verne. Godwin primarily teaches graduate public administration courses and has extensive experience in local government administration in Southern California. She has contributed chapters on other senatorial and congressional campaigns in previous editions of *The Roads to Congress*. Research interests include electoral politics, innovation in government, and development of the next generation of public managers. Godwin's current research examines local government financial reserves and policies in light of the Bell, California scandal and cut-backs due to the recent recession.

William K. Hall is a Professor Political Science at Bradley University. His teaching and research focus on American national government and politics as well as state and local government and politics. He is the author of *The New Institutions of Federalism*. Hall has contributed chapters to various edited collections and has edited *Illinois Government and Politics*. He has authored articles on judicial retention elections and also on cumulative voting and city council elections for a number of professional journals.

Jeffrey Kraus is the Associate Provost and Professor of Government and Politics at Wagner College, where he has been on the faculty since 1988. Before coming to Wagner, Kraus taught at Kingsborough Community College (1980–1987) and Baruch College (1987–1988). Kraus has written about elections and campaign finance. He received his Bachelor's degree from Brooklyn College (1978) and his Masters (1980) and Doctorate (1988) from the Graduate School of the City University of New York.

Tom Lansford is the Academic Dean, Gulf Coast, at the University of Southern Mississippi and a Professor of Political Science. Dr. Lansford is the author, coauthor, editor or coeditor of 31 books, including most recently, the edited volumes *America's War on Terror* (2003; second edition 2009), *George W. Bush: A Political and Ethical Assessment at Midterm* (2004), and *Judging Bush* (2009). Dr. Lansford is the author of more than one hundred essays, book chapters, and reviews.

Jerry McBeath is Professor of Political Science at the University of Alaska Fairbanks, where he has worked since 1976. He received an MA from the University of Chicago (international relations, 1964) and a Ph.D. from the University of California, Berkeley (political science, 1970). His research interests are in the areas: Alaska politics/government, federalism, circumpolar northern politics, ethnic politics, domestic and foreign politics of China and Taiwan and environmental politics, both domestic and international. His most recent publication on Alaska (co-authored) is *The Political Economy of Oil in Alaska: Multinationals vs. the State* (Lynne Rienner, 2008). Currently, he and his spouse, Jenifer Huang, are writing a book on "Environmental Education in China."

Bob N. Roberts is Professor of Political Science at James Madison University, where he reaches courses on public administration, the legal environment of public administration, and state and local government. Roberts has published numerous articles in such journals as *Public Administration Review*, *The International Journal of Public Administration, and Public Integrity*, and he is the author or coauthor of *White House Ethics; From Watergate to Whitewater: The Public Integrity Wars; Public Journalism and Political Knowledge;* as well as the encyclopedias *Ethics in U.S. Government: An Encyclopedia of Presidential Campaigns, Slogans, Issues, and Platforms.* Professor Roberts is also a frequent media commentator on politics.

Josh M. Ryan is Assistant Professor of Political Science at Bradley University. His recent research focuses on the bargaining process between the House and Senate, including bicameral resolution procedures and the effect of ideology on bargaining success. His other research interests focus on the role of elites in campaigns and elections.

Carl Shepro is a Professor of Political Science at the University of Alaska Anchorage. He has concentrated his research and writing on rural Alaska education and government. His most recent publication is a chapter on Alaska Campaigns and Elections included in *Alaska Politics and Public Policy,* edited by Clive Thomas from the University of Alaska Press (forthcoming). He is currently writing and doing research on policy issues in the circumpolar North, on the influence of communication patterns in local government, and on local participation in resource management in rural Alaska.

Daniel E. Smith is an Assistant Professor of Political Science at Northwest Missouri State University. A former practicing telecommunications attorney, his primary teaching and research interests include Judicial Politics, Jurisprudence, and Constitutional Law, with emphasis on personal rights and the First Amendment. He also has interests in Political Theory and scholarship of educational innovation.

Anand Edward Sokhey is an Assistant Professor of Political Science at the University of Colorado at Boulder. Anand specializes in American politics, and his work examines the role that social influence plays in voting behavior, political participation, and opinion formation. His work has appeared in journals such as the *American Political Science Review*, the *American Journal of Political Science*, and *American Politics Research*.

Joshua Whitney holds an M.A in History from Western Illinois University and an M.A. in Political Science from Eastern Illinois University.

CPSIA information can be obtained at www.ICGtesting.com
Printed in the USA
BVOW031827081011

273127BV00001B/3/P